The Origins
of American
Strategic Bombing
Theory

Titles in the Series

*Airpower Reborn: The Strategic Concepts of
John Warden and John Boyd*

*The Bridge to Airpower: Logistics Support for Royal Flying
Corps Operations on the Western Front, 1914–18*

Airpower Applied: U.S., NATO, and Israeli Combat Experience

The History of Military Aviation

Paul J. Springer, editor

This series is designed to explore previously ignored facets of the history of airpower. It includes a wide variety of disciplinary approaches, scholarly perspectives, and argumentative styles. Its fundamental goal is to analyze the past, present, and potential future utility of airpower and to enhance our understanding of the changing roles played by aerial assets in the formulation and execution of national military strategies. It encompasses the incredibly diverse roles played by airpower, which include but are not limited to efforts to achieve air superiority; strategic attack; intelligence, surveillance, and reconnaissance missions; airlift operations; close-air support; and more. Of course, airpower does not exist in a vacuum. There are myriad terrestrial support operations required to make airpower functional, and examinations of these missions is also a goal of this series.

In less than a century, airpower developed from flights measured in minutes to the ability to circumnavigate the globe without landing. Airpower has become the military tool of choice for rapid responses to enemy activity, the primary deterrent to aggression by peer competitors, and a key enabler to military missions on the land and sea. This series provides an opportunity to examine many of the key issues associated with its usage in the past and present, and to influence its development for the future.

The Origins
of American
Strategic Bombing
Theory

CRAIG F. MORRIS

Naval Institute Press
Annapolis, Maryland

Naval Institute Press
291 Wood Road
Annapolis, MD 21402

Library of Congress Cataloging-in-Publication Data
Name: Morris, Craig F., author.
Title: The origins of American strategic bombing theory / by Craig F. Morris.
Description: Annapolis, Maryland : Naval Institute Press, [2017] | Series:
    The history of military aviation | Includes bibliographical references and
    index.
Identifiers: LCCN 2017025943| ISBN 9781682472521 (alk. paper) | ISBN
    9781682472538 (epdf)
Subject: LCSH: Bombing, Aerial—United States—History—20th century.
    | Strategic bombers—United States—History—20th century. | Military
    doctrine—United States—History—20th century. | World War, 1914–
    1918—Aerial operations, American. | Aeronautics, Military—United
    States—History—20th century.
Classification: LCC UG703 .M67 2017 | DDC 358.4/14—dc23 LC record
    available at https://lccn.loc.gov/2017025943

The views expressed in this book are those of the author and do not reflect
the official policy or positions of the United States Air Force, Department
of Defense, or the U.S. Government.

CONTENTS

ACKNOWLEDGMENTS

A work of this magnitude can never be the sole effort of just one person. I am grateful for the help, guidance, and support of many individuals in the pursuit of this book. I know this short list can never be complete and I apologize for anyone who may be overlooked in this formal thank-you. From detailed guidance and editing to suggesting new avenues for examination through informal conversations, this book would not have come to fruition without the help of a myriad of people. If there are any errors or misstatements, they are solely my responsibility.

I want to start out with my primary adviser Dr. William Trimble. Bill was a complete joy to work with from the start of my time at Auburn until the completion of my PhD. He took a green Air Force lieutenant colonel on a very short timeline and with only a general concept of a dissertation topic and guided him along a path to ensure not only graduation, but also a relevant research effort. His keen guidance and tireless efforts to improve my substandard grammar are deeply appreciated.

The other members of my committee also deserve high praise. Drs. Alan Meyer, Mark Sheftall, and David Carter proved outstanding teachers, mentors, and friends. Each played a large role in shaping my thoughts on how outside influences affected the evolution of strategic bombing theory during the often-chaotic World War I and interwar eras. A special thank-you goes to Dr. Alan Meyer for his many coffee breaks with me, where he helped this tired old military officer understand the academic process and keep him on track in his research.

Finally, I must mention Mr. Thomas Wildenberg. On countless occasions, Tom's expert subject matter knowledge and kindly guidance helped keep me on focus. I am deeply indebted to him for constantly reminding me to look beyond the accepted story line of my own military service and seek a deeper understanding of what was going on inside the minds of the key theorists and in their writings.

As with any project of this size and scope, I had to rely on a great many researchers to help me gather data for this project. The staff at the Air Force Historical Records Agency became almost a second family to me during the process, as they helped me find documents, pointed out other potentially valuable resources, and most important, kept up my morale with their always-friendly banter. While the whole staff deserves praise, Tammy Horton deserves special acknowledgement for her help in garnering electronic copies.

Of course, this project would have fallen flat without the tireless support of my family. I especially want to thank my two children Joseph and Virginia for enduring far too many "vacations" centered on exploring museums and archives. Along these same lines, my ever suffering wife Kelly should be proclaimed an angel for her support and acceptance of a military officer with an addiction to history. Long before this book, she suffered through vacations to battlefields, museums, and historic sites. Her loving support and sense of humor have enabled me to pursue this dream and I am forever grateful.

Finally, I cannot end this section without dedicating this book to my father. Lawrence Morris kindled my love of history at an early age. Some of my fondest memories are watching documentaries on the World Wars with him. He has been a tireless supporter and I wish to thank him for all he has done to get me to this point.

The Origins
of American
Strategic Bombing
Theory

INTRODUCTION

It was a blustery English day on May 12, 1942, when the first B-17 Flying Fortresses of the 97th Bomb Group arrived in High Wycombe airfield northwest of London. The landings heralded the beginning of a massive buildup of American airpower in Europe. Less than a month earlier, on April 24, Maj. Gen. Carl Spaatz of the United States Army Air Forces (USAAF) had provided the strategic direction for these bombers when he established the headquarters of the 8th Army Air Force (AAF) just thirty miles away at Bushy Park.[1] At the time, the 8th AAF contained only a bomber group, a fighter group, and a transportation group, but eventually these forces would be expanded to form the "Mighty Eighth"—the massive air fleet that attacked and helped destroy the Nazi war machine.

The deployment of the first American bomber group to England marked the first step toward realizing the dreams of a generation of airpower advocates dating back to World War I. Their vision had centered on a bold new concept: that the strategic use of aircraft could radically transform traditional warfare. To forward-thinking aviation theorists, the advent of aircraft promised to cast aside the limitations that had been imposed on ground and naval forces by geography, warfighting capabilities, and operational reach since the dawn of organized warfare.

Propelled by the new technology and enhanced production capacity of the modern industrial nation, aviation seemed to offer armed forces the ability to strike strategically. No longer would a country's military be forced to engage directly with an enemy's army or navy to win a war. By relying on aircraft it could avoid those costly operations and use long-range bombers to attack directly at an enemy's industrial heart. It was nothing less than a revolutionary vision of warfighting.

Yet in these early stages the vision was constrained by some serious challenges. First, not everyone agreed that air would be transformational. Many military and political leaders regarded aircraft as just another weapon in the traditional naval and ground warfare arsenals. In their minds the expansion of military aviation would not change warfare; it merely offered new capabilities that could be used to support tried-and-true conventional strategies. Second, as occurred with almost any new technology, the initial design evolutions often failed to meet advocates' expectations—falling far short of what was needed to "transform" warfare. Finally, the theorists' conceptions would have to be turned into a set of well-crafted principles. Although author H. G. Wells might imagine large airborne fleets laying waste to enemy cities, military professionals knew that for airpower actually to become revolutionary would require organization, training, funding, and logistics that would be provided reliably as part of an accepted strategic doctrine.

Thus the long-running argument over the role of airpower in helping to ensure national security began early in the American military's experimentation with aviation. The debate turned on two equally important questions: should the Army's fledgling Air Service be independent, and what would be the best way to employ airpower in war? This dilemma was evident in the first formal Army Air Service doctrinal manual, written by Maj. William C. Sherman in 1921. "In deriving the doctrine that must underlie all principles of employment of the air force," he wrote, "we must not be guided by conditions surrounding the use of ground troops, but must seek out our doctrine . . . in the element in which the air force operates."[2]

This viewpoint may explain some of the apparent confusion over the early phases of the development of American airpower. For decades, historians struggled to explain how the two components of the Air Service's doctrine worked together, first in the Air Service itself and the succeeding Army Air Corps, and later in the formation of the postwar (fully independent) U.S. Air Force. To close the gap, they credited both Brig. Gen. William "Billy" Mitchell and

Maj. Gen. Benjamin Foulois as important influences in the early Air Service, and that both had championed the independence of the aviation branch and the use of strategic bombing.

There are three major flaws in this explanation. First, it falls victim to what Brandeis University Professor David Hackett Fischer has called the "historian's fallacy," where chroniclers assume that decision makers of the past had acted having the same views about unfolding events that historians would adopt years later.[3] For example, because World War II spawned an Army Air Force that was both essentially independent and committed to strategic bombing, then the founders of the postwar United States Air Force must have been early advocates of both. Second, the explanation often obscures other truly important figures who do not quite fit the stereotype. The attention given to Brigadier General Mitchell and Major General Foulois hides the work of quieter, less well-known, but truly innovative thinkers. Finally, the approach misses the importance of broader social factors in shaping the thinking of both the men who created the doctrine of strategic bombing and of the military organizations that carried it out.

In truth, the evolution of the strategic bombing doctrine was neither the work of one man nor the result of a natural progression. Rather, it stemmed from an intricate interaction among developments in airpower theory, aircraft technology, organizational dynamics, and political forces. Indeed, as late as 1938 the status of strategic bombing was highly in doubt. The Army had all but halted purchases of heavy bombers, and talk about the theory of strategic bombing was confined largely to the backwaters of the Air Corps Tactical School (ACTS) in Montgomery, Alabama.

Unfortunately this complex narrative conflicts with the Air Force's own version of its beginnings and with historians' accounts of the same events and factors. The divergence is evident in the service's own early analyses of the success of strategic bombing and in more recent revisions of those assessments. Mostly written between the 1950s and 1980s, the documents depict the expansion of strategic bombing as an unstoppable force that was at least partially choreographed by the central players—a notion that is clearly observable in the early histories of American aviation in World War I and the interwar years. But these documents tend to miss the larger inter-play among key factors that ultimately helped transform technological advances into military strategy.

Four well-known books form the basis of the linear analysis championed by the Air Force. First, historian Maurer Maurer's *U.S. Air Service in World War I* sets the stage by chronicling the British influence on key aviation advocates as a major factor in employing aircraft to attack an enemy's industrial infrastructure. Maj. Gen. (Ret.) and military historian I. B. Holley Jr.'s *Ideas and Weapons: Exploitation of the Aerial Weapon by the United States During World War I: A Study in the Relationship of Technological Advance, Military Doctrine, and the Development of Weapons* supports the linear history with his argument that aviation's unfulfilled promise during World War I guided American military thinking in the interwar years, as Billy Mitchell pushed for increases in bomber production, the strategic use of airpower, and Air Service independence. Robert Futrell's *Ideas, Concepts, and Doctrines: Basic Thinking in the United States Air Force, 1907–1960* takes up where Holley leaves off. Futrell portrays the interwar years as a competition for dominance between the Army and its Air Corps, where the lessons of World War I merged with the technological advances of that period to push airpower toward a doctrine based on strategic attack. Finally, Robert Finney's *History of the Air Corps Tactical School, 1920–1940* describes the ascension of strategic bombing theory through the lectures, theoretical debates, and officer interactions at the Air Corps' doctrinal training ground.

Together, the authors present a familiar—and at times contradictory—narrative of the development of airpower doctrine: American aviators, fascinated by the concept of strategic bombardment, brought the idea back from Europe after World War I. The new movement grew inside the nurturing environment of ACTS, where aviators linked strategic bombing theory with the new capabilities of the latest aircraft. In the lead-up to World War II, political support and military necessity ensured that strategic bombing would become the grand aerial strategy used to degrade German war industries.

But later studies by a new group of military historians who revisited the subject during the 1990s and 2000s showed that this officially accepted narrative was flawed. The most important of the new volumes was Tami Davis Biddle's *Rhetoric and Reality in Air Warfare: The Evolution of British and American Ideas About Strategic Bombing, 1914–1945*. Biddle pursues a more nuanced understanding of bombing. Exploring the wildly inaccurate predictions about the effectiveness of airpower in the interwar period, she compares the theoretical progressions in Britain and America to gain a better understanding of how military institutions create and implement new ideas. In doing so, she sheds light on the role of organizations in the development of strategic bombing theory.

Similarly, Mark Clodfelter's *Beneficial Bombing: The Progressive Foundations of American Air Power, 1917–1945* also explores other causes to explain the rise of strategic bombing. Instead of a writing a linear history, Clodfelter looks at how social and economic progressivism directed the way strategic bombing advocates and political leaders thought—and ultimately helped shape their theories. Although Clodfelter's work may leave room for argument, his introduction of social factors as a major influence is an important step in understanding the history of strategic bombing.

Stephen McFarland's *America's Pursuit of Precision Bombing 1904–1945* bolsters the new rethinking about the rise of strategic bombing by exploring the technological advances as a factor. He contends that far from being a linear process, the interwar search involved a back-and-forth attempt to find an acceptable airpower doctrine based on the introduction of greater precision in bombing. While this was most often associated with strategic bombing, McFarland argues that it just as easily could have sought more precise operational airpower as the primary tool. Indeed, he suggests that doctrine development took a back seat to technological change during those years, with the real story focused on designing a bombsight that could take account of speed, altitude, wind, and bomb aerodynamics—a step that would make strategic bombing even more attractive.

Finally, in *Air Power in the Age of Total War*, John Buckley argues that geography and political policies played a large part in determining aviation war strategy during the interwar years. In the United States and Britain, a desire to bring the fight directly to the enemy without the need for ground invasions prompted even more interest in strategic bombing. By contrast, both Germany and France held fast to the need for a ground war, effectively relegating aviation to providing operational support for such efforts. Finally, both the Japanese and United States navies preferred a more tactical aviation doctrine that would center on deploying dive-bombers and torpedo-bombers to help fight the anticipated great naval battles in the Pacific.

Although these books have contributed greatly to a better understanding of the evolution of strategic bombing, there still is something missing: a more detailed, broader look that explores how outside factors such as political pressures, economic stresses, and organizational conflicts intertwined to shape strategic bombing during its evolution in World War I and the interwar years.

This book will attempt to provide that. Using British aviation historian Neville Jones' masterpiece, *The Origins of Strategic Bombing: A Study of the Development of British Air Strategic Thought and Practice Up to 1918*, as a model, it uses a chronological approach, interspersing the actions of critical individuals against the backdrop of larger contextual factors and world events. In this way, it seeks a new understanding of the origins of American strategic bombing.

Chapter one explores how the Mexican Expedition of 1916 prepared the United States Army and its air component for the trials of World War I. The deployment of the 1st Aero Squadron to Mexico was a wake-up call that alerted the nation's leadership to the poor state of military aviation. The chapter explores how this alert led not only to increased spending, but also to a theoretical awakening about the potential value of strategic bombing.

The next chapter broadens the scope to show how the nature of World War I influenced the development of strategic bombing theory in Europe. It investigates the theoretical foundations established by air combat between 1914 and 1917, which the United States inherited when it entered the war. Chapter three builds on this work by exploring how the Americans created their own version of strategic bombing theory in the summer and fall of 1917. By tracing the linkages between the early American aviation leaders and their British, Italian, and French confidants, the chapter demonstrates how the Air Service aviators absorbed the lessons the Europeans had learned.

After building the theoretical foundations for American strategic bombing, chapter four analyzes how men such as Mitchell and

Col. Edgar S. Gorrell attempted to turn theory into workable plans for air campaigns. It delves into Mitchell's vision for American air-power and Colonel Gorrell's bombing plan of November 1917 as the beginning of the attempt to establish a strategic bombing campaign. Despite their efforts, shortcomings in aircraft design and production, along with conflicting leadership visions, forced America's military leaders to shelve their strategic bombing plans until 1919. As a result, the war ended before advocates of strategic bombing could see their plans tested in combat.

Chapter five explores how, with strategic bombing still an untested theory, these advocates kept the concepts alive after the war by incorporating bombing theory into operational manuals and into the official history of the Air Service. Most influential was Gorrell, who, having been appointed AEF Air Service chief of staff, took on the responsibility of completing the official history and used the opportunity to ensure that the core elements of strategic bombing theory survived. The report that resulted conspicuously included a chapter on his strategic bombing plan, along with a survey of Allied bombing efforts against German industry. Together, they would provide future strategists with the background information and statistical data that they needed to support their own concepts. In retrospect, his efforts appear to have been a masterstroke, since the push for the creation of a strategic bombing force was all but abandoned in the military drawdowns and tight budgets of the 1920s.

Chapter six spells out the political factors, economic pressures, and interservice rivalries that shifted American thinking in the early 1920s and pushed strategic bombing out of the military spotlight. The idea of someday establishing a long-range bomber force was still part of the discussion, but with no adversary threatening U.S. security the strategic bombing issue waned and coastal defense became the primary role for America's remaining bombers. Instead Billy Mitchell's fight for Air Service independence took center stage.

Many historians consider the Air Corps Act of 1926 as the turning-point for strategic bombing, contending that the autonomy opened the way for a revival of the plan for a long-range bomber force. Chapter seven argues that this interpretation is misguided. In reality, the concept of strategic bombing was almost entirely absent from

Army policy during the Air Corps era. The lack of adequate budgets, a defensive national security policy, and rapid technological change coalesced to stymie that push for a strategic bombing doctrine. Instead, the Air Corps Act created small, independent planning groups, focused mainly on using bombers in coastal defense. Only in ACTS and the Air Corps Material Division—free from the realities of budgetary and political constraints—were theorists and engineers free to explore how long-range bombing might be used as part of a strategic force. Even so, that was all they needed for the moment. The Air Corps' vision of strategic bombing began to edge back toward center.

Chapter eight completes the book by turning the traditional strategic bombing story line on its head. Where the conventional version of events describes the late 1930s as a period of triumph, it was actually the time of the greatest trial for the strategic bombing concept. With the support of a new chief of staff, the Army refocused on rebuilding its long-standing conventional components, virtually eliminating the primary weapon required for strategic bombing—the heavy bomber. It was only the advent of World War II and the political support of President Franklin D. Roosevelt that saved the day. Luckily for the Air Corps, the men who had developed the concepts behind strategic bombing while assigned to ACTS as middle-grade officers in the early 1930s now stood ready to promote their ideas in this new political environment. In August 1941 a combination of global events, new technology, political support, and a well-prepared staff of military aviation experts helped turn strategic bombing theory into a strategic bombing plan in just nine short days when the men of the Air War Plans Division wrote AWPD-1, the first comprehensive strategic bombing plan for the defeat of Nazi Germany.

Thus, the book traces the history of a technology and a concept. When the United States Army acquired its first airplane it had little inkling of how this new technology would one day challenge the traditional understanding of warfare. As the machinery evolved in both America and across the Atlantic, airplanes sparked the imagination of military thinkers and civilian dreamers alike. During the horror of World War I, airpower promised to break the deadly trench war stalemate through terror bombing and destruction of critical production facilities. Although the war ended before the technology would be able to prove the theory, the concept survived to influence a future generation of aviation leaders—and to become a dominant force in World War II. The process was slow at first, but both the bomber pilots and military aviation leaders proved flexible enough to settle, temporarily, for more acceptable missions—such as coastal defense and hemisphere security—enabling the idea to survive until America once again needed a strategic theory to use in countering a major peer competitor.

While many histories search for simplicity or primary causal factors, this book embraces the complexity of reality. Within the twists and turns of those conflicting priorities and evolutions is a story of technological transformation that turned a new invention into an effective weapon and later into a strategy that forever changed how America exercised its military might.

Aeronautical Division, U.S. Army Signal Corps (1st Aero Squadron—first operational squadron formed March 1913)	August 1907–July 1914
Aviation Section, U.S. Army Signal Corps	July 1914–May 1918
(Air Service, American Expeditionary Forces)	September 1917–May 1919
Air Service, United States Army	May 1918–July 1926
U.S. Army Air Corps	July 1926–June 1941
U.S. Army Air Forces	June 1941–September 1947
United States Air Force	September 1947–present

Author's note: Through the evolution of U.S. airpower from its beginnings in 1907 to the creation of the United States Air Force in 1947, the American military has changed the organizational structure and the name of its major aviation component several times. Here is a list of those names and the dates that they were in effect.

CHAPTER 1

A Late-Night Wake-Up Call in Mexico

It was a cold, brisk spring evening on March 19, 1916 when U.S. Army 1st Lt. Edgar S. Gorrell found himself hopelessly lost in the ever-darkening skies of northern Mexico. It had only been a few hours since his unit, the 1st Aero Squadron, had received orders to deploy to Nueva Casas Grandes as part of a U.S. invasion to punish a band of paramilitary border-raiders led by Mexican brigand Francisco "Pancho" Villa. When the orders arrived, it seemed like a simple task to prepare and fly eight Curtiss JN-3 aircraft the 71 air miles from Columbus, New Mexico. But things started to go awry almost immediately. By the time the pilots took off, the evening sun was already low on the horizon. With only one of the pilots experienced in night flying, the stage was set for a calamity.

Fortunately, the pilots' skills, combined with a considerable measure of luck, enabled them to avoid any fatalities that night. Still, four of the eight aircraft lost sight of the formation and landed on their own in the opaque Mexican desert, with one of the planes damaged beyond repair.[1] First Lieutenant Gorrell had perhaps the worst experience that evening. After attempting to turn back to Columbus, he encountered engine problems in his JN-3 and settled down deep inside enemy territory. He spent the rest of that night wandering around until the combination of money and brandishing his service revolver persuaded a local farmer to help him link up with the nearest American soldiers.

This event forever changed the young lieutenant's mindset. He realized that he had been so focused on joining the Air Service and learning to fly that he had spent little time thinking about the larger state of aviation. What exactly were the roles and missions for aircraft in the Army? How should the aviation section organize itself to conduct those missions? Was the technology now on hand sufficient? These were all questions that he had largely ignored in his zeal to get into aviation. As Gorrell pondered the events of March 19 along with his other experiences in Mexico, he began to question both his own preparedness and that of his squadron for military operations.

Gorrell was not alone in this self-reflection. Newspaper reporting from Mexico indicated that most U.S. pilots had similar concerns. Even the 1st Aero Squadron's commander, then–Capt. Benjamin Foulois, submitted multiple critiques of the equipment, the organization, and the way the squadron was being used during the campaign.[2] In effect, the unit's experience in the Mexican Expedition was proving to be a wake-up call, not only for the Air Service, but also the Signal Corps, the Army leadership, and eventually the U.S. Congress about the problems that America's flying forces were facing on the eve of their entry into World War I.

In some ways, Captain Gorrell's own frustrations before, during, and immediately after the Mexican conflict are a metaphor for the challenges faced by the fledgling Air Service. His reflections provide insights into the thinking, organizational difficulties, and technology problems that were impeding the young aviators. The solutions fashioned by these young men would lay the foundation on which strategic bombing theorists would build after the United States entered World War I in April 1917.

SHAPING THE MAN: WEST POINT TO MEXICO (1912–16)

Edgar Staley Gorrell was born in Baltimore on February 3, 1891. By all accounts, he was a smart, quiet lad with a knack for numbers and a keen sense of exploration. The combination of intelligence and adventurism served him well when he entered Baltimore City College at the tender age of thirteen. Yet, young Gorrell's sense of adventure pushed him toward a military career. In February 1908 he joined the freshman class at the United States Military Academy. Classmates remember him as slender and a bit shy, but they also recalled that he was an avid sportsman and a surprisingly good athlete.

They affectionately called him "Nap," based on his diminutive stature and reticent demeanor. Overall, Gorrell fit nicely into the structured academic and military lifestyle of the Academy. He ended his time at West Point as the captain of a cadet company and graduated in the top third of his class in June 1912.

Perhaps the defining moment of Gorrell's life occurred on May 29, 1910. On that morning, he joined his West Point classmates on a hill overlooking the Hudson River as they waited for aircraft designer and manufacturer Glenn Curtiss to pilot his airplane over the area on a flight from Albany to New York. As the group cheered, Curtiss struggled to keep his plane aloft in the turbulent air over the river valley.[3] Then–Cadet Gorrell stood mesmerized by the spectacle of Curtiss' flight, the longest city-to-city flight recorded so far. The moment captured everything that Gorrell found exciting—the thrill of flying, the adventure of a new frontier, and the technical challenge of aeronautics. From that point on, he was determined to seek a career in aviation.

Army rules then required West Point graduates to serve two years in a combat arms slot before they could transfer to a support branch, so Gorrell's dreams of flying were delayed. He served his first tour of duty with the infantry at Fort Seward, Alaska, where he spent a couple of years as a junior officer in Company L of the 30th Infantry. Then he sought reassignment to the Signal Corps.[4]

His dreams of becoming an Army aviator finally came true with his transfer to the Aviation Section in December 1914. Gorrell arrived at Coronado, California, later that month itching to learn to fly. He joined a growing list of Air Service pioneers who were trained at the military's West Coast center for aviation on North Island, next to Coronado. Gorrell proved to be an avid student and a steady pilot, receiving Expert Pilot License No. 39 in 1915. Later that year, he joined another small, but growing coterie of international aviators who had earned a pilot's license from the Fédération Aéronautique Internationale (FAI).[5]

With his training completed, the Army assigned Gorrell to the 1st Aero Squadron. The unit had started out in September 1914 at North Island, but quickly deployed to Galveston, Texas, as part of the Army's response to the strained relations with Mexico. When border tensions did not explode into fighting in 1915 as strategists had expected, the 1st Aero Squadron moved to Fort Sill, Oklahoma, which offered better flying conditions. Soon after, it received its new Curtiss JN-3 aircraft. To the pilots' disappointment, the JN-3 proved underpowered and difficult to fly. After several accidents—and injuries—many of the artillery officers who had been designated as spotters refused to fly unless "during war and in the case of absolute necessity."[6]

Gorrell entered this atmosphere in November, when he joined the squadron, shortly after it moved from Fort Sill to Fort Sam Houston, near San Antonio. By the time he arrived the unit was hard at work building an airfield and conducting training sessions.[7] But the construction work disrupted the pilots' training schedules, leaving the aviators insufficiently prepared when the conflict along the Mexican border broke out again.

On March 9, 1916, a band of men under the command of Pancho Villa raided Columbus, killing seventeen Americans. The United States responded swiftly by ordering then–Brig. Gen. John J. Pershing to lead a force of 15,000 troops to Mexico to capture or kill Pancho Villa.[8] Pershing took what was then a radical step in planning for the expedition. He decided to use trucks to transport and resupply his combined cavalry and infantry forces. He also tapped the 1st Aero Squadron for an unusual, twofold mission—to help his ground units search the vast desert for Villa's troops, and to maintain communication with fast-moving independent cavalry units.

His rationale for both decisions made sense. Unlike many areas where the U.S. Army had fought recently, northern Mexico lacked any major railroad lines that might have been commandeered for military use; trucks were a natural subsitute. And for reconnaissance and communication, aircraft would enable the Army to operate at speeds and distances well beyond what his cavalry units could achieve. The airplanes not only could search for Mexican bandits, they could also locate the kind of fast-moving U.S. Army columns that were operating independently along the border. When they did, the pilots could land with urgent messages from the expedition commander and return with up-to-date reports from the field. The system promised an effective backup for wireless sets, which often proved unreliable in the cold, wet conditions of the Sierra Madre mountains.

The day after the Pancho Villa raid, then–Captain Benjamin Foulois, the 1st Aero Squadron's commander, received word that his unit would join Pershing's expedition.[9] Foulois was well aware that his squadron was underprepared for the harsh terrain in which it would operate, but he also knew that this was an important time to prove the worth of airpower in combat conditions. To deploy the aircraft, to operate from remote locations, and—most important—to keep the squadron supplied would be a monumental task. Luckily Foulois had Gorrell as his adjutant and supply officer. Between March 10 and 12, Gorrell oversaw the acquisition of nineteen thousand dollars' worth of parts and ten new trucks to haul the unit's men and equipment. The trucks included seven new Jeffrey "Quad" one-and-a-half-ton, four-wheel-drive trucks, and three others leased from local businesses in San Antonio.[10] This proved fortuitous. The 1st Aero would arrive in theater as the only American unit fully mechanized. It not only had the aircraft, but also the trucks needed to transport the fuel, equipment, and personnel that would be required to keep the airplanes flying.

Gorrell completed the preparations in just two short days. When the orders finally arrived, on March 12, 1916, the squadron left by rail for Columbus, with eight aircraft, eleven officers, eighty-two enlisted men, and ten trucks.[11] By the time the unit got to Columbus, on the fifteenth, however, the ground forces had already left for Mexico. The late arrival meant that Foulois could not coordinate his unit's initial flights directly with the ground column commanders. Yet, it did not hinder the 1st Aero for long. The squadron immediately uncrated its aircraft and made ready for support missions. Just a day later, on March 17, the group flew its first combat observation mission, confirming that there were no enemy forces near the advancing American cavalry formations.

The 1st Aero Squadron's early contributions were not just in the air. Logistics problems plagued Pershing as he hunted for Villa. The trucks that Gorrell had bought before leaving San Antonio ended up being a rare commodity in the confusion of the expedition's advance. Gorrell often drew double duty, flying on one day and commanding truck convoys on another. On March 15, for example, he led a truck convoy assigned to carry replacement officers and supplies to Las Palomas, Mexico. "What an experience it was, driving this original truck train into unfriendly territory, with a guard consisting of airplane mechanics," he said, recalling the day in an article later.[12] Yet, once again, the 1st Aero was splitting its duties at a time when it should have been focusing on its primary mission of flying. Why were untrained mechanics serving as convoy security? Why were qualified pilots—an extremely rare quantity then—traipsing around the desert leading truck convoys? These distractions almost certainly played a role in the troubles that beset Gorrell and the squadron. They also underscored the inadequacy of the command structure, the doctrine, and the technology of the squadron and of the fledgling Army Air Service.

SHAPING THE AIR SERVICE

The problems facing Gorrell and his fellow pilots in Mexico were not sudden developments. They stemmed from a long string of decisions made at many levels. As aviation became more widely accepted in the Army, it found itself shaped by myriad political, economic, and service-culture issues.

Although the Wright brothers, Wilbur and Orville, made their first successful fight on December 17, 1903, the Army, cautious and parsimonious, did not buy a plane until August 2, 1909, after the Wrights completed two trial flights and received approval from a specially convened Board of Officers.[13] Even then, the aviation program remained experimental and underfunded for years before it was granted operational status. Indeed, the birth and infancy of military aviation displayed a long, almost-flat trajectory from roughly 1903 until 1912, when the Army formally established a command structure, a staff, and a training school for the air component.

During this period, both the Army and Congress made important decisions—primarily in funding, technology, and organizational structure—that proved instrumental in shaping military aviation. Not all of these choices were military-related, yet together they would set the parameters for the early Air Service and have long-lasting effects.

Perhaps the greatest issue was funding. Partly because of the low level of military spending in general, the aviation component had suffered a budgetary squeeze from the start. Yet other factors also played important roles. Most notable was the public outrage that followed the failure of a costly attempt by the Smithsonian Institution to develop a heavier-than-air flying machine. In 1898 the War Department granted $50,000 to Samuel P. Langley, the institution's secretary, to design and build a workable model, but the prototype, which Langley had dubbed the "Great Aerodrome," crashed into the Potomac River twice and never achieved what the secretary had promised. The flop sparked a backlash in newspapers and set Congress to questioning how the Army could spend so much for such a disappointing result. After that, Army leaders were reluctant to seek any more funding for aviation research. Instead, the cost of developing new aviation technology would have to be financed indirectly by individual Air Service units or be borne by private aircraft builders.

The burden on individual aviators in the wake of the Langley fiasco was almost laughable by today's standards—reflecting the Army's refusal to seek special funding for experimental aviation programs. For example, after the government accepted the Wright Model B biplane, the Army tasked a lone Signal Corps officer, then–Lieutenant Foulois, to take the aircraft, along with eight enlisted mechanics and one hundred fifty dollars, to San Antonio and "teach yourself to fly and evaluate the military possibilities of aviation."[14] The reason for the unusual assignment was simple: the Army had no money to pay aviators or test aircraft. Foulois' unit got its funding from the Signal Corps budget—or the part of it that was left over after the branch had paid for its normal communications support activities. So branch commanders were pressed to use some of any surpluses to pay for aircraft testing and training.

As Foulois continued to make strides in Texas, aviation began to win some converts within the Signal Corps leadership. Brig. Gen. James Allen, the chief signal officer, requested $200,000 for aviation in both 1910 and 1911, including the purchase of twenty new aircraft. There also was increasing public support for military aviation, spurred by growing numbers of aircraft enthusiasts across the

country. Yet Congress continued to balk at allocating funds specifically for aviation, continuing to finance aeronautics through the Signal
Corps' general operating account of $250,000 a year.[15] Just as much as
the Army's budget policies, the lawmakers' approach slowed progress
and fostered the perception of aviation as the realm of tinkerers and
experimenters—at least for the time being.

The budget problems also exacerbated another dilemma for the
early air service: how to improve current technology. With barely
enough money available to keep aircraft flying, Army planners gave
little thought of improving aircraft design for military use. Instead, technological change came through trial and error, as mechanics and pilots
in the field suggested modifications that they could make on their
own to improve their ability to train and take part in public demon-
strations. Foulois' own memoir describes one of these do-it-yourself
opportunities. Almost immediately after arriving in San Antonio, he
decided that the catapult sled launching system for the Wright brothers' airplane was hindering his ability to choose where to take off and
land. Foulois wanted to replace the catapult with a mechanism that
would enable him to operate from any level field. Working feverishly,
he devised a tricycle landing gear that would alleviate the need to
reposition the catapult ramp for each flight. But he had long ago spent
his one-hundred-fifty-dollar budget on replacement parts for several
earlier accidents.[16] So he was forced to delay the improvement until
after the Signal Corps made additional funds available.

Finally, the treatment of aviation as a low-budget experiment
created organizational and staffing issues that hindered early aviation
operations. Not only did the Signal Corps have only a tiny budget to
share, it was also a relatively small branch itself within the Army. In
1908 the Corps consisted of only 118 officers, who were assigned to
filling staff billets in Washington, carrying out activities at all major
Army bases, and conducting day-to-day operations in three field
companies.[17]

With no surplus manpower to tap, the Signal Corps had to look to
other branches to provide pilots, most of them lent under temporary
duty assignments. But the shortcomings of the system became apparently almost immediately with 1st Lts. Frank P. Lahm and Frederic

E. Humphreys, the first two Army pilots to be trained by the Wright brothers. The two underwent training from Wilbur Wright in October and November 1909, but as soon as they had completed the assignment they were pulled back by their own branches—the Corps of Engineers in the case of Lieutenant Humphreys and the Cavalry for Lieutenant Lahm, who had been a highly experienced airship pilot and was now an airplane pilot.[18] Their departure left the Signal Corps with no trained pilots for its only aircraft, resulting in the unusual set of orders to Foulois to take the aircraft and one hundred fifty dollars to San Antonio and "teach yourself to fly."

Still, by the end of 1911, Foulois' work in Texas was starting to pay dividends. His aerial feats had helped fuel public fascination with flying, which meant more money for aviation in the larger intraservice budget battles. On March 3, 1912 the annual War Department appropriation bill included its first allocation for aviation, totaling $125,000, of which $25,000 was made available immediately for the purchase of two new aircraft.[19] Between 1912 and 1916 military aviation in the United States grew at an exponential rate, both in numbers and in capabilities. The money also financed technological improvements.

The new funding also created both strategic and tactical advances. First, the Signal Corps bought two new aircraft from different builders—a Wright Model B and a Curtiss Model D—a step that introduced the first cross-pollination of aircraft design into Army procurement. Next, the Signal Corps began to experiment with onboard technological advances that paved the way for improved aviation capabilities in future designs. Foulois later described some of these advances, citing 1914 as a year of experimentation. He recalled how pilots in the newly formed 1st Aero Squadron broke new ground by equipping aircraft with wireless telegraphs, cameras, machine guns, and primitive bombs.[20] And as the young pilots gained more flight time, they began to think about still more new ways to use aircraft as weapons.

Improved funding also gave military authorities the ability to improve the organizational structure for Army aviation. Buying more new aircraft meant training more pilots to operate them. That required special units to plan and carrying out pilot training, supervise the acquisition of more aircraft, and supply the equipment needed to operate them. The first step was to create a staff office within the Signal Corps to oversee the growth of Army aviation. The Corps' new Aeronautical Division began as a three-person staff in 1907. Within five years it had expanded to take over the management of the branch's fifty-one personnel and $125,000 aviation budget.

The next step was to organize a system to recruit and train the rapidly growing numbers of pilots. The Signal Corps had established a flight training school at College Park, Maryland, and recruiting had proven fairly easy; by this time, the War Department already had collected a number of applications from eager officers who wanted to become aviators. What was missing was a formal scheme for training pilots. With that in mind, the school's new commander, Capt. Charles deForest Chandler, put together a training syllabus designed to ensure that aviation candidates would learn the prerequisite skills. The result was a program that required pilots to qualify for the Fédération Aéronautique Internationale certification before they would be awarded their Army wings.[21] The requirement served as the bedrock of pilot training as the school moved first to Augusta, Georgia, and then to North Island, near San Diego, which offered more advantageous flying weather.

As the flight school settled into daily operations, it also became a crucible for new ideas and experimentation. As early as the fall of 1911 the school began to participate in technology development. One of the most interesting experiments, in October 1911, involved the testing of a new bombsight by the Coastal Artillery Command. At the suggestion of a lieutenant named Riley E. Scott, the school mounted a 64-pound telescopic device on one of its Wright Model B aircraft and conducted multiple drops of two eighteen-pound bombs to test the accuracy of the bombsight.[22] Although the equipment showed that achieving bombing accuracy would require much more work, it also demonstrated how the Corps' new aviation component was already thinking about operational requirements. This mindset continued in 1914 through further trials of airborne cameras, wireless sets, and machine guns.

Aviation also showed its potential value during operational maneuvers. A detachment from the flight school made an impression on senior leaders during maneuvers in Connecticut in July and August of 1912. Foulois led seven pilots and four aircraft from College Park to the maneuvers. His own words best describe the effect of the mission: "We proved that airplanes could replace the cavalry and could prevent surprise mass attacks by providing information on enemy troop buildups and movements much faster than ever before."[23] While Foulois' own recollections of the event may not have been the accepted Army position on aviation, the participation in maneuvers like these opened the eyes of many senior leaders to the possibilities of aircraft as a military tool.

By 1914 both Congress and the Signal Corps realized that military aviation needed its own place in the Army's organization and a dedicated budget and manpower allocation to go with it. On July 18, Congress passed House Resolution 5304, "An Act to Increase the Efficiency of the Aviation Section of the Army," which provided all that and created a formal staff component within the Signal Corps to manage it.[24] The legislation also spurred other changes within the Army. With a permanent budget now in place, the Signal Corps determined it was time for an operational aviation unit dedicated to preparing for military operations. On August 5, Signal Corps General Order No. 10 created the 1st Aero Squadron, with Foulois as its commander.[25]

Taken together these two developments marked a great leap forward for military aviation. The guaranteed funding meant that Army aviation leaders could now make medium-term plans with some semblance of stability. Although some argued that the dollar amounts were still insufficient, aviation activities no longer had to depend on leftover funds from whatever surpluses the Signal Corps accumulated. The creation of a staff, training school, and operations component enabled leaders to refine aviation doctrine and prepare pilots and equipment for combat. Finally, the combination of funding and organization helped create a system for properly testing and acquiring new airframes and equipment for the fledgling service. Although the U.S. Aviation Section still was small compared to that of European nations, it now contained all the required elements needed to prepare for combat.

Even with these dramatic changes, problems remained. Contained within the law were the kernels of new difficulties that the 1st Aero Squadron would face in Mexico and during the buildup of the

American Expeditionary Force Air Service in World War I. The first involved personnel policies. From the beginning aviation was regarded as the realm of youth. This played a large part in the Army's initial policy of only providing flight training to junior officers who were assigned to temporary duty. H.R. 5304 codified this policy into law by limiting assignment to the Aviation Section to unmarried lieutenants under thirty years old. Foulois describes the unintended consequence: "[t]he result was that the section was being filled with young, inexperienced second lieutenants, leaving no one with age and experience to command an aviation organization."[26]

In practice, the personnel policy spawned two other problems: First, it forced the Army to fill the operational commands at the training school and the 1st Aero Squadron with junior officers who lacked the experience that an equivalent commander in the more-robust infantry, artillery, or cavalry would have gained at that point in his career. As commander of the 1st Aero Squadron, for example, Foulois had never been assigned to a general staff post—a tour that would have helped him acquire more planning and coordination skills before he was deployed to Mexico. Second, the policy helped foster a bias against placing non-aviators in command of aviation organizations. In an interesting irony, Foulois complained in 1916 that the choice of Billy Mitchell, a longtime staff officer and then a major, to replace veteran pilot Col. Samuel Reber as head of the Aviation Section on grounds that Mitchell did not have operational experience in solving the practical problems that aviators faced. (Mitchell later would voice similar objections about naming non-aviators to command positions when an Army engineer, Maj. Gen. Patrick Mason, was selected by Pershing, his former classmate, to command the AEF Air Service in May 1918.)

Second, by creating a separate identity for military aviation, the new personnel policies reinforced the elitist cultural attitudes that encouraged pilots to believe they were different from traditional Army officers. To them, their world was special, filled with daredevil feats and danger. Congress bolstered this attitude when it awarded pilots a 50 percent pay increase for the months they were assigned to flying duty. It was a mixed blessing. On one hand, the sense of individuality bred a willingness to innovate that served the air arm well in later years. When young pilots were faced with troubling situations, they often turned to innovative technology or else devised new strategies to overcome them.

At the same time, the creation of a separate aviation component would intensify a third problem: the difficulty of integrating aviation operations with the rest of the Army. The distinct aviation culture, combined with the fact that so many aviators held junior ranks, impeded coordination between the Aviation Section and other commands. Meanwhile, commanders of ground forces too often did not understand what aircraft could do for their troops. Misperception of aviation's capabilities and roles abounded. The disparity resulted in poor cooperation between the air and ground components that often led to operational problems for the pilots.

Some of this was evident in the immediate runup to the Mexican Expedition. Gorrell's own writing describes a shortage of flight training in Texas because the 1st Aero Squadron was occupied with building its own living quarters, operational buildings, and maintenance structures.[27] Interstaff coordination could have alleviated the situation, but the combination of separate command chains, different cultures, and split operations ended up limiting cooperation. When it came to operations, many field commanders lacked any understanding of how to use aircraft properly, while the junior aviators did not have either the rank or the doctrinal backing to advise those commanders on the use of airpower in their ground tactics. One saving grace was that pilots deployed to the Mexican Expedition were young and open to new ideas.

THE WAKE-UP CALL

Flight training, administrative duties, and social obligations had filled Gorrell's military aviation career before Mexico. His busy schedule left the young pilot with little time to concentrate on policy or doctrinal issues. Even when the 1st Aero Squadron prepared to deploy to Mexico, he was so busy with supply duties, convoy commander missions, and training that he had little time to think about anything else. That all began to change in March 1916, when the squadron began flying

combat missions. Gorrell and the other pilots soon became dissatisfied with both their aircraft and the missions they were assigned.
While ordinarily such grumblings might have been kept within the
squadron, they eventually made their way to the halls of power in
Washington via the national newspaper reporters who were traveling
with the new aviation squadron. Thus, Mexico served as an warning-
bell, not only for the pilots, but also for senior leaders, about the poor
state of preparedness in military aviation.

The alarm first rang on March 19, 1916, when the 1st Aero
Squadron received orders to deploy to Nueva Casas Grandes. Anxious
to complete the move that night and resume observation missions the
next morning, Foulois ill-advisedly ordered his pilots to fly to Nueva
Casas Grandes that day while the enlisted men packed the trucks and
drove overnight to meet them. But the plan almost ended in disaster.
With both the captain and his squadron so inexperienced, both flight
planning and equipment packing took much longer than expected.
The pilots did not leave Columbus until 5:10 p.m., meaning they
were forced to fly much of the mission after dark. Although a few of
the aviators had done some night flying, none had done so for long
distances over sparsely inhabited territory.

For Gorrell, the flight to Nueva Casas Grandes became another
life-changing event. Weighed down with fuel and personal baggage,
his aircraft barely cleared a fence at the end of the field.[28] As darkness fell, he lost sight of the other aviators in his formation. He
tried to navigate alone, but became hopelessly lost over the darkened
desert. When he realized his predicament, he turned back north to
return to Columbus, but his JN-3 had reached its limits. When the
engine started to overheat, he made a forced landing inside enemy-
controlled territory. Realizing his extremely dangerous position, he
gathered up a pistol and a few supplies and headed into the desert.
He spent the rest of the night in the wilderness until just before
dawn, when he happened upon a Mexican national. Gorrell used
his weapon and eight dollars in silver coins to persuade the reluctant
man to lead him back to American forces. After an arduous trip, he
finally made it back to the squadron on March 23, bedraggled and
the worse for wear.[29]

The Nueva Casa Grandes fiasco was not the only incident that demonstrated how badly prepared military aviation was at the time. It was the first of a series. Problems involving technology, planning, and doctrine surfaced increasingly as the squadron flew more hours and embarked on more difficult missions. As before, the independent and resourceful aviators often developed work-around fixes, but in the end the complications were visible not only to the Army but to the public and political leadership.

For the 1st Aero Squadron technology was a problem almost from the beginning. Although the Curtiss JN-3 proved adequate for training, the air operations in Mexico—particularly in the Sierra Madre mountains—revealed its true limitations. Pilots discovered that the aircraft, hampered by low power and unable to fly very high when fully loaded with fuel and equipment, could not clear the ten-thousand-foot ridgelines. To make matters worse, the JN-3 proved difficult to control in the high winds and snow. On March 22, 1916 Foulois sent a memorandum to the chief of the Aeronautical Division in Washington asserting that the present model JN-3 was incapable of meeting mission requirements. He already had lost two of his eight aircraft in crashes, so when he asked for replacements this time he recommended that the Army buy new aircraft from five different companies—two each from Martin, Curtiss, Sturtevant, Thomas, and Sloane.[30] Unfortunately the Signal Corps was not set up to buy and deploy airplanes rapidly, and Foulois had to sustain operations as best he could.

The squadron continued to lose aircraft to accidents through the end of March and into April, and by April 20 it was down to just two functioning JN-3s. Two days later, Pershing ordered the 1st Aero back to Columbus to refit and receive new equipment. Waiting for them when they arrived was the first of twelve new JN-4 aircraft, part of the Army's 1916 purchase of ninety-four such planes that it had ordered for the air service. But that, too, went awry. During flight testing, the men of the squadron disliked the JN-4 so much that Foulois complained directly to Maj. Gen. Frederick Funston, commander of the Army's Southern Department. Funston in turn interceded with Secretary of War Newton Baker, and the Army withdrew the JN-4s and replaced them with the 160-horsepower Curtiss R-2s, equipped with machine guns and bomb racks. Still, this took time, and the first two Curtiss aircraft did not arrive until May 1. Even then, teething problems with the propeller required additional delays as squadron mechanics developed a way to build propellers that would be able to operate in dry desert climates.[31] The delays effectively ended the squadron's operational role in the Mexican Expedition.

The 1st Aero Squadron's problems went beyond just the aircraft. It also was hampered by Army doctrine, which seemed to exhibit no understanding of how to use aviation in concert with ground forces. Initially Pershing had seen two roles for his aviation squadron: reconnaissance and communications. Not only could the aircraft search for Villa's forces, but they also could locate independently operating U.S. columns and deliver orders from the commander. It was a reasonable approach, not only to Pershing but also to Foulois, who voiced support for the plan. Yet, because the squadron's JN-3 aircraft demonstrated difficulty with reconnaissance missions in the Sierra Madres, it was increasingly relegated to simple courier duty. During the heart of the expedition from March 26 to April 4, the squadron flew seventy-nine missions carrying mail and dispatches along Pershing's line of advance and only two reconnaissance missions.[32]

The operational imbalance drew additional complaints from many of the pilots. Not only were they risking their lives flying underperforming JN-3 aircraft, but the vast majority of their efforts were spent delivering mail. Foulois addressed the issue in his summary report of August 28, 1916. One of his recommendations was to confine flight duties to military applications and avoid risking the lost of aircraft and flight time on routine missions that could be better carried out by trucks or other ground transport.[33]

Such complaints might not have created a call for change outside the squadron had it not been for the work of newspaper reporters attached to the expedition. On April 3, 1916, an article in Joseph Pulitzer's *New York World* claimed that several pilots had complained to reporters about airplane deficiencies and poor Signal Corps oversight of aviation.[34] Almost immediately, a backlash occurred in the Army leadership. Who were these young, brash pilots questioning Army and Signal Corps leadership, especially in the open press?

The Army launched an investigation into the matter and sent officers to interview the men of the 1st Aero Squadron. Most pilots denied talking to reporters, but Gorrell admitted that he had discussed "foreign aviators, the lack of engine power in the aeroplanes of the First [Squadron], and military aeroplanes, past and present" with the reporter, Webb Miller.[35]

Interestingly this admission did not hurt Gorrell's standing or career. Despite the initial anger at the newspaper article most Army leaders, especially Pershing, recognized the value of aerial observation and were aware of the technical and logistics problems the infant branch faced. In this environment Gorrell's criticisms became a rallying cry for more investment in the air service rather than a black mark on his record.

Despite the best efforts of the 1st Aero Squadron, Pershing could not locate and capture Pancho Villa. Still the squadron's pilots accomplished much in this early test of airpower. They flew five hundred forty missions, greatly aiding in intelligence gathering and facilitating communications between Pershing's often widely separated forces.[36] The expedition also wakened the American public and its leaders to the overall weakness of the nation's aviation forces. With the European war threatening to draw in the United States, Congress acted to bolster the armed services. In June 1916, it took the first step, with the National Defense Act. In addition to other funding increases, the act provided thirteen million dollars to expand the Army Air Service to eight squadrons and to buy more capable aircraft.[37] Although this was still a drop in the bucket compared to what the military would need in World War I it was a timely step in preparing the nation for war.

EDUCATION AND PREPARATION

The Mexican Expedition also led to internal changes in the air service. The Signal Corps' leaders decided they needed to build the novice Aviation Section on the Army's traditional branch model. This required them to recruit talent from within their own ranks and provide younger officers with the experience they would need to guide the new Air Service. The Signal Corps began focusing on educating its officers and developing doctrine on how to use military airpower.

One of the key beneficiaries of this new focus was Gorrell. On a personal level, he emerged from the Mexican Expedition with a heightened reputation. He had become a recognized figure in the Air Service, the Signal Corps, and the Army as a whole. Gorrell was not just a talented flyer, but also a keen intellect, a proficient planner, and a technical expert. Even if he had a reputation for being too candid, his skills outweighed the negatives. In what became his third life-changing event, the Army rewarded these attributes with an assignment to the Massachusetts Institute of Technology (MIT), where Gorrell pursued a master's degree in aeronautical engineering.

MIT had a long history in aeronautical research that both the Army and Navy supported with funding and students. Six years before the Wright brothers' pioneering flight, MIT built its first wind tunnel as part of a student thesis. Still, it was not until 1909 that the school's aeronautical engineering program truly started to expand. That year, a U.S. Naval Academy graduate, Ens. Jerome C. Hunsaker, enrolled at MIT. Ensign Hunsaker applied his passion for aviation to his studies in engineering. By the summer of 1913, he had helped create the core of an aeronautics program at MIT. This program blossomed into a government-funded endeavor when Hunsaker and Donald Douglas built a permanent research wind tunnel in 1914, the first structure on MIT's new Cambridge campus.[38]

Gorrell entered this new program in September 1916 and once again proved a stellar performer. Detached from military operations, Gorrell focused his attention on the science behind flying. His graduate thesis, "Aerofoils and Aerofoil Structural Combination," became a noted pioneering work in the field, receiving accolades from military, industrial, and academic sources.[39] By June 1917, only two months after the United States entered World War I, Gorrell had graduated with a Master of Science degree and returned to the Army as a captain with an assignment to the chief signal officer's staff.[40] His job on the staff was to recommend the operational structure and technology that would be required for the Air Service if the United States entered World War I. Members of the staff remember Gorrell spending his days working out personnel, aircraft, and budget requirements on large sheets of wrapping paper spread out on the floor of his office.[41]

These calculations became the core of the original appropriations for U.S. military aviation in World War I.

Gorrell also played a major role in overcoming the second short-coming that emerged from the conflict in Mexico: the need to develop a doctrine for military aviation—a plan that would set down the most effective way to use military aircraft in combat operations. Luckily Gorrell and other U.S. planners had the perfect laboratory for discovering what worked and what would not work in military aviation—the war in Europe. From the outbreak of hostilities the American Army received steady reports on the growing importance of aviation in the European war effort. The Signal Corps' 1915 annual report included information on the air war and demonstrated how it already had influenced operational thinking. The report described how airplanes were proving their value in reconnaissance and artillery fire-control. And it chronicled the growing importance of a new type of aircraft, a combat machine that could be used in both a pursuit and a bombing role.[42] Yet, at this early stage in the war the Americans were focusing less on technology than on planning and funding. As a result the report's conclusions emphasized the additional monies that the Air Service would need should the United States enter the war—not on the types of aircraft and missions that it would fly.

After the experience in Mexico, the focus began to shift. Although cost was still the Army's primary concern, there was a greater appreciation for planning and operational lessons. The Signal Corps sent observers to Europe to garner as much as possible from the British, French, and Italian air services. The most famous of these observers was then–Colonel Billy Mitchell, who left for Europe on March 17, 1917 with orders to investigate what was being done in French aviation. When Colonel Mitchell arrived in Europe, he discovered that the United States was now an active participant in the conflict, having declared war on April 6. Invigorated, he toured French factories and aeronautical schools and even flew over the front with French pilots.

Mitchell's most dramatic experience occurred when he visited the headquarters of Maj. Gen. Hugh Trenchard, commander of the Royal Flying Corps (RFC). Mitchell arrived during one of the many mini-crises that often beset a combat command headquarters. When

Trenchard's aide tried to reschedule the visit, Mitchell complained vociferously. When the RFC commander came out of his office to see what the noise was about, Mitchell blurted out that he would "like to see your equipment, your stores, and the way you arrange your system of supply. Also, I need to know all you can tell me about operations, because we will be joining you in these before long."[43] Luckily, the usually quick-tempered Trenchard found the American's impudence charming and coordinated a three-day demonstration of the RFC's training, supply, and flying operations. The results led Mitchell to prepare a memorandum for the soon-to-arrive Pershing, describing his concept for the organization and the creation of American Expeditionary Force (AEF) air service.

While Mitchell was developing these concepts, Gorrell participated in another study group that was tasked with learning from European examples, deciding which technology was worth pursuing, and securing the initial support agreements from the allied nations. The group, led by U.S. Colonel Raynal Bolling, included Gorrell and played a key role in the development of American strategic bombing theory. As the two Americans met with their British, French, and Italian counterparts they developed an appreciation of the airpower theories propagated by each nation. The summer of 1917 became a period of intensive learning, thinking, and strategy development for the small, but important band of American aviators in Paris.

With this broad experience behind him, Gorrell became the model for the new breed of aviator the Air Service needed as the United States entered World War I. He had grown not just into a steady pilot but also a proven academic, a gifted planner, and a talented logistician. The transition had not occurred overnight, but rather was a gradual move from the adventure-seeking young cadet to the open-minded military expert who was ready to make his mark. Key moments along the way shaped Gorrell and prepared him for the great challenges that lay ahead. West Point taught him discipline, but it also kept his sense of adventure alive. Aviation focused that pioneering sense toward a new military specialty that offered great possibilities. His experiences in Mexico tempered his adventurism and taught him skills in the more mundane, but equally important areas of logistics, engineering, and planning. Perhaps even more important, his Mexico stint taught Gorrell to think for himself and to remain open to new ideas and concepts. Finally, MIT cemented his professional credentials. In this way, Gorrell emerged as a model of the combination of aviator, engineer, and planner that the Army needed to prepare its Aviation Section for entry into the war in Europe.

CONCLUSION

Although most people probably do not think of 1903 to 1916 as a formative time for U.S. strategic bombing theory, the era was remarkably important. The early stage laid the technical, organizational, and doctrinal foundations on which air strategists built when the United States entered World War I. Like any other foundation, this one had advantages in some areas and limitations in others.

With regard to technology, the era was a mixed bag. Funding problems delayed both the acquisition of new aircraft and the modification of designs to meet military needs. This led to a weak aircraft industry and a military aviation procurement system that proved to be severely overtaxed when asked to produce large numbers of more capable aircraft. Even after 1916, when funding was no longer an issue, problems with aircraft production remained. Military aviation clearly felt the impact of this lost opportunity. Aircraft producers simply could not ramp up production fast enough to fill the growing Air Service requirements of World War I. As a result, Army leaders had to choose which types of aircraft to build first. They gave observation and pursuit aircraft the highest priority; bomber production remained low until 1918.

Organizational overhaul fared better. The era saw the formation of an aviation staff and command structure capable of growing as the Air Service expanded in World War I. More important, the experience in Mexico convinced the Signal Corps to develop its own expertise to manage the structure. When the United States finally did enter World War I, a core of experienced and educated pilots was ready to expand the fledgling service—in size, capabilities, and strategy. Gorrell was a perfect example of this newly minted scholar aviator. Given a baptism of fire in Mexico, shaped by MIT, and finally polished on the general staff, he represented an ideal officer, learning from the Europeans and helping to craft an American vision of aerial warfare.

Finally, the development of a doctrine during those years was a small, but important early step in the formation of American military aviation thought. The experience in Mexico forced the Army to recognize that a well-thought-out concept of how aircraft could be used in combat was the core building block of airplane design, organizational structure, and operational integration. No longer sidetracked by the need to fight for funding, the young aviators turned for inspiration to the great air war being fought over Europe. Just as the air war itself was evolving at a lightning pace, so too did the appreciation of strategy in the newly minted AEF Air Service. As the first officers arrived on the Continent, they experienced a learning curve akin to drinking from a fire hose. Yet, in a handful of key American theorists this overwhelming situation produced new strategic insights.

In this way, the early aviation era and the Mexican Expedition in particular were critical events in the development of strategic bombing theory. The era is best summed up as a long, slow period of initial learning, followed by a wake-up call about the poor state of American military aviation, which in turn spawned a brief, but important period of sharp growth. This scenario did not evolve from a planned strategy. Instead, it resulted from the combination of internal and external decisions that shaped the very nature of aviation, the Signal Corps, and the Air Service. The decisions often had lasting effects—if not always those for which policymakers had hoped—as the American flyers entered the Great War.

CHAPTER 2

The War in Europe

The development of military aviation in the United States and Europe followed similar paths in the early part of the twentieth century and revolved around the same three issues—technology, organization, and doctrine. But the pace at which the new warfighting component advanced on each side of the Atlantic differed dramatically, primarily because of geopolitical factors. The United States, protected by two oceans, took a much slower and less costly approach, focusing on improving technology rather than acquiring aircraft, building an organization, or drafting doctrine.

By contrast, the Europeans, alarmed by mounting hostilities only a short flight away from their respective homelands, moved more rapidly in these other areas. Both government and military leaders in Europe recognized that conflict was imminent and expected from the start that aviation would be playing a major role. Although the response differed from country to country, Europe's early acceptance of aviation as a military weapon instilled new thinking that soon shifted the Continent to a different course.

Yet, the Europeans fell short in dealing with technology development and organizational challenges. At the start of the war, most European militaries had adequate aircraft inventories and organizational structures to support the limited use of aviation for observation missions, but they lacked long-range bombers and agile pursuit aircraft. The onset of actual air combat rapidly altered their outlook. By 1916, technology and command structures in Europe had begun to catch up, and the next year all three elements of airpower—technology, organization, and doctrine—were largely in place. All that was needed to broaden the use of military aviation beyond mere support of ground and naval forces was political commitment. Into the middle of this dramatic period the first American aviators arrived in the late spring of 1917, eager and ready to learn.

STRATEGIC BOMBING: THE CONCEPT

The notion of strategic bombing originated long before the outbreak of World War I. Both Europeans and Americans had been entertaining images of aerial bombardment since the first balloon flights in the late eighteenth century. As the historian L. T. C. Rolt pointed out, although the most obvious use for military balloons was for surveillance, growing numbers of early airpower theorists had envisioned airships flying over enemy cities and dropping bombs on the civilian population.[1] Still, it was not until the turn of the twentieth century that strategic bombing finally caught the public's attention, and that was largely through the work of popular novelists.

Authors such as Jules Verne, H. G. Wells, and R. P. Hearne excelled at playing on the fears of the time. Verne's 1893 novel, *Clipper and the Clouds*, depicted a mysterious aviator named Robur using a zeppelin-like airship to influence national leaders. While Verne's work left room for interpretation, Wells' 1908 *The War in the Air* was more direct. Wells wrote about a fictional massive German aerial flotilla destroying New York in a surprise bombing attack. Despite Verne's and Wells' fame, perhaps the most influential of the three was Hearne's 1909 *Aerial Warfare*. In this analytic evaluation of airpower, Hearne claimed that all of Britain was at the mercy of German zeppelins. Hearne's warning soon became widely accepted in the public and government ministries. Historian John Morrow even credits Hearne with turning a general fascination with bombing into a full-fledged airship scare that lasted well into World War I.[2]

Although the futuristic literature may have generated a sizable readership and instilled fear in the public, the reality was that current aviation technology then could never fulfill the visions of the early authors. Even Hearne's clarion call lacked any evidence that Germany might be able to carry out the destruction that he depicted. In the end, though, it did not matter; fear overcame rational thought. Public anxiety created pressures that both excited and frightened military professionals. The German ballooning authority H. W. L. Moedebeck best described this disconnect in an 1886 paper on the value of bombing, asserting that "while the physical effects of bombing were almost nil, it undoubtedly produces a depressing effect to have things dropped on one from above."[3] In that simple statement, Moedebeck captured the dichotomy of early strategic bombing. The current technology promised little in actual physical destruction, yet the psychological fear of bombing raids was a primal force in creating public pressure.

The trepidation eventually worked its way into the thinking of government leaders. Initially, they tried to control the threat through international accords. In the Hague Conference of 1899, the European governments agreed to prohibit the discharge of any projectiles from balloons or similar devices for five years.[4] Yet, international agreements could not stop technological advances. As heavier-than-air flight became a reality, European militaries began to see the value of airplanes in their arsenals.

By the time the prohibition on bombing came up for renewal at the Hague Conference of 1907, a great deal had changed. The majority of European countries refused to renew the articles. Their decision was based on one of three rationales. First, the newly invented airplane showed frighteningly strong potential as a military weapon. Although no country had plans for a bomber force at this early stage, none of them wanted to forgo the advantages that airplanes might provide in future years. Second, most countries expected to use aircraft, both lighter and heavier than air, at least as observation platforms. Surely any enemy would defend itself against this threat with antiaircraft fire. If pilots were fired upon from the ground, should they not be able to fire back? Extending the 1899 agreement would have prohibited that. Finally, all agreed that restrictions then in place on assaulting undefended cities already applied to aircraft as well as artillery, so technically there was no need to limit airplanes and zeppelins specifically.[5]

The catalyst for this major shift in international public opinion proved to be the stunning advances in aviation technology that captured the public's imagination during the decade. On October 23, 1906, Brazilian aviator Alberto Santos-Dumont made the first fully powered takeoff and landing in a heavier-than-air aircraft in Europe—a success that prompted British newspaper magnate Alfred Lord Northcliffe to declare that England was "no longer an island" now that airplanes had come of age. On July 1, 1908, Count Ferdinand von Zeppelin completed a record twelve-hour flight in a balloon that gave people a glimpse of the possibilities of long-range aviation and created both excitement and apprehension throughout Europe.[6] Both the public and key politicians now regarded military aviation as a potential terror, capable of threatening their peaceful lives miles behind the front lines. For their part, military professionals saw it as an effective means of destroying distant industrial and political centers.

How each country viewed the possibilities depended on its particular circumstances. In Germany, long-range aviation offered a means to attack directly the previously untouchable British homeland. That bolstered growing German nationalism, which saw zeppelins as a symbol of German power. The heightened self-confidence carried over to the Germans' international negotiations. At the May 1910 International Conference on Aerial Navigation in Paris they proposed that "the navigation of the air above a foreign country should be free in principle, and that foreign airships should not be treated less favorably than those of nationals."[7] Although the other European nations roundly rejected the proposal, it helped define Germany's attitude toward aviation in the run-up to World War I. Military aviation represented a critical strategic threat that Germany could use to show its strength.

The change in Germany's outlook produced some unintended consequences. In 1911 the country faced a critical choice between developing airplanes or airships. Even at that early date, aeronautical advances suggested that aircraft might soon offer a cheaper, more flexible tool than the decidedly more costly zeppelins. Yet, the zeppelin had become a critical component of the German national identity. On October 25 Prussian War Minister Josias von Heeringen convinced Kaiser Wilhelm II that Germany must preserve airship superiority over the other European countries rather than place its bets on heavier-than-air craft.[8] The decision channeled huge amounts of money into zeppelin production at the expense of aircraft development, while German military strategists began thinking about zeppelin raids as the nation's primary method of attack. As a result, Germany began the war with ten zeppelins, but only two hundred forty-five airplanes, none of which was capable of conducting long-range bombing raids.

The French public followed the Germans in its enthusiasm for aviation. Airships and airplanes became both a fascination and a cause for fear. French historian Edmond Petit summed up the period as a time when aviation became a "universal preoccupation" in France.[9] As with Britain, the exuberance influenced government policy. The French War Ministry used its relatively larger aviation budgets to set the standard for airpower development. The army became an active part of the aviation industry by directly financing aircraft designers. Besides underwriting important technological advances, the investment program created valuable connections between the military and the aviation industry that helped foster an understanding of airpower absent in most other countries. The most notable example was the future French military commander, Gen. Joseph J. C. Joffre, who chaired a commission on aviation experiments in 1905.[10] His interaction with the industry introduced Joffre to the potential for airpower and likely made him more open to innovative uses for aircraft.

Nonetheless, some French aviation enthusiasts, like their American counterparts, often met resistance when dealing with senior military leaders. In March 1913 Ferdinand Foch, the future allied commander in chief, commented blithely that "Aviation is a fine sport. I even wish officers would practice the sport, as it accustoms them to risk. But, as an instrument of war, it is worthless."[11] Foch's attitude demonstrated the suspicion with which many senior military leaders held aviation at the time. Yet, it also highlighted a major difference between European and American views prior to World War I. In France, aviation fit perfectly with the offensive spirit and esprit de corps that French military leaders wanted instilled in all their officers. In America, on the other hand, early aviators were often considered eccentric daredevils who behaved outside the norm expected of an Army officer. The more accepting attitude in France helped create perhaps the best-prepared air service in August 1914, with one hundred forty-one combat planes organized into twenty-one squadrons and another one hundred seventy-six in reserve or training roles.[12]

Where the Germans and French adopted straightforward approaches to military aviation, the British attitude was more complex. In October 1908 Britain's Committee on Imperial Defence set up a subcommittee headed by Reginald Baloil Brett, the 2nd Viscount of Esher, to investigate the dangers that military aviation posed to Britain and what advantages the country might gain by developing its own airships and airplanes. Lord Esher's report reflects the guiding principles behind early British policies. "[T]he evidence before the Committee tends to show that the full potentialities of the air-ship, and the dangers to which we might be exposed by their use, can only be ascertained definitely by building them ourselves," he wrote. "This was the original reason for constructing submarines, and in their case the policy has since been completely vindicated."[13]

The Esher report formed the basis for one avenue of expansion of military aviation in Britain. A strong desire to match the German zeppelin program pushed the country toward developing its own airships and strategic airpower. As was the case with building warships, the aerial arms race offered security through parity as a means of deterrence. As might be expected, the Royal Navy favored this model for aviation, itself focusing on traditional naval strategies of attacking an enemy's means and will to resist through blockades and direct attacks.

Yet, airships were to become only one element in British military aviation. A second focus evolved around the growing importance of heavier-than-air flying machines. On February 17, 1912, the Committee on Imperial Defence Sub Committee on Aerial Navigation recommended the formation of an airplane-equipped flying corps to support army operations. The subcommittee even set priorities for the missions of such a new component: reconnaissance, reconnaissance protection, communications, artillery spotting, and bombardment.[14]

This dual nature of airpower in England both shaped and was shaped by the divide between the army and navy. The army's steadfast concentration on ground support drove technology, organization, and doctrinal thinking in its air service, the Royal Flying Corps (RFC). Technological development moved toward slow, but highly stable aircraft well suited for observation missions. Organizational structure centered on squadrons directly tied to army commands, with little latitude for independent operations. Finally, doctrine mirrored the thinking of ground officers, who saw aviation as a tool to augment the cavalry in reconnaissance or support the artillery in guiding and correcting gunfire.

These early changes set the tone for future RFC air operations. They not only ingrained the new corps' way of thinking, but more important they created foundations that proved difficult and costly to change. A good example is the first widely produced RFC aircraft, the Royal Aircraft Factory Be2a. While the plane's inherent stability was an asset for its reconnaissance mission, its top speed of seventy miles an hour and its bombload of only one hundred pounds severely limited its use as a pursuit aircraft or bomber.[15] Moreover, designing a new airplane took time. As a result, the RFC had to manage with poorly suited designs for much of the early part of the war.

By contrast, the Royal Navy viewed airpower in a strategic light. Naval thought centered on using airplanes to help maintain sea control through direct attacks on enemy ships, ports, and support facilities. This vision of airpower led to different technologies, organizations, and doctrinal concepts. From the start, the navy pursued aircraft designed for long over-the-water flights and for bombing. While navigation in the Royal Flying Corps meant map-reading, by 1913 the Royal Navy led the world with the first published manual on air navigation, the first compass specifically designed for aircraft, and a circular slide-rule for calculating wind drift.[16] The navy also adopted a different organizational structure, incorporating the concept of the independent wing, which offered more latitude for aerial operations. Finally, it adopted the idea promoted by Winston Churchill, then First Lord of the Admiralty, for a combined offensive and defensive doctrine. Churchill advocated attacks on the zeppelin bases as the best means of preventing the Germans from using airships against England. At first, his policy called for eliminating the zeppelin threat by destroying airship bases and support facilities. As the war progressed, though, it required only a small jump to apply Churchill's (and the Royal Navy's) idea of launching strategic attacks against German industry as well.

As result Britain entered World War I with what amounted to two separate and quite different military air components. When the conflict began, the Army had an inventory of fifty airplanes to provide direct ground support for the British Expeditionary Forces (BEF). The Royal Naval Air Service (RNAS) had ninety-three long-range airplanes and six airships at its disposal.[17]

Two other nations merit consideration in the run-up to World War I. Farsighted aircraft designers in both Italy and Russia helped steer technology toward long-range aviation. The most important of the two was Italy. Italian aircraft designer Giovanni Caproni led the way with his three-engine 260-horsepower Ca-1. The plane, which first flew in late 1914, had a range of 344 miles and carried a crew of four and up to 460 pounds of bombs.[18] It also fit nicely with Italy's strategic challenge. If the Italians joined the war, they almost certainly would have to mount a long and costly ground offensive through the Alps against Austria-Hungary.

Employing long-range aircraft seemed to offer the possibility of averting this grueling land campaign. As Caproni argued, his bombers could fly over the Alps to strike at important Austro-Hungarian military targets. At the very least they could act as super-long-range artillery to support the ground offensive. Yet, some Italian airpower advocates, including the aggressive aviation battalion commander Giulio Douhet, envisioned a new, more exciting possibility: with a sufficient number of long-range bombers, Italian aircraft could attack Austro-Hungarian war industries directly, potentially even forcing the enemy to cease hostilities for lack of armaments.

The Russians had their own visionary aircraft designer in Igor Sikorsky, a pioneer aircraft designer who built fixed-wing planes and helicopters. His Ilya Moromets Type A, which flew its maiden voyage on December 11, 1913, was originally designed for commercial passenger transport. But its 113-foot wingspan, four engines, and fully enclosed cabin held immense military potential, particularly for long-range bombing and reconnaissance roles.[19] The airplane was ideally suited to Russia's military needs. With long distances separating Russia from German industrial and logistics facilities, Moscow required such a plane to have any hope of attacking German strategic targets. Unfortunately, the size and complexity of the Ilya Moromets limited production speed. Only twenty Type A models were available for operations in 1916. Still, the bomber succeeded in flying more than four hundred missions between February 1915 and Russia's departure from the war—primarily against the German army.[20]

Other European countries almost certainly would have welcomed a chance to buy long-range bombers that offered the advantages of the Ilya Moromets, but Russia's remoteness tended to shield its technology and doctrine from aviation strategists in the West. Although Sikorsky eventually licensed production of his aircraft to the British and French, by 1916 the cost of the Russian bomber and the versions developed by the two Allied countries precluded their building large numbers of them themselves.[21]

THE EARLY MONTHS OF THE WAR

When war broke out in August 1914, many waited apprehensively for the predicted aerial assaults, but none of them took place. The gargantuan military efforts of both the German and the British-French forces severely limited strategic air operations. Airpower on both sides was focused on defeating the enemy's ground forces, precluding the acquisition of fleets of long-range bombers that fiction writers had envisioned would be deployed to attack European cities. Instead, most bombers were sent to destroy operational targets such as railyards and supply depots.

Even so, the fear of bombing remained among the civilian populations of these countries. The wariness was evident even in Germany's declaration of war against France. As part of the rationale, the Germans cited the French bombing of Nuremburg on August 2, 1914—an interesting reference, since the Germans knew well that no aircraft in the French inventory could fly as far as Nuremberg.[22] Some historians attribute this to a combination of fear and rumors that had gripped the German government. Another possibility is that the Germans realized the fear that the threat of bombing would spread and used the reports to galvanize their population.

Either way, instead of the predicted aerial bombardments of national capitals, the early bombing efforts were limited to small independent raids. On August 6, the Germans launched their first zeppelin attack on Liege, Belgium, with minimal results. Perhaps a more accurate harbinger was an August 30 raid on Paris by a small German Taube airplane. Lt. Ferdinand von Hiddessen broke Paris' usual quiet Sunday morning routine when he dropped five small bombs along with a note warning that "the German army is at the gates of Paris."[23] Von Hiddessen's raid marked the start of a mini-bombing campaign. Individual Taube pilots visited the city ten times between August 30 and October 12. The raids did not intensify public panic as many prewar visionaries had predicted. Despite eleven deaths, most Parisians considered the raids a spectacle and jockeyed for positions from which to watch the aircraft drop their bombs.

The irony of these early raids was that they were not part of any organized effort. For their part, the Germans likely saw them as a diversion to keep pilots' morale high during dangerous reconnaissance missions. Meanwhile, the French and British were too preoccupied with the Battle of the Marne to think much about raids by single aircraft. All sides were too involved in the all-consuming early battles on the Western Front to consider strategic bombing.

This situation in France began to change after the Battle of the Marne. Once the Germans had halted their race to the sea and had established trench lines, Allied aviation units had more freedom to return to prewar doctrines. The first such effort was by the British RNAS. Winston Churchill, then first sea lord, had long been concerned about the zeppelin threat, and this new phase of the war provided the opening he needed to launch the first RNAS long-range aerial attacks against zeppelin bases. With the bulk of the RFC now based in France, the British government gave the navy the task of defending English airspace. Convinced that the best defense was a good offense, Churchill argued that the most effective way to stop the German air raids was for Britain to take control for one hundred miles around the RNAS base at Dunkirk and attack the zeppelin sheds from there.

Despite Churchill's plans, for much of August and September the overwhelming needs of the ground forces required that the RNAS spend all of its combat time supporting the ground effort. Even when the navy could break away from its ground-support mission, the next set of priority targets on its assignment list were submarine pens and port facilities. It was not until the end of September that the RNAS finally ordered its bombers to attack the zeppelin bases. The service conducted four raids between September 22 and December 25, 1914. Three of these were traditional counterforce missions, aimed at destroying zeppelin sheds and the airships inside them. The most important demonstration of strategic bombing was a November 21 raid targeting the Zeppelin factory at Friedrichshafen. It required the RNAS to move secretly four new single-engine Avro 504s to Belfort on the Swiss border. The aircraft then flew low over Lake Constance, attacked the airship works, damaged a zeppelin under construction, and created a tremendous explosion at the factory's hydrogen gasworks.[24] Despite the drama and heroism, the real importance of the mission lay in the selection of the target. For the first time, airpower had attacked an industrial source of an opponent's military power.

This must have seemed like a foreign concept to the RNAS' sister service, the RFC. The Corps' prewar focus on ground support meant that its units in France had only limited long-range assets and capabilities. The army's decision to deploy its most experienced officers to France only exacerbated the situation. The decision meant that the critical staff functions that were required for the RFC to grow were held primarily by relatively green young officers.[25] The task of buying aircraft and training thousands of new pilots rapidly overwhelmed these men. In the melee of staff work, they all too often ignored questions involving technology development, aerial strategy, and pitfalls discovered in earlier action at the front.

Accordingly, British historian Neville Jones describes this early era as critical for strategic bombing. On one hand, the RNAS laid a foundation that enabled it to expand to meet the needs of strategic bombing in the later stages of the war. On the other, the RFC failed to set a solid footing for future operations. Failure to heed lessons from the front meant delays in technology, organization, and doctrinal change, which created long-term problems for the RFC.

THE FIRST STRATEGIC BOMBING CAMPAIGNS, 1915

While the story of strategic bombing in 1914 revolved around the British RNAS, 1915 saw the French and then the Germans take the lead. Their air forces introduced new technologies, organizational schemes, and planning methods into strategic bombing. In doing so, they added to the foundation laid in the prewar era and tested by the RNAS.

In late 1914 the new French director of aeronautics, Col. Joseph-Edouard Bares commissioned a specially designed air unit focused on strategic attack. The result was Groupe de Bombardement No. 1 (GB 1), consisting of eighteen single-pusher engine Voisin bombers divided into three escadrilles placed under the direct control of General Joffre, then commander in chief of French forces on the western front.[26] Here the early French efforts to develop experienced senior leaders who were familiar with aviation paid off. Joffre's background on the 1905 Aviation Commission opened him to new airpower ideas, and he supported Bares' concept to use the group to strike German communications lines and critical industry. With the full support and protection of Joffre, GB 1 flew its first mission against the railway station at Freiburg on December 4.

Although this was an important first for French strategic bombing, Bares must have understood that for bombing to succeed it required a well-thought-out targeting strategy. In December and January, he developed a new strategic campaign plan for 1915 containing a target-selection model based on weighing a target's importance against its vulnerability to French raids.[27] The formula proved invaluable in enabling Bares to counterbalance the need to strike critical industries with the reality of limited aerial resources. Perhaps more important, it provided a way for strategists to change their priorities as new technologies made their way to the battlefield.

Joffre approved the plan in late January and even went one step further, earmarking twenty-one out of the seventy-one new escadrilles planned for 1915 to serve as bomber units. Thus, GB 2 came into being in January and GB 3 was established in March.[28] Throughout 1915, the expanded force conducted raids primarily on chemical plants and iron-works in Karlsruhe, Trier, and Saarbrucken. Initially, the French met with some success, but their relatively primitive Voisin bombers proved difficult to navigate and lacked adequate bombsights, often missing their targets by miles. Moreover, as the Germans became more skilled in air defense, French aircraft losses mounted. By late 1915, the French turned to night bombing and limited their efforts.

Historian John Morrow sums up the early French strategic bombing campaign: "Aware that the war was becoming a conflict of material, GQC selected industrial targets for a strategic bombing campaign intended to shorten the war. Unfortunately, their simple and robust Voisin aircraft, modified artillery shell bombs, and primitive techniques proved unsuitable."[29] Still, the French campaign broadened the strategic bombing foundation upon which future advocates built. Bares' targeting scheme, especially, survived to play a major role in later British and American strategic campaigns.

The French were not the only country to set their sights on strategic bombing. In late 1914 the German command revived its prewar vision of zeppelins terrorizing French and British cities. Kaiser Wilhelm II initially resisted these efforts, leery of the consequences if the bombing were to kill a member of the British royal family or destroy an important historical site.[30] But the French campaign against German cities that began in December led him to discard such inhibitions. After an especially destructive raid against Freiburg, he finally relented. On January 15, 1915, he granted the army permission to target British coastal ports, a relatively cautious first step. As soon became obvious, however, in this escalating cycle of violence, London could not remain unscathed for long. Finally, in an Imperial Order of February 12, Wilhelm designated the London docks a valid military target. Almost immediately, the German Naval Airship Division launched a mission with London as its target, but unfavorable weather prevented its success. It was not until May 31 that Zeppelin LZ38 finally reached the city, dropping thirty small bombs and ninety incendiary devices in northeast London.[31]

The attack was the first of nineteen raids over the year in which German zeppelins dropped a cumulative thirty-seven tons of bombs and killed two hundred nine persons. The following year (1916) began with an even more destructive bombing run. On January 31, nine zeppelins converged over Liverpool and dropped their explosives. Although the airstrike resulted in little physical destruction, it had some important consequences in both countries. In Germany, it enabled Capt. Peter Strasser, the commander of the Naval Airship Division, to convince the Kaiser that his zeppelins eventually could force Britain to surrender if he could only overcome current technological shortcomings in navigation and bombing—a decision that led Germany to continue diverting much of its increasingly scarce resources to airships rather than boosting outlays for airplanes. Hence, at a critical moment, Germany continued to split its limited resources between the two types of aircraft. In Britain, the zeppelin raids sowed widespread panic among night-shift workers, many of whom refused to come to work for as long as a week.[32] The resulting threat to war production focused the British government and military on the effect that bombing raids could have on civilian morale. It also showed the British that they, too, could use strategic bombing to dampen the spirit of the German population.

The year also saw a small but important foray by the Italians. When Italy joined the war on May 23, 1915, it was the only nation to have acquired an airplane that had been specifically designed for long-range bombing—the three-engine Caproni Ca-1.[33] Yet, the Italian army's initial need for ground support operations overwhelmed hopes of carrying out strategic bombing raids. For most of the year the big Capronis flew ground support and reconnaissance missions. By late summer, this began to change, mainly through the efforts of Giulio Douhet.

Born near Naples in 1869, Douhet entered the Italian army as an artillery officer in 1888. Throughout his career, he remained a controversial figure. On one hand, he was admired as a man of a keen intellect and an infectious enthusiasm for new technology, who became an outspoken advocate of increased mechanization. On the other, his unapologetically candid public criticism of military planning and

funding decisions sparked anger and resentment among his superiors. As a result, his career fluctuated wildly between prestigious
commands and menial staff jobs.[34]

Perhaps these same characteristics led to Douhet's fascination
with aviation in 1908. While still attached to the artillery, he wrote
a series of articles advocating airpower as a powerful military tool.
When Italy formed its first aviation element in 1910, Douhet used
his connections to secure a transfer to the newly formed Aviation
Battalion. where he continued to deepen his knowledge of airpower
and wrote articles advocating increased funding.[35] By 1914 Douhet
had become the battalion's commander and had begun a life-
long campaign to expand the service's strategic bombing capability. He worked feverishly on a plan that called for large multicrew
Caproni bombers to operate independently against industrial targets.
Unfortunately, Douhet's personality got in the way of his dreams.
After he overreached his authority by authorizing the purchase of
Caproni bombers on his own, the Italian army removed him from
command and exiled him as chief of staff for the Lombardy Division.

Before leaving the Aviation Battalion, Douhet wrote a series of articles in *Gazzetta del Popolo* advocating a strategic bombing campaign
designed to destroy Austria-Hungary's industrial capability and will to
resist.[36] Although these ideas did not gain much currency in the Italian
military at first, eventually they worked their way into the growing
cross-pollination of Allied thinking about strategic bombing. Douhet
addressed some of the key problems that the early French and British
bombing efforts faced. Both countries realized that the crew of small
single- or two-seat bombers became overwhelmed by navigation,
bomb aiming, and self-defense during long missions, which inevitably led to poor results. Douhet suggested that assigning a dedicated,
large, multimember crew to a bomber like the Caproni could solve
this problem.

The year 1915 marked a critical first step in strategic bombing. The
French took their first tentative steps toward adopting the concept,
while the Germans attempted their own strategic bombing operations, centered on their zeppelin fleet. The results of both campaigns
were modest, but the doctrinal changes were long-lasting. The Bares

targeting strategy became a basic element in all later French, British, and American strategic campaigns. Meanwhile, the Germans learned from their earlier mistakes and put in place a plan for preparing their air services for a new and larger effort against England. Even the British, who had steered clear of strategic campaigns in 1915, learned from the German raids. The panics that set in when the bombs fell during the zeppelin raids on England highlighted the importance of the effect that bombing raids would have on civilian morale. Finally, the Italians provided an important element by showing that successful strategic bombing operations would require large, multicrew bombers.

VERDUN AND THE SOMME INTRUDE

What had begun as a promising year for strategic bombing advocates in 1916 quickly turned into a setback. First, the modest results from French and German bombing efforts of 1915 prompted many military and political leaders to turn away from strategic bombing as a way to win the war quickly. At the same time, the major ground battles of Verdun and the Somme once again required a full commitment of military aircraft, leaving few resources available for strategic bombing. Still, there were some success stories, such as the experience of the British RNAS' 3 Wing, which shaped bombing technology, organization, and doctrine.

The year began with a difficult situation for the French. On February 21 the Germans launched their effort to bleed the French army white at Verdun. As part of the offensive, the German air service conducted a massive aerial assault designed to seize the initiative in the skies. The French knew they had to act swiftly. On February 29 Bares decided to focus the French air forces on Verdun in an effort to win back the skies. Included in the group were fifteen elite fighter squadrons.[36] But Verdun turned into a death-mission for French pilots just as it was for the common foot soldier, imposing an even bigger strain on French resources and on the country's already-beleaguered aviation industry. By June 1916 the French had amassed 1,120 aircraft in the Verdun sector.[37] Unfortunately for the pilots, the Germans had fielded a comparable force. In the daily air battles over the trenches, the French lost pilots and airplanes at almost unsustainable rates. To meet this need, in the spring of 1916 the French revamped their aircraft production priorities. Where manufacturing observation aircraft and bombers had been given top billing in 1915, the new schedule called for rapid production of observation aircraft and pursuit planes.

To be sure, that did not spell the end of strategic bombing for the French. Both GB 1 and GB 2 continued raids on German economic targets early in 1916, striking the railroad station at Metz, the iron-works in Lorraine, and munitions factories in the Saar region. Yet as Verdun consumed more resources and the Somme offensive began, the French bomber units increasingly found themselves pulled aside to provide tactical support. The fatal blow occurred on October 12 when the French air service conducted a joint raid with the RNAS against the Mauser arms factory at Oberndorf. Losses from the mission were high, with seven out of twenty-four aircraft shot down.[38] With facto-ries unable to make up the bomber losses and still fill demands for new pursuit planes, the French limited bombing to night raids, despite their poor performance on accuracy.

A major lesson that the French drew from their setbacks in 1916 was the need for a dedicated strategic bomber. Their two-seat Voisin bombers lacked the range and sturdiness to penetrate enemy defenses and bomb strategic targets, and the Caproni bombers built under license from Italy proved too underpowered for sustained combat operations.[39] The country's previous failure to develop more-advanced bombing technology, combined with the downgrading of bombers in the nation's aircraft production priorities, had forced military author-ities to rely on night raids, which were notoriously ineffective. The setbacks of 1916 focused the attention of French politicians and mili-tary leaders on the urgent need to win air superiority over the front before ground operations could be successful.

Meanwhile, across the Channel, the RNAS' success in its early bombing raids had heightened British interest in mounting a strate-gic bombing campaign. New long-range aircraft such as the Sopwith 1½ Strutter, along with the advent of more accurate bombsights, increased the capabilities of available bombers, while growing coop-eration with the French offered the possibility that the two coun-tries might conduct a joint strategic bombing campaign. Finally, the establishment of a dedicated strategic bombing wing with the backing of Gen. Douglas Haig, commander of the British Expeditionary Force, suggested that Britain finally might have mustered the political will to embrace strategic bombing as a major component of its arsenal.

Here, too, however, the effort was sidetracked by the ensuing ground fighting, which demanded the full attention—and resources—of the British military. As had happened in France, competition for funds—in this case between the RNAS and the RFC—intensified in the face of the battle of the Somme, confronting policymakers with urgent decisions involving critical technology, organization, and doctrinal issues.

The RFC spent the early part of 1916 preparing for the Somme offensive. Virtually all of its attention was focused on building up forces, preparing the battlefield through interdiction missions, and conducting reconnaissance activities. This left strategic bombing to the RNAS, which was prepared to expand its anti-zeppelin campaign into a much larger strategic bombing effort.

In May the Admiralty ordered Capt. W. L. Elder to establish RNAS 3 Wing at Luxeuil, twenty-five miles northwest of Belfort, but the location proved inadequate so the unit moved to Ochey, near Nancy, in late June.[40] The new site was within easy range of many industrial targets in western Germany, but it also was surrounded by a bevy of French and RFC bases.

The idea of a sixty-aircraft naval wing operating the new Sopwith 1½ Strutters in central France was certain to touch sensitive nerves in the RFC. The Admiralty fully understood the danger and only allowed the unit to become operational after the navy obtained General Haig's consent. On 3 June, the GHQ released this statement: "The C-in-C sees no need to object in any way to long distance bombing being undertaken by the Royal Naval Air Service, with the proviso that any such bombing undertaken in the area behind the German lines in front of the British Army shall be subject to his concurrence."[41]

Despite Haig's official acceptance of 3 Wing, the RNAS effort faced opposition from both internal and external critics. As expected, the external opposition came from the RFC's former commander, Lt. Gen. Sir David Henderson, who now, as director-general of military aeronautics in the War Office, saw 3 Wing as a direct rival, competing for valuable aviation resources. He now used his connections to the Joint War Air Committee (JWAC) to challenge the RNAS plans.

The JWAC had been established to limit overlap and waste in the often-competing army and naval air forces. Henderson seized on the overlap issue in a memorandum to the JWAC on February 4, 1916, stressing that the competition for long-range engines was hampering the RFC's ability to acquire sufficient observation aircraft for the Somme offensive.[42] He followed up later that summer with two memos arguing that long-range bombing operations from land were an RFC mission and therefore a duplication of effort.

The internal opposition to 3 Wing came from an unexpected source, Adm. Sir Reginald H. Bacon, the commander of the Dover Patrol, who wrote on June 1 that "warfare in the air, to be useful, has to be entirely subservient to warfare on land or sea."[43] Because Admiral Bacon controlled all naval activities at Dunkirk, 3 Wing could expect only limited support from the primary British naval base in France.

Bacon's complaints could not have come at a worse time. The start of the Somme offensive on July 1 had created a logistical and organizational nightmare for 3 Wing. Still in the process of setting up the wing, Captain Elder found himself without strong command support just when he needed it most—at a time when he was facing three major problems that had no obvious solutions.

First, in order to acquire basing rights and encourage Anglo-French cooperation, the Admiralty had agreed to allocate twenty of the first sixty arriving aircraft to the French so they could create a bomber force that could be used for joint campaigns with 3 Wing.[44] That plan backfired, however. The Sopwith 1½ Strutter had proved itself to be not only a good long-range bomber, but also an effective observation and tactical bombing aircraft. As a result, the army began to divert an ever-increasing number of the new deliveries for use as observation planes and ground-support aircraft, leaving 3 Wing with a critical bomber shortage and postponing the operational status of the new joint force until October.

The second problem was the lack of a carefully thought-out campaign plan. Since the RNAS did not have a command structure for strategic bombing, there was no senior staff to develop targeting priorities, coordinate operations, and evaluate mission results. To get around that problem, the Admiralty agreed to place 3 Wing under the French, who already had set up a staff support structure to oversee the operations of their own bombardment groups.[45]

There was an inherent logic in the decision. The French had more experience than the British in commanding larger bomber units. The targeting scheme they put together in September 1916 was far ahead of its time. It called for selecting industrial targets based on their importance to the German war effort—a priority-ranking system that left French operations planners free simply to weigh the relative importance of iron, chemical, or munitions industries without having to rank the worth of individual factories. Finally, the French continued Bares' system of balancing the importance of individual targets against the risk that Allied forces might run in carrying out an attack against them. In the end, the French system enabled operational planners from both allies to make rational choices on which sites to attack, while at the same time reducing the risk to their own severely underequipped bombing units.

The third problem that RNAS commanders faced was the impact of the fiercer-than-expected war in crowding out strategic bombing from the wartime wish list of top British policymakers.

Despite their numerical inferiority, the Germans quickly reinforced their aerial forces in the Somme region. By late 1916 casualties in the skies over the Somme reached critical levels, with the British losing 782 aircraft from July to November, almost twice the number with which they started the campaign.[46] With the RFC constantly demanding higher priority for its own aircraft acquisition needs, the British government disbanded the JWAC in October and replaced it with a new Air Board under Lord George Nathaniel Curzon. The government tasked this new committee with determining the priorities for aircraft production, the best strategy for military aviation, and the most effective organizational structure it should use.[47]

The Air Board set about its work immediately. Unfortunately, with such prohibitive aircraft attrition rates it was difficult for any government organization to limit the number of new airplanes allocated to the RFC. After receiving a memorandum from Haig describing the RFC's urgent need for aircraft replacements, the board ruled against the Admiralty and gave production priority to the army. Board members even went one step further: they recommended that the navy lend both aircraft and pilots to the RFC during the new service's time of crisis. Not wanting to appear adversarial, the Admiralty ordered 3 Wing to provide nineteen pilots and six aircraft to augment the RFC.[48] The double whammy not only slowed the arrival of new aircraft at 3 Wing, but it also transferred existing navy aircraft and personnel to the army.

Even so, the story of 3 Wing is not one of failure. Despite the delays and setbacks, the wing achieved some operational successes. By the time its pilots flew their last mission on April 14, 1917 they had conducted eighteen raids, including four night missions with the new four-engine Handley Page 0/100 bombers.[49] While these numbers were low compared to the fifty-two tactical raids conducted by 1 Wing from Dunkirk in the same period, 3 Wing had many more logistical, distance, and command challenges to overcome than other aviation units.

A better method of assessing the wing's success might be to examine its contribution to the advancement of strategic bombing technology, organization, and doctrine. In the area of technology, 3 Wing's operations reinforced the need for dedicated multicrew bombers. The performance of the Handley Page bombers demonstrated the advantages that such planes provided in improved navigation, bombing accuracy, and defensive capabilities. Meanwhile, the wing's use of the Sopwith 1½ Strutter demonstrated the overwhelming requirement for a two-seat daylight bomber, leading to the highly capable DH 4. Organizationally, 3 Wing highlighted the need for an independent bomber force. The operational delays caused by logistics and interservice fighting impeded the wing's operations. When government attention once again turned toward strategic bombing as a priority, the lessons from 3 Wing informed their thinking. Finally, the unit's work with the French ingrained their target selection and prioritization schemes into British doctrine. When the time came to develop a British bombing plan, the French concepts provided valuable guidance.

All in all, 1916 was a disappointing year for advocates of strategic bombing. The costs of two massive ground offensives put strategic bombing on the back burner for all countries engaged in the war effort. The French, caught off guard at Verdun, rapidly switched all but abandoning long-range bombing to enable their forces to meet the German onslaught. The British meticulously prepared for the Somme, but poor aircraft technology, combined with Trenchard's aggressive offensive plan, produced extremely high attrition rates. In the face of this reality, Britain delegated its strategic bombing program to an under-supported wing that operated without strategic guidance. Finally, the Germans, overwhelmed by the tactical air war, largely eschewed strategic campaigns outside of a few raids.

Still, the year was not a total loss for strategic bombing. The hard-won lessons of the previous year remained intact and survived into the renewal of strategic bombing in 1917. The British also learned important concepts from the limited operations of 3 Wing; these shaped British aviation strategy when the government once again called on its long-range bomber forces.

THE RENEWAL OF STRATEGIC BOMBING, 1917

Although the great offensives of 1916 exhausted all sides, the relentless attrition continued into 1917, with air forces of all countries preparing themselves for even more sacrifice as the war dragged on. Nevertheless, change was in the wind. On the Allied side, April brought a major psychological setback for the French when their army mutinied following their abortive attack on Chemin des Dames. Meanwhile, the entry of the Americans into the war on April 6, 1917, seemed finally to offer the hope of overcoming aircraft shortages. Indeed, the Germans realized beforehand that they could not win a war of attrition once the Americans arrived in force, so they had to strike at the very heart of the Allied Alliance before the full weight of the U.S. military intervention became a factor. On the ground this translated into heightened preparations for a new offensive, but in the air it meant trying to knock the British out of the war once and for all.

Throughout 1916, the German navy never forgot about its plan to attack Britain directly. Led by the energetic Captain Strasser, the navy continually pushed for larger zeppelins and more raids on England.

Following the success of his Liverpool raid on January 31, 1916, Strasser proposed a new strategic campaign against England to be carried out by larger and higher-flying zeppelins.[50] Unfortunately for him, this time the cost of the war disrupted Germany's plans to engage in strategic bombing. The all-out conflicts in Verdun, the Somme, and Jutland required the services of many of his zeppelins.

By autumn the situation had started to change. With Germany's High Seas Fleet unable to break the British blockade and the German army locked in a battle of attrition, the zeppelin seemed to offer a possible way for the Germans to break the stalemate. Strasser seized on the moment on 10 August when he wrote to Fleet Admiral Reinhard Scheer, the fleet's commander, that "the performance of the big airships has reinforced my conviction that England can be overcome by means of airships."[51] With Scheer's full approval, Strasser set out on one last effort to break the British economy and their will.

The German attackers ran into a hornet's nest. Britain also had spent 1916 working on improvements to its air defense system. Better tracking, more-capable interceptors, and new incendiary bullets drew a heavy toll on them. Of the 187 zeppelins that the Germans launched against England that year, only 111 reached their targets. During the height of Strasser's all-out offensive the Germans lost 6 costly zeppelins in combat.[52]

The heavy losses, combined with a stunning technological breakthrough, prompted the Germany military to shift its strategic bombing program from zeppelins to heavy bombers. The turning point came in the autumn of 1916, with the successful testing of the new Gotha bomber, a twin-engine, long-range heavy bomber that offered a means of striking England without the heavy cost or high risks of the more vulnerable slow-flying zeppelins. The army decided to invest its future in this new technology and canceled its zeppelin program in January 1917.

With this dramatic shift, the commander of the German Air Service, General Ernst von Hoeppner, proposed to create a squadron of thirty Gotha bombers to carry out a strategic campaign against Britain. The German High Command approved the plan and ordered Captain Ernst Brandenburg to establish Kagohl 3, the England Squadron, in February at St. Denis Westrem in Belgium.[53]

The squadron was ready for operations in May, and on the twenty-fifth it flew its first mission. Twenty-one Gothas took off for London, but ran into bad weather and ended up bombing Folkestone, a small town in southeast England, instead. Despite the disappointing results, the initial raid presaged a new aerial campaign against London, for which the British were not fully prepared. Lulled into a false sense of security by the dwindling zeppelin raids, the British had relaxed their defenses. The lapse was soon laid bare on June 13, when fourteen Gothas dropped seventy-two bombs on London, killing 168 persons. Equally telling, although the British launched ninety-two aircraft to intercept the bombers, they recorded no aerial victories that day.[54]

Shock over the German successes sparked a public outcry and a call for increased protection. On June 20, Haig and Trenchard were called to testify to the cabinet. Predictably, Trenchard advised that the best defense was to occupy Belgium and push the German bases back beyond the range of the Gotha bombers.[55] Unmoved by his logic, the cabinet ordered Haig to release two pursuit squadrons from the Continent to bolster homeland defenses. Trenchard acquiesced, but when no new raids appeared by the end of June he began steps to return the squadrons to the front.

Trenchard's move coincided with a new raid by the Germans, who sent twenty-one Gothas over London on July 7, causing fifty-four deaths and more than 200,000 pounds' worth of damage.[56] The new round of bombing propelled the previous clamor into an uproar and spread fear throughout the British public. By midsummer some 400,000 Londoners either had left the city or were seeking air-raid shelters at night. London newspapers were calling the Gotha campaign an aerial siege of the city.[57]

The public panic soon spurred action. On August 7 Prime Minister David Lloyd George appointed a commission, headed by South African soldier and statesman Lt. Gen. Jan Smuts, to investigate the status of aviation and aerial defenses. The Smuts Commission released two important findings that summer. On July 19 it called for a revamping of the aerial defense system—a move that led to the creation of a single command system that integrated observers, command and control, antiaircraft artillery, and interceptor aircraft.[58] Although this was important, the panel's second report, released on August 17, had even greater implications. First, it recommended the formation of an independent Royal Air Force (RAF) that would combine the resources of the RFC and RNAS. It also assigned the new service the primary mission of carrying out strategic bombing raids.

Section seven of the document declared:

> The magnitude and significance of the transformation now in progress are not easily realized. It requires some imagination to realize that next summer, while our Western Front may still be moving forward at a snail's pace in Belgium and France, the air battlefront will be far behind on the Rhine, and that its continuous and intense pressure against the chief industrial centers of the enemy as well as on his lines of communication may form the determining factor in bringing about peace.[59]

The report created a firestorm in both the army and navy as senior commanders fought to keep control over their own aviation components. Nonetheless, in the wake of the Gotha raids on London, the public clamor for revenge permeated the British government, which accepted the Smuts proposals and immediately began fashioning an independent RAF. The newly formed service would be tasked with supporting the army and navy when needed and with creating and conducting a strategic bombing program.

As part of the formation of the independent force, Capt. Arthur Vyell Vyvyan, the assistant director of the Royal Naval Air Service, asked Lord Hardinge Goulborn Goffard Tiverton, the 2nd Earl of Halsbury, to submit a paper on bombing to the newly revamped Air Board describing the best method for the pursuit of a strategic campaign against Germany. As a Royal Navy aviator, Tiverton had served as the armaments officer of 3 Wing during its truncated bombing effort. The position was far more important than it seemed. Tiverton's interest in bombing theory had led to his assignment to work with the French on strategy issues.[60]

In his role as an insider on strategy development, Tiverton garnered a deep appreciation for Bares' targeting methodology, which he modified to his own needs. Bares' influence is clearly seen in a paper that Tiverton submitted to Vyvyan on September 2, 1917, in which he recommended stationing an independent bomber force in the Verdun area that would target the critical ironworks and chemical plants in Dusseldorf, Cologne, Mannheim, and the Saar region.[61] Even considering the French dominance in this field, Tiverton produced a uniquely British vision of a strategic bombing campaign. Most notably, he recommended a combination of daylight and nighttime operations to maximize physical destruction and lower citizen morale.

Thus, the first half of 1917 saw the rebirth of strategic bombing after the horrendous year of 1916. With a war of attrition settling over the trench lines, all sides sought a new means to bring a close to the war. Strategic bombing advocates leaped at the chance to test their theories. Although neither side had had the political will in 1916, the disheartening outlook for the Germans and the British reaction to Gotha raids sparked widespread support for strategic bombing both in Germany and among the Allies. Still, even with the newfound support, there were challenges to meet. Logistical and production problems plagued everyone. The Allies worried about how to integrate the soon-to-arrive American forces. Nevertheless, the future of strategic bombing looked promising.

CONCLUSION

Into this turbulence of aviation growth, new thinking, and political pressures the first American aviators stepped in the late spring of 1917. The British were moving toward an independent RAF, with a strong strategic bombing element. Yet, it was far from a done deal. Just because the Air Board recommended the policy did not mean that the leaders of the RFC and RNAS would drop their long-held opinions and rivalries. Instead, advocates on both sides of the strategic bombing argument sought support for their ideas among their new allies, the Americans.

Meanwhile, the French and Italians had their own concepts that they wanted to stress to the Americans. Beset by losses in 1916 and mutinies in 1917, the French were more focused on maintaining the morale of their people during that critical summer. General Maurice Duval, the head of the French Air Service, noted to General Pershing that Britain's bombing plan had "come to draw lightning, which would then strike their host."[62] The criticism reflected the concern of the French political leadership in 1917 that Britain's bombing of German cities would lead to German retaliation against French and British cities in an ever-intensifying war of terror. As a result, French military officers sought to convince their American counterparts to employ aviation in a more traditional role of supporting ground forces and achieving air superiority.

The Italians still viewed strategic bombing as a possible war-winning strategy, but acknowledged that the distances and terrain in the Alps made that impossible, at least with current technology. Still, the Americans could easily use the Italians' Caproni bombers to attack German industry from more suitable bases in eastern France. Indeed, American visitors often were given a dual sales pitch—for strategic bombing *and* for the Caproni bomber.

In the end, it was left up to a select group of U.S. aviators and strategists to sort through the complex mix of technology, political pressure, and operational lessons. Luckily, the Americans had spent the year between the Mexican Expedition and their entry into the war trying to prepare such a group. Men such as Billy Mitchell, Raynal Bolling, and Edgar Gorrell soon found themselves faced with a series of grand decisions. It became their role to select the best elements of each nation's aerial strategy and merge them into a uniquely American doctrine.

CHAPTER 3

The Birth of American Strategic Bombing Theory

The second half of 1917 proved pivotal for the United States, its Army, and especially its Air Service. The technological, organizational, and doctrinal shortcomings that had beset the fledgling U.S. military aviation effort between 1903 and 1916 became critical issues as the United States entered World War I. Lax planning had left the Air Service far short of the number of suitable aircraft that it needed—especially bombers, which historically had been assigned a low priority. A haphazard organizational structure had forced Army authorities to fill important leadership positions with inexperienced junior officers, who often found themselves with little or no guidance in making important decisions. The lack of a solid, well-thought-out doctrine for military aviation further intensified the other problems that the service faced and frequently resulted in competing, sometimes contradictory plans. Finally, the evolution of a separate, elitist culture in the aviation component made coordination between these newly promoted flyers and senior ground commanders difficult at best. Together, these deficiencies left the Army with an air arm that was rife with confusion, inefficiencies, and misdirection—factors that would have a profound effect on the size, structure, and missions of the rapidly expanding Air Service as a component of the new American Expeditionary Force (AEF) in Europe.

Adding to the difficulty was that preparing for an overseas combat deployment demanded that almost everything be classified as high priority, from ramping up aircraft production to rapidly training massive numbers of new pilots and—most important—developing workable strategy and tactics. Uncertainty and redundancy seemed to rule the day. Still, the actions taken following the Mexican Expedition alleviated the worst of the effects. Bright, energetic, and highly motivated young aviators worked tirelessly to achieve success in the critical deployment and training phases of 1917. General John Pershing, the AEF's commander, reflected the combination of frustration and empathy that Army leaders felt toward the Air Service when he described its senior staff in a letter as "good men running around in circles."[1]

Perhaps no other element of the new AEF Air Service felt the frustration as keenly as the advocates of strategic bombing. Long-range bombing had been all but ignored in the pre-1917 American Air Service and its advocates faced a difficult challenge in trying to convince Army leaders to consider it seriously. As a concept long-range bombing had many proponents, both within the U.S. Army and among the European allies, but the lack of an established bombing doctrine meant that each of them was free to press for his own vision of what should be done.

American thinking about aerial bombing at the start of the war fell into two distinct categories—*strategic* bombing and *strategical* bombing. Historians often overlook the difference, perhaps thinking of it as a semantic nicety, but it actually defines one of the core strategy debates that guided the early development of American bombing theory. Ironically, in the end the doctrine that U.S. forces finally adopted did not represent a victory for either of the two competing approaches, but was an amalgam of both, influenced by European ideas and the realities of war.

STARTING FROM SCRATCH

For all of the technological advances in aviation during the early 1900s, as the United States entered World War I American generals and admirals still had not yet reached agreement on what the role of airpower in military operations should be—clearly a necessity before they could determine the size, the mission, and the aircraft inventory of the new AEF Air Service. That there might be a role for strategic bombing was even farther from the planners' minds.

Aviation had always been a secondary consideration for the Army. Military leaders acknowledged that aircraft had a role to play in warfighting, but most thought it should be subordinate to the primary missions of the infantry, artillery, and cavalry. The Army's gospel on military operations, the *Field Service Regulation of 1914*, cemented that notion. Although the manual devoted a full section to aviation, the missions it prescribed for aircraft were limited to reconnaissance, observation, and aerial artillery spotting. The only mention of a direct combat role for aviation was a single sentence in section 31: "Aeroplanes are also used to prevent hostile aerial reconnaissance."[2]

The United States was not alone in such thinking. In 1914 most European army leaders also believed that aviation's primary role should remain one of observation and artillery support. Few theorists saw an independent combat mission for the often-fragile aircraft. But the war, which began earlier on the Continent, had forced European pilots, air service commanders, and eventually the armies' leaders themselves to reassess their views about airpower, and, in the process, about strategic bombing as well. The turning point came in the critical summer of 1917, after the German Gotha bombardments of London destroyed buildings and killed large numbers of civilians. The massive public outcry for revenge bombing against German cities gave British advocates of strategic bombing an opening as their government reconsidered the possibilities of this new kind of warfare.

Isolated from the fighting in Europe before 1917, the U.S. Army continued to hew to a narrower view of what airpower could achieve. Asked during a hearing of the House Military Affairs Committee in December 1914 whether aircraft had developed any practical value for offensive military operations, Brig. Gen. George P. Scriven, the chief of the Signal Corps, responded: "No sir, I believe not." He then went on to describe how recent tests in San Diego had shown that U.S. military aircraft could carry only about one hundred twenty pounds of bombs and had difficulty hitting selected targets. He conceded that although "in a few isolated cases bomb-dropping may do harm," he added that "as a fighting machine the aeroplane has not justified its existence, except aeroplane against other aircraft."[3] With this simple statement, he effectively ranked observation as the primary mission for U.S. military aircraft, pursuit as the second, and bombing last. And he effectively shelved the role of strategic bombing for the next two years.

Just the same, as the conflict in Europe widened even the Americans could not ignore the rapidly developing air war. In March 1915 the Army War College began a study on the proper size, composition, and missions of the Army if it should enter World War I. The military aviation section of the report demonstrates that thinking on airpower was slowly changing. Although the study still relegated bombing to a tertiary role, for the first time it recommended a dedicated bomber force. Section sixteen of the study called on America to adopt the European model, where "a special type of aeroplane has been developed for dropping bombs, these machines are sent in flotillas of from thirty to sixty machines. Against railways, roads, bridges, and hostile parks of various kinds, this method of attack has given considerable success."[4]

In April 1917, when the United States entered World War I, the rapid expansion of American military forces quickly changed the dynamics of the debate over aviation doctrine. Indeed, for airpower planners, the first challenge seemed to be to decide where to begin. There simply was no accepted concept for the mission, size, or structure of the soon-to-be-created AEF Air Service. That changed on May 24, when President Woodrow Wilson received a telegram from French Premier Alexandre Ribot spelling out the French vision for American airpower. Premier Ribot's cable is important enough that it deserves a full review.

It is desired that in order to cooperate with French aeronautics the American government should adopt the following program: The formation of a Flying Corps of 4,500 aeroplanes to be sent to the French front during the campaign of 1918. 2,000 planes should be constructed each month as well as 4,000 engines by the American factories. This is to say that during the first six months of 1918, 16,500 aeroplanes (of the latest type) and 30,000 engines will have to be built. The French government is anxious to know if the American government accepts this proposition, which would allow the allies to win supremacy of the air.[5]

The request from the French soon became the guiding principle behind American airpower planning. On April 3, the secretaries of the Navy and War and the chairman of the National Advisory Committee on Aeronautics created a six-member Joint Army-Navy Technical Board (JANTB), which was assigned to coordinate the development of aircraft by the two services.[6] With no other guidance, the board decided to accepted Ribot's request as a starting point for planning the size and makeup of the American air contingent.

There was one major shortcoming in embracing the French request: Ribot's cable did not address the doctrinal roles for the American air forces. This is an interesting quirk of history, since the cable was based on a French general staff analysis of the structure that American air forces would require for the Allies to win the war. In what was almost the mirror image of accepted American policy, the French suggested that the United States establish these priorities: first, aircraft designed to search for submarines; second, aircraft capable of pursuit and bombing; and finally, observation and artillery-spotting aircraft for direct ground support.[7] Had the strategy portions of the French study been reflected in Ribot's cable, American doctrinal thinking might well have taken a different course.

Instead, as historian I. B. Holley suggests, in drafting his cable Ribot likely relied more on a clarifying memorandum from the commander of the French Armies of the Northeast, who recommended that the American offensive group proposed in the general staff study comprise thirty pursuit groups and thirty bomber groups, or about 4,320 aircraft—an easily defined number that the premier could have used in his own request for ramping up U.S. aircraft production.[8] Without the corresponding general staff study, however, the doctrinal guidance got lost in the transatlantic communication.

Lacking direct guidance on aircraft acquisition priorities from anywhere else, on May 29 the JANTB sent a production plan to the secretaries of War and the Navy that recommended a ratio of three observation aircraft to five pursuit planes to one bomber.[9] This decision had two major ramifications for the development of strategic bombing. First, it formalized the long-held Army vision of using airpower primarily for observation and pursuit missions. Second, by setting bomber production at such a low priority, the board ensured that if there were any delays in aircraft construction, they would exponentially affect the deliveries of bombers to combat units.

Even so, the board's actions contained one bright spot for advocates of strategic bombing. The panel took on newly promoted Army Capt. Edgar S. Gorrell as the Air Service member of the JANTB—a move that introduced him to doctrinal debates. Freshly returned from his MIT master's studies, Gorrell was one of the few aeronautical engineers in the military, making him an ideal choice for the post. Moreover, the JANTB's president—now—Brig. Gen. Benjamin Foulois, who had been Gorrell's old squadron commander in the Mexican Expedition—quickly secured his assignment to one of the Air Service's senior staff billets. In this role Gorrell became an integral part of the stateside planning effort, providing him with direct experience in dealing with the aircraft production challenge and enabling him to observe the impact that the absence of an airpower doctrine would have.

At the time, the board's recommendation was the most comprehensive vision available for American aviation expansion and it immediately became the core of the War Department's emergency appropriation request of $640 million for aircraft acquisition. Since the appropriation was the largest single amount ever approved by Congress for aircraft acquisition, the Army sweetened the deal with assurances that the 4,500 new aircraft would be delivered to the front by May 1918. Persuaded, the House approved the bill on July 14, the Senate passed it a week later and the president signed it on July 24.[10]

Although the JANTB's production numbers were sufficient for budgeting, they told little about how America planned to build or use those airplanes. The Signal Corps rapidly saw the problem and took steps to fix it. On May 16, the cabinet-level Council on National Defense created an Aircraft Production Board to serve as a liaison between the Army and the civilian aircraft industry. Its first chairman, Howard E. Coffin, a Detroit businessman who had had experience in the field, transferred the board to the Army, with the mission of advising the Signal Corps on aviation technology.[11] Coffin had begun his professional career in the automobile industry, gaining a reputation for standardizing parts and production processes. As board chairman, he promptly decided that the two sides must accelerate production dramatically if the United States was to meet its goal for delivering the 4,500 planes to the front. To do that, he declared, industry would have to pare back the variety of aircraft that it would manufacture.

As the Aircraft Production Board and the Signal Corps began to ponder which aircraft to produce, the need for an overall aviation strategy to help them make those decisions became apparent. The guidance that had been provided earlier from the JANTB and an old Army War College study were outdated and of limited value, so many key leaders advocated their own visions for American airpower.

One such example of this was a joint interview with Maj. Gen. George O. Squier, the Army's Chief Signal Officer, and Coffin in the June 6, 1917 edition of *The Sun*, a New York newspaper. Although Squier generally hewed to the Army's narrower view of what doctrine should be, focusing on the important missions of observation and pursuit, he also provided a small, but telling reference to the role that bombing potentially could play in achieving victory, noting that "the Allies so far have not been able to develop and use bombing machines to the needed extent because they could not secure enough airplanes to carry out this work on a great scale." Having said that, Squire asserted that the problem wasn't insurmountable. "[O]nce furnished with all necessary numbers of airmen and aircraft," he continued, "we can speed victory by carrying out bombing and observation work unhindered."[12] The article is evidence that the vision of bombing as an offensive tool was gaining acceptance among key aviation leaders inside the Army.

As the debate continued, Signal Corps leaders concluded that they needed to know substantially more about the air war in Europe before they could decide what types of aircraft to buy for use at the front. The result was a joint fact-finding mission to Europe that included the Corps' own senior leaders and members of the Aircraft Production Board. The move was not unusual. Teams of U.S. Army officers already were on the Continent studying the situation with plans to make recommendations and start the process of buying war materiel and equipment.

Signal Corps aviators also were tapped for a mission to Europe led by then–Maj. Raynal Bolling, a New York National Guard aviator and successful corporate lawyer, to study the French, British, and Italian air services and recommend which types of aircraft the United States should buy. The team included two Army pilots, two naval aviators, two civilian automobile executives, and ninety-three civilian aircraft industry experts.[13]

With such a critical mission, the Signal Corps had faced a tough decision on who should accompany Bolling on the mission. Lt. Col. John B. Bennet, the head of the Signal Corps Aviation Section, realized that the two nominees would need an unusual set of skills. They must be experienced aviators, but they also should be technical experts in aeronautics and aircraft design. Who could be a better choice than Gorrell as the combat-proven new graduate of MIT's aeronautical engineering program and member of the JANTB? The fact that he was then working on the estimate for the air service's $640 million funding request only reinforced those qualifications. Gorrell's combination of aeronautical engineering expertise, planning experience, and growing reputation as an intellectual secured him one of the two Army positions on the Bolling Commission.

On June 16 Gorrell joined the other military members of the panel on the White Star passenger liner *Adriatic* as she departed from New York for Liverpool.[14] The ten-day crossing proved useful, enabling members of the team to socialize and share their backgrounds and thoughts on aviation. As Holley rightly points out, Bolling left New York before the JANTB finalized its recommendations. As a result, Holley infers that Bolling had to rely on the Ribot cable and on what doctrinal guidance he had garnered from the board's initial report.[15]

Yet Holley missed a unifying element in Gorrell's appointment. As a member of the JANTB and of Foulois' team drafting the Air Service appropriations request, the captain offered a wealth of information on which Bolling could draw. He and Bolling developed a strong professional bond during the Atlantic crossing. Commission members recalled that the two stayed up far into the night discussing their flying experiences, aeronautics, and the proper use of aircraft.[16] These late-night discussions may have steered Gorrell's thinking beyond the narrow question of how to manage aircraft production to the more fundamental problem of how to use airplanes in combat. Although

Gorrell's own records do not shed much light on this, it is reasonable to assume the discussions rekindled the interest in aerial strategy that he had shown during the Mexican Expedition.

Still, the panel had a task to accomplish and not much time to do it. Once Bolling arrived in England his team split into two groups. The civilian experts, under the supervision of Rolling I. Mowry of the Cadillac Motor Company, fanned out to aircraft factories around Europe to learn how best to integrate American manufacturing into those processes.[17] Meanwhile, the military members conducted a whirlwind tour of the Allies' aviation forces to gather information on their aircraft designs, production capabilities, and potential for supporting U.S. aircraft needs. Bolling's own report on the trip provides a hint of the frenetic pace that the commission members kept during that early summer: "[L]anded at Liverpool June 26, 1917, proceeded to London, remained there about a week, proceeded to France and to Paris, remained there about two weeks, proceeded thence to Italy, remained there about ten days, returned to Paris and remained there about ten days."[18]

By late July the commission's leadership was once again in its Paris headquarters at 45 Avenue Montaigne, near the Arc de Triomphe. Here Bolling began work on his final report. The report, released on August 15, set priorities for what panel members considered to be the three basic elements of American airpower. The first was to build a sufficient number of training aircraft to produce the required numbers of new pilots. The second was to build aircraft for direct support of ground forces. Finally, in a new turn for American airpower development, Bolling recommended that the U.S. build more aircraft than it needed for tactical operations in support of Allied ground troops and also produce additional fighters and bombers for use in independent military operations against Germany.[19]

Bolling was not yet recommending a move toward strategic bombing, which was still a nebulous concept in the AEF Air Service. Indeed, he reinforced that point in a memorandum to Coffin on October 15 in which he described strategic bombing as still a widely debated concept throughout the Continent. He depicted the British government as beginning to support bombing as a weapon for revenge, but he balanced that against the British Army's continuing resistance to anything beyond a ground-support role. Bolling portrayed the French as hesitant to embrace strategic bombing, due to concerns over possible German retaliation and to a "temporal lack of interest" among French military leaders. In his view, only the Italians fully supported long-range bombing, but he scoffed that their claims about its potential were overblown. As an example, he quoted the commander of aerial operations with the Italian 4th Army, as having told him that "with systematic and sustained bombing . . . he could force a retreat of the Austrian Army within fifteen days."[20]

Despite these conflicting assessments, Bolling predicted that bombing could succeed if it were carried out in a systematic, thorough, and consistent manner. Because this was difficult to do with the limited assets on hand, Bolling indicated that "the Allies must combine toward certain definite operations for which the preparation should be begun at once."[21] Bolling seemed to peer into the future when he predicted that the only obstacle to success in strategic bombing would be if individual countries refused to participate in joint operations and would hold back their airpower for exclusive use in their own raids and attacks.

Although the work of the Bolling Commission was important, its members were not the only Americans proffering recommendations for American aerial strategy and policy in Europe. Even before April 1917, American airpower theory had been changing rapidly as more and more U.S. military observers were dispatched to European aviation units. For the Americans, the most important of these was then–Lt. Col. William "Billy" Mitchell. On March 17 the chief of the Signal Corps ordered him to visit and report on the status of French and British military aviation.[22]

Arriving in Europe, Mitchell threw himself into learning as much as he could about both countries' aviation efforts—sometimes in unconventional fashion. Ignoring U.S. Army regulations, he flew over enemy lines with the French. Overlooking military decorum, he visited Maj. Gen. Sir Hugh Trenchard unannounced, essentially demanding that he be given a tour of British aerial operations. Despite his brief stay, Mitchell emerged as the most experienced American aviator in theater.

His contacts helped ensure that he was part of the group welcoming Pershing on June 13, when the AEF commander arrived in Paris.[23] Nor did Mitchell wait long to get his ideas about aviation into Pershing's hands. He quickly submitted a paper on air policy and organization to Pershing's chief of staff, Maj. Gen. James G. Harbord.

Mitchell's paper was a study in vagueness, mixed with contradictions. What appears to be a discussion about setting priorities for aircraft acquisition hides a subtle doctrinal subtext. The overall structure of the document suggests that the colonel was pressing for greater focus on strategic bombing, yet his definition of that concept is not consistent with his later references to it. It seems likely that he was still forming his vision of strategic aviation when he wrote. At one point he talks about "the air attack of enemy material of all kinds behind his lines," hinting at something broader than damaging an enemy's industrial capability or harming morale. By contrast, his description of tactical aviation is somewhat more informative: "to ensure observation for fire and control of our own artillery . . . airplanes and balloons observe the fire while others fight off hostile aircraft which attempt to stop it."[24]

Despite such ambiguities, the memorandum provides insights into two important aspects of Mitchell's thinking at this early stage that historians often misinterpret. The first relates to the independence of the air component now being revamped. Twice Mitchell clearly suggests that airpower ought to be an independent element in the Army's combat structure. Early on he proposes that the entire AEF Air Service be placed on an equal footing with the Army's other combat branches. Later he specifically addresses strategic forces, writing that "strategic aviation must be organized, separate from those directly attached to army units."[25] The wording marked a clear break from the previous Signal Corps position, which had held that the mission of airpower was purely to support ground combat operations. Mitchell was hinting at a separate, possibly independent role for the AEF Air Service.

Second, the white paper brought up an interesting conundrum: was Mitchell truly advocating strategic bombing at that time? On one hand, he talked in general terms about using airpower to attack the enemy's war making matériel. Some of his own wording can even be interpreted as supporting the kind of strategic bombing that we recognize today. For instance, his claim at the end of the white paper that "with this class of aviation the United States may aid in the greatest way and which, it is believed if properly applied will have a greater influence on the ultimate decision of the war than any other one arm" seemed to hint at a war-winning role for independent strategic bombing.[26]

Read another way, however, Mitchell's broad use of the term "strategical" aviation was more in line with the modern definition of aerial interdiction. His statements such as "they would be used to carry the war well into the enemy's country" could be interpreted to mean interdicting the flow of supplies and reinforcements well behind the front lines. Indeed, this application of airpower was more consistent with Mitchell's appreciation of the British model, which he acquired during his meetings with Trenchard, the RFC commander. By the summer of 1917 Trenchard regarded the primary role of airpower as one of supporting offensive ground operations by repeatedly attacking the enemy deep in his own territory.[27] Mitchell's memorandum appears to support Trenchard's viewpoint more than advocating anything close to our current understanding of "strategic" bombing.

On closer examination, it seems most likely that Mitchell's memorandum actually advocated a twofold mission for airpower. On one level it described a tactical force conducting observation and artillery spotting missions in direct support of a ground commander. On another Mitchell was pressing for a semi-independent "strategical" element that would attack the enemy's war materiel behind the front lines. It is quite likely that a misunderstanding of Mitchell's use of the term "strategical aviation" explains the belief of many historians that Mitchell was advocating what would later evolve as the twenty-first-century concept of strategic bombing.

Still, Mitchell's radical proposal caused concern in the AEF staff. Even if he was not advocating strategic bombing as a war-winning weapon, he seemed to support an independent role for the AEF Air Service, which many senior ground commanders viewed as threatening. It is likely that the Mitchell memorandum was fresh in the mind of Harbord, the AEF chief of staff, when less than a week later, on June

19, he convened a Board of Officers to draft recommendations on aviation-related issues. The board contained a mix of aviators, combat arms officers, and staff officers. At its first meeting the panel assigned individual members to research specific aviation areas and propose specific steps that the Allies should take. The task of reviewing the section on bombing went to Maj. Frank Parker.

Although Parker was a cavalry officer, he had close ties to military aviation. He had married the daughter of now–Lt. Col. Frank S. Lahm, the first Army officer to fly in a Wright airplane—a connection that gave him entrée into the ever-widening circle of military aviators.[28] He also had a keen intellect and a sense of military propriety, a combination that would prove useful in carrying out his assignment.

Parker's report, delivered at the board's meeting on July 4, redefined aerial bombing in a way that was acceptable to the AEF's leadership. He deftly suggested broadening the mission of strategic aviation without seeming to overstep the Army's narrower vision of the airplane's military potential. He proposed setting as the objective of bombing "to attack the supply of an enemy army, thereby preventing it from employing all of its means of combat."[29] He even proposed an initial list of objectives and target types, including enemy depots, factories, and communication lines. As such, Parker's vision of airpower was more in line with army expectations than anything proffered previously. It provided for aerial support for ground forces while omitting the controversial language about Air Service independence that had been contained in Mitchell's original memorandum. At the end of the meeting, the board approved Parker's recommendations and forwarded them to Pershing.[30]

Pershing's system of compartmentalizing the pre-combat planning for the new aviation component ensured that the AEF commander and his staff were receiving a wide variety of inputs on what it should look like. The recommendations were hammered out by four different working groups, which effectively built on one another. The JANTB provided a plan that focused heavily on the numbers of observation and pursuit planes needed. The Bolling Commission modified this slightly by adding an extra offensive aerial force to be used primarily to support ground forces. Then, Mitchell added a Trenchard-inspired concept of an independent aerial offensive. Finally, through Parker, the Board of Officers redefined bombing into something more acceptable to senior American military leaders. All of these options had to be filtered through the lenses of Pershing and his senior staff, many of whom held deep convictions on the use of airpower to support infantry troops. Still missing from the mix was a strategic bombing option similar to the earlier French proposals of 1915 or the British plans that were working their way through Parliament in the summer of 1917.

SOWING THE SEEDS OF STRATEGIC BOMBING

As the Bolling Commission's efforts drew to an end, Pershing sought to keep the best and brightest staff officers in Europe for the cadre of his rapidly forming AEF. Between August 1 and August 15, Pershing promoted Gorrell to major, made him the chief engineer of the AEF Air Service, and put him in charge of the technical section. This new position not only kept Gorrell in Paris, but it also gave him responsibility for executing the aircraft acquisition and support recommendations that he had helped draft as a member of the Bolling Commission. Between August 1 and September 15 Gorrell oversaw the acquisition of approximately $80 million worth of aircraft, engines, radios, guns, buildings, and even whiskey for the AEF Air Service.[31]

Although the job was demanding, Gorrell rose to the occasion. In an unpublished article on Gorrell, retired Maj. Gen. Orvil Anderson jokingly posited his importance: "at the end of this hectic period an entire boatload of people landed in France to take on the jobs that Gorrell had been holding down."[32] Gorrell's success quickly got him noticed by senior leaders in Europe, who admired his sharp mind and ability to think strategically.

Gorrell's success also came to the attention of senior leaders in Washington. In an October 9 memo to Brig. Gen. William L. Kenly, chief of the AEF Air Service, Bolling opposed a request to send Gorrell back to the capital to represent the Signal Corps on the General Staff. His wording reflects his high esteem for Gorrell. "Frankly, I do not see how we can get along without Maj[or] Gorrell in France as his knowledge goes far beyond mere technical matters, Bolling said. "He does not confine his work merely to technical matters, but is my chief advisor on all matters requiring knowledge of military aviation."[33]

Consequently, when Foulois, now a brigadier general, arrived with senior personnel for the AEF Air Service staff, Pershing moved Gorrell to the AEF Air Service operations directorate. In this new position, Gorrell led the development of aerial strategy for the service's impending combat operations. In this way, his duties transferred from the daily grind of logistics to more cerebral, but no less critical, planning responsibilities.

From late September to December 1917, Gorrell focused on developing a strategic plan for the AEF Air Service. As an experienced staff officer, he sought guidance from previous Army studies and international sources. He built on the ties that he made during his travels with the Bolling Commission and later as chief engineer of the Air Service. At the same time, he began to organize his thoughts about a strategic bombing doctrine.

Two influences helped shape Gorrell's views on strategic bombing. First, the internal debate about the role of airpower within the United States Army provided him with a historical knowledge and framework on which to base his study of the issue later. Second, British, French, and Italian aviation strategists expanded his thinking beyond the narrow scope with which U.S. Army leaders viewed the choices. The result was a fusion between the changing American views on strategic bombing and the more advanced European perspective in 1917.

Indeed, Gorrell may well have been the best-placed officer in the U.S. Army to keep tabs on the evolution of the internal debate on aerial strategy. His membership on the JANTB and on Foulois' staff gave him a detailed knowledge about the size and structure of the forces needed. When Gorrell arrived in Europe, he was perfectly situated to observe the doctrinal evolution of the AEF Air Service. In Paris he had frequent contact with both Mitchell and the Board of Officers. His role on the Bolling Commission and later as chief engineer of the AEF Air Service provided him with myriad opportunities to discuss strategy with key staff members and to read the findings of the various other official discussion panels.

Finally, Gorrell's contacts with foreign military aviators and theorists played a major role in molding his thoughts on airpower. The
most important of these was his close relationship with Lord Tiverton.
In 1917 Tiverton was a Royal Navy aviator assigned to the British
Aviation Commission in Paris. The British commission was only a few
blocks from the offices of the Bolling Commission in a requisitioned
apartment house near the Arc de Triomphe.[34] In both his time as chief
engineer of the AEF Air Service and as an operational strategist on the
Air Service's staff, Gorrell often sought Tiverton's advice. Their official
exchanges blossomed into a friendship and Tiverton became a leading
confidant and adviser to Gorrell on the question of strategic bombing.

Born in 1880, Tiverton enjoyed a typical British upper-class child-
hood. As a young man, he attended Eton and Oxford, and became a
barrister in 1906. His life changed abuptly, however, in 1914. When
Britain declared war on Germany, Lord Tiverton left his law practice and entered the Royal Naval Air Service. After serving briefly as
an armament-training officer, he moved to 3 Wing at Luxeuil in the
summer of 1916.[35] Although 3 Wing had been created primarily to
hinder zeppelin production, the RNAS soon expanded its mission to
include bombing German industrial targets; the Royal Flying Corps
(RFC), which had held that job before, had been overwhelmed with
demands that it support ground troops participating in the Somme
offensive. As 3 Wing's armament officer, Tiverton was closely involved
in the planning and target selection for the unit's Sopwith 1½ Strutters
and Shorts bombers.[36] The mission suited Tiverton, who quickly
evolved into the unit's primary strategist.

Unfortunately for Tiverton and the 3 Wing, the RFC successfully blunted the RNAS expansion. Its opposition centered on two
elements. The first was traditional interservice rivalry. The RFC
did not look favorably on the notion of naval aircraft flying from
ground bases in central France against targets deep into enemy territory. Although RFC leaders had not yet embraced the idea of strategic bombing in itself, they regarded it as their territory and viewed
3 Wing's expansion as an unwanted incursion into their domain. A
greater factor behind the RFC's opposition, however, was the issue of
aircraft inventories. The combination of continuing heavy losses from

the RFC's high-risk Somme operations and of production problems with the new Sopwith 1½ Strutter bomber had left the Corps with an uncomfortable shortage of suitable aircraft. Trenchard had complained to the Air Board that "if the Navy obtained large numbers of engines and machines that the Army required, the effect will be seriously felt."[37] In the end, both factors won the day, and 3 Wing was doomed.

By June 1917 the Royal Navy had decided that Tiverton's planning capabilities were needed elsewhere. The RNAS transferred him to the Aviation Commission in Paris to work on a strategic bombardment policy.[38] Tiverton worked closely with the commission's RFC officers and the French air staff to develop recommendations for the equipping, training, and planning of a major bombing campaign to take place the following year. Shortly after they began, however, the French started to focus more on tactical aviation. So Tiverton turned to the new aviators in town—the Americans. He worked hard to cultivate friendships with members of the Bolling Commission and with early AEF Air Service staff officers alike.

Tiverton and Gorrell had met during Bolling Commission discussions on the feasibility of buying British bomber aircraft for the fledgling AEF Air Service, but their shared interest in strategic bombing built a friendship that went far beyond that. In many respects, the more senior Tiverton served as a mentor to the young Gorrell. Tiverton had spent most of the summer of 1917 working on the strategic bombing policy for the RNAS. In September, he shared this policy memorandum with Gorrell.[39] The four themes of strategic bombing that Tiverton identified struck a chord with Gorrell; they continually show up in his later writings. It would be too far a leap, however, to say that Gorrell simply took Tiverton's ideas as his own. The themes of objectives, offensive force, concentration, and morale effects of bombing all were well known to Gorrell and were key concepts in Mitchell's and Parker's policy recommendations.

Perhaps it is best to think of Tiverton as an inspiration for the overworked young staff officer. As many historians have noted, Gorrell copied large parts of Tiverton's memorandum. Yet, that does not necessarily mean he simply stole Tiverton's ideas. In the time-honored world of military staff work, copying others' writing that bolsters one's own argument is simply good time management. Borrowed statements such as "unquestionably, the greatest morale effect is by day, compared to night attacks when German workers are in their own houses" cannot be considered solely a British idea. All air services held similar beliefs. Thus, while there is a clear amalgamation of some of Tiverton's work into Gorrell's, to claim that it is plagiarism seems a stretch.

The British were not the only source of international inspiration for Gorrell. From his first visit to Italy with the Bolling Commission, Gorrell maintained a close relationship with Count Giovanni Battista Caproni, an aircraft designer and close friend of the Italian bombing theorist Giulio Douhet.[40] During his initial trip to Italy in June 1917, Gorrell formed a relationship with Count Caproni. Like Gorrell's friendship with Lord Tiverton, the count took on the role of a mentor to the young major. Both men shared an interest in bombing, which they discussed numerous times when Gorrell was in Italy. Caproni's journal mentions several conversations over dinner where he and Gorrell discussed air warfare and the role of bombing in destroying an enemy's ability to fight.[41]

Caproni seems to have captured Gorrell's imagination during these sessions. In a memorandum to Bolling dated October 15 Gorrell adopted many of Caproni's ideas in suggesting how the United States should approach strategic bombing. "This is not a phantom nor a dream," Gorrell wrote, "but is a huge reality capable of being carried out with success if the U.S. will only carry on a sufficiently large campaign for next year, and manufacture the types of airplanes, that lend themselves to this campaign, instead of building pursuit planes already out of date."[42]

As the memorandum suggests, Gorrell's friendship with Caproni did not end when the Bolling Commission concluded its business. The two men continued to correspond through the end of 1917. Sometime before October 31, Caproni gave Gorrell a book, *Let Us Kill the War; Let Us Aim at the Heart of the Enemy.*[43] The volume, reprinted in English, described how strategic bombing could destroy an enemy's industrial base and civilian morale. On November 17 Gorrell wrote to Caproni asking for more copies to share with his fellow aviators. Tellingly, in the same letter, he also called on Caproni to recommend targets inside Germany for an American strategic bombardment campaign.[44]

The two men's influences on internal American debates are visible in Gorrell's first two formal reports from Europe. The Bolling Report on August 15 specifically highlighted the need to buy long-range bombers to sustain a strategic effort. Meanwhile, Gorrell's companion memorandum to Brigadier General Scriven, chief of the Signal Corps, dated September 27, provided still more information on the possibilities of bombing.[45] In that one, Gorrell set the stage for his later proposal by outlining the state of British, French, and Italian bombing efforts. It is less a policy recommendation than a description of the current technology, tactics, and strategy used by each country's military air component. Still, the memorandum demonstrated the strong influence from the British and Italians that formed the basis of Gorrell's seminal *Strategic Bombardment Plan* of November 1917.

Together, these show clearly that there were many influences guiding Gorrell's thinking about strategic bombing during that period. Yes, he did borrow heavily from Tiverton's work for his own writings, but they were leavened with elements of American and Italian thought. It is difficult to say exactly where Gorrell got each idea, since his strategic bombing theory was just coalescing then. Most likely he borrowed heavily from Tiverton because his lordship's paper contained three important elements that resonated with Gorrell. First, the Tiverton papers closely matched Gorrell's own vision of strategic bombing. Second, Tiverton's work often mirrored the ideas that Caproni proffered in his correspondence with Gorrell. Finally, because Tiverton's work was written in English, it was readily available and easy to include as the basis of his report. This last consideration surely had a strong appeal for Gorrell.

THE AMERICANIZATION OF STRATEGIC BOMBING

Major Gorrell's strategic bombardment plan began to form as early as August 15, 1917, when Pershing selected him to lead the Air Service's technical section.[46] In this post, Gorrell led efforts to buy the combat aircraft required by the newly arriving American squadrons. On the surface this may seem like a simple task, but the AEF had no accepted procedures for airpower acquisition then. As Gorrell wrestled with the issue of what types and how many of each aircraft to buy, he rapidly discovered that he had first to determine how America would use airpower before he could make decisions about numbers and types of aircraft.

Gorrell's links with the Bolling Commission, the Board of Officers, and foreign aviation theorists helped guide his thinking. The observation and pursuit missions were well developed, and the AEF leadership held definite opinions on those missions, so the task in those categories was straightforward—to buy the best European aircraft for each of the accepted mission sets. Bombing was another issue. Although most nations employed tactical bombing, strategic bombing was still largely theoretical, but that was changing rapidly. The summer of 1917 saw an increase in strategic bombing planning, especially after May 25, when the Germans began the Gotha raids against England.[47]

The fact that bombing was so new most likely appealed to Gorrell's sense of adventurism. Yet bombing might have remained just a personal fascination for him had it not been for the structural changes that the AEF was undergoing at the time.

When Pershing took command of the American Expeditionary Force in April 1917, he thought long and hard about whom his subordinate commanders should be. For the Air Service, he favored Foulois. The two had built a professional relationship when Foulois served under Pershing as the commander of the 1st Aero Squadron in the Mexican Expedition. Regrettably, only one month before the AEF's start, Foulois had begun a critical assignment as chairman of JANTB in Washington. In June 30, 1917, his portfolio expanded when he became chief of the Aviation Section of the Army Signal Corps—a job that placed him in charge of all production, training, and deployment of Air Service forces inside the United States.[48] Even with Pershing's influence, the Aviation Section post was too important to remove Foulois during the critical buildup.

Even so, that only delayed Pershing in tapping Foulois; it did not dissuade him. By late October, the situation had stabilized enough for Foulois to head to Europe to replace Kenly as chief of the AEF Air Service. Word spread quickly that a new commander was on his way with a large staff to take over operations, and Gorrell must have real-ized that his own relatively junior rank would mean that he would lose his posting to a more senior officer. A memorandum from Bolling to Coffin just two days before Foulois' arrival supports this assessment. In it, Bolling indicated that his staff was looking forward to having the new officers, since it had been severely undermanned. Yet, at the same time there was apprehension over the prospect that the move might also entail placing new senior officers into key staff billets.[49] With this air of uncertainty as a backdrop, Gorrell began consolidating his thoughts into a formal proposal to present to Foulois on his arrival.

As many expected, Foulois showed up in November with a large cadre of senior officers to supplant the existing command structure. On November 21 seven new officers arrived at the technical section and one of them, Lt. Col. Halsey Dunwoody, replaced Gorrell as the chief of the section.[50] This might have been the end of Gorrell's vision, but Foulois was concerned about the lack of operational and strategic employment planning in the AEF Air Service. Amid the heavy workload of buying aircraft, setting up airdromes, and train-ing personnel, the staff had paid scant attention to how to use the Air Service in combat.

Gorrell was ready to meet this concern. Following Mitchell's example, he presented his proposed strategic bombing plan on November 28, only a day after Foulois assumed command of the AEF Air Service.[51] The plan must have met Foulois' intentions because he approved it immediately and included it with other proposals to forward to Pershing. Foulois' own note to AEF Chief of Staff Harbord on December 1 reported that his staff had been working on "the air policy to be recommended for adoption by the American Forces for the past ten days and would forward it to HQ AEF soon."[52] Gorrell's proposal was part of the overall air policy package that arrived at Pershing's office in early December 1917.

Although much of the document borrowed heavily from Tiverton's British bombing proposal, there were noteworthy differences. Aware that senior Army leaders still viewed airpower as primarily a support function for ground operations, Gorrell used a two-pronged approach to getting their attention.

His introduction read like a sales pitch to the AEF senior leadership. First, he argued that that bombing could help the U.S. Army win the war. Historian George Williams best describes his logic: "land battle is in stalemate; artillery is the key to the land battle; ammunition production is the key to artillery; factories are the key to ammunition production; therefore, aerial bombardment should attack munitions factories, thus influencing the land battle."[53] Although Gorrell's argument was not expressed quite as succinctly, he made a similar point on how strategic bombing might facilitate victory.

Then he invited the leadership's attention to the impact of the recent Gotha bombings in Britain—especially in London—which were changing the way military leaders and politicians on the Continent viewed airpower. The Trenchard and Mitchell vision—of the *strategical* use of aircraft primarily for behind-the-front-lines interdiction missions to support ground offensives—was being challenged by a new *strategic* vision of airpower to help break an enemy's industrial might and its will to fight, potentially ending a war without the need for a ground victory. Although the British led the way in this thinking, mainly due to the clamor for revenge after the Gotha bombings, other countries were beginning to see the value of strategic bombing as well.

Gorrell was one of the first Americans to discuss the strategic implications of the Gotha campaigns. His memorandum stressed three points about the German offensive. First, if the Allies did not respond the Germans would be able to destroy European industrial targets with impunity while their own factories and supply depots remained intact. Second, with the front lines now positioned in France, geography was giving the German pilots an advantage. German aircraft based in Belgium and France were only a short flight away from French and British industrial areas, while Allied pilots targeting German cities would have to endure long, dangerous flights to reach them— which made long-range bombers more important to the Europeans and Americans. Finally, the Germans had the biggest advantage of all: They had a head start on their enemies in developing strategic bombing forces. "[T]he Germans' words were being rapidly turned into deeds."[54] In effect, Gorrell created two rationales for America pursuing strategic bombing: it would help win the war, and the Allies had no choice but to respond to the German bombing campaign.

The plan that Gorrell outlined was a four-pronged program that borrowed heavily from Tiverton's four themes, but couched them in terms that resonated with American military leaders. First, he proposed that the AEF Air Service separate its strategic bombing units from its tactical forces—a division that he argued was necessary to ensure that the strategic units would be able to focus solely on their primary mission without interference. Second, he called for the strategic forces to identify and prioritize target areas that would cause the most damage to enemy war production. Next, he said the Air Service should position bomber bases so it could launch concentrated attacks against those targets. Finally, he recommended that the Allies structure their operations to focus attacks on a single target each day so as to maximize both the physical destruction to enemy infrastructure and the impact of the bombing on civilian and military morale.[55] Embedded in these steps were the foundations of what would become American strategic bombing doctrine for the next hundred years—independence, targeting, and concentration.

There was one key difference between Gorrell's recommendation and what Lord Tiverton had advocated. In keeping with the earlier recommendation of the Board of Officers, Gorrell proposed a system of round-the-clock bombing against German targets in order to "give the Germans no rest from our aerial activities and no time to repair the damage inflicted."[56] The British had favored night operations to limit losses from antiaircraft fire.

Gorrell's position on daylight bombing may have seemed out of place, considering the high aircraft losses that Allied aviators experienced from earlier rates. Indeed, that same problem prompted the Germans to move to night bombing by the fall of 1917.[57] Still, as U.S. Air Force historian George Williams points out, the American position may have been a combination of theory and real-world practicality.[58] From his time as the chief of the Air Service Technical Section Gorrell must have understood the realities of bomber aircraft production and delivery timelines for the AEF Air Service. The Americans' choice for their primary daylight bomber, the DH-4, was already in production in Britain, with allotments scheduled for delivery to the AEF Air Service, but the Handley Page night bomber production was delayed to await the delivery of Liberty engines from America and was not scheduled to arrive in the AEF Air Service operational units until May 1918.[59] This meant that daylight bombers would be arriving at the front months before the nighttime bombers. On the other hand, starting daytime operations first would not only take the fight to the enemy sooner, but it also would provide pilots with experience in navigating far behind the front lines without the extra complication of darkness. Although daylight losses might be higher, the Americans felt this trade-off was worth the cost.

Gorrell returned to his salesmanship in the conclusion of his proposal. Although this last section was brief, it was a clarion call to action. A single sentence in the section underscores the urgency of the entire proposal: "Unless a decision is made to commence it immediately, we cannot hope to operate during 1918."[60] This warning apparently resonated with Pershing. The plan was dated November 28. Pershing approved it on January 5, 1918.

The strategic bombing proposal instantly won support within the AEF staff and enhanced Gorrell's career in the process. Recognizing him as the American expert on strategic bombing, Pershing promoted him to lieutenant colonel and gave him command of Strategical Aviation in the Zone of Advance on December 3, 1917.[61] Gorrell immediately began preparations for the strategic bombing offensive. Although he could not control the pace of aircraft deliveries, he took steps to ensure that the facilities, training plans, and bombing doctrine would be ready when they arrived.

CONCLUSION

Out of this maelstrom of a rapidly expanding AEF, a newly appointed Air Service staff, the influences from the experiences of allies, and the pressures of war emerged the first clearly defined American vision of strategic bombing. Years later U.S. Air Force Gen. Laurence S. Kuter, who spent much of his career in strategic bombing posts, described the Gorrell plan as the "earliest, clearest, and least-known statement of the American conception of the employment of air power."[62] Yet

Kuter's description understates the complicated mixture of historical precedent, new thinking, and wartime realities that underlay the plan. Although the Gorrell plan is often viewed as the work of a single theorist, it is more accurate to recognize it as the amalgamation of many ideas—from both inside and outside the U.S. Air Service—shaped by the realities of combat and brought together by Gorrell.

The groundwork for Gorrell's work was laid in the early development of the Air Service from 1903 to 1916. The foundation proved sturdy, but was limited at first by the Army's narrow vision of airpower. The process accelerated, however, with America's entry into World War I, which enabled men such as Billy Mitchell, George Squier, and Frank Parker to burnish the doctrine through their early writings.

At the same time, European airpower strategists, such as Caproni, Trenchard, and Tiverton—influenced their new allies by sharing their visions of strategic air power and their experience with members of the new AEF Air Service who were preparing for imminent U.S. combat operations.

Finally, the realities of the battlefield played a role in shaping American strategic doctrine. By 1917, senior leaders understood that the war would be won in large measure by the ability of the combatant countries to keep their armies fed, supplied, and able to fight. The importance of attacking the enemy's factories and transportation system was understood by almost all leaders. Still, aircraft were a limited asset that required careful management to ensure that they were available when needed. The Gotha raids on England during the summer of 1917 helped spur changes to this traditional way of thinking. Without a response, the Allies risked letting the Germans gain the advantage in this new form of industrial warfare. Consequently, leaders slowly became open to risking airpower in deep strikes against enemy resources.

For Gorrell, too, all three factors came together at the right place and right time. His background not only opened him to the possibilities of strategic aviation, but also positioned him to address the problems at hand for the American air service. His connections with key strategists in the American, Italian, French, and British air services guided his intellect during those critical days. Finally, the imperative to get his ideas presented in the turmoil of changing staffs in the fall of 1917 secured his reputation as a superior air planner and eventually led to his own combat command where he could test his ideas.

Unfortunately for Gorrell, the technological, organizational, and doctrinal problems facing the AEF Air Service were a long way from being solved in December 1917. In later months he faced delays in aircraft deliveries, organizational infighting, and failures in senior leadership support that dramatically hindered his ability to execute his vision. These trying times led Gorrell to modify his visions of strategic bombing and altered the AEF Air Service's perceptions of proper airpower doctrine.

CHAPTER 4

The Hard Realities of War

In the fall of 1917 two separate forces propelled the expansion of strategic bombing theory. In Britain, public demand for a response to the recent German bombings of London and other cities revived the debate over long-range bombing. Meanwhile, the newly arrived American aviators received a quick education in airpower doctrine. For the young Americans, who had spent little time thinking about the role of airpower in a war, the tutelage must have been like drinking from a fire house. In this situation, however, their inexperience proved to be a positive factor. They were able to keep open minds to the new methods of warfare that their French, British, and Italian allies were espousing. Edgar Gorrell, Billy Mitchell, Frank Parker, and others took readily to these doctrines, immersing themselves in the debates and actively seeking out the European experts.

In this way, early American bombing strategy became an amalgamation of European ideas and American theories. Gorrell's strategic bombing plan of November 28, 1917, was the best example of this new vision. His proposed bombing campaign seemed to win quick support from the AEF leadership; both Foulois and Pershing rapidly approved the plan. On December 3 Foulois appointed Gorrell commander of Strategical Aviation in the Zone of Advance, with orders to oversee the preparations and execution of his plan.

By January 1918 it seemed that Gorrell, now a colonel, was a rising star in the AEF Air Service. Yet the hard realities of war were about to affect his plans. Just as the earlier French and British strategic bombing advocates were thrown off course by the competing demands for close air support in the great battles of Verdun and the Somme, so too would the Americans be diverted by the Ludendorff Offensive, a series of successful German ground attacks along the western front that began in March 1918. The tremendous expenditures of military might—first to stop the Germans and then to begin the slow process of pushing them back—effectively precluded any strategic bombing campaigns during 1918.

Still, the idea of a strategic bombing campaign never died in the American Air Service. Instead, its advocates continued to work with their allies and soon proposed new plans to the AEF staff. Finally, with the help of British pressure for mounting a bomber offensive, along with projections that the Allies soon would have a surplus of aircraft if the war effort continued to go in their favor, were able to turn their attention back to planning for long-range bombing missions. What would have happened in such an air campaign remains a mystery, however. On November 11, 1918, the major combatants signed an armistice, ending the war before their new bombing strategy could be tested.

GORRELL'S STRATEGIC BOMBING PLANS

After Gorrell's assignment as strategic aviation commander he imme-diately began work to turn his bombing proposal into a functioning plan. The timing must have seemed ripe, what with the heightened British pressure for such a campaign and the growing interest within the AEF leadership. Yet Gorrell was to learn once again that not all senior leaders were open to potentially radical new airpower theories. Many of them remained steadfast in believing that the only viable role for aircraft was in direct support of ground forces.

Still, in December 1917 Gorrell appeared to be perfectly situated to turn American strategic bombing into a reality. Upon assuming his new command, he had quickly surrounded himself with highly capable deputies, beginning with Maj. Harold S. Fowler as his execu-tive officer. An American, Fowler had joined the British Army in 1914 as an artillery officer before shifting to the Royal Flying Corps, first as an observer and in 1916 as a pilot. When the United States entered the war, he transferred back to the Air Service and helped develop

America's pilot training program.[1] Gorrell used his talent to speed the construction of bomber bases and the training of bomber crews. Next he hired Maj. Millard F. Harmon as his pursuit-support planner. Even at this early stage, most aviators understood that bombers required protection if they were to reach their targets without excessive losses. Harmon's background in pursuit aviation made him a good candidate to plan escort missions. Finally, Gorrell looked to a British officer who was on loan to the AEF Air Service to become his strategic bombing planner. In October 1917, after suffering injuries that limited his ability to fly, Wing Commander Spencer Grey was assigned to assist the American flyers.[2] Gorrell had pushed hard for the transfer, calling Grey, who had commanded both day and night bombing squadrons in the Royal Naval Air Service, "the world's greatest authority on aerial bombardment."[3]

The British readily agreed to the request, since they also were moving toward implementing a new vision of strategic bombing. After the confusion and fear of the July 7 Gotha raid on London, the public outcry had forced the British government to explore new options. At a cabinet meeting four days later, the government agreed to set up a two-man committee with Prime Minister Lloyd George as the chair and Lieutenant General Smuts as the primary investigator to explore how best to counter the German raids.[4] This led to two major recommendations. On July 19 Smuts suggested placing the coordination of air defense under a single joint command as a way of improving the protection of London against air raids. On August 17 he took another leap forward by proposing a complete restructuring of the air services into a single independent air force that would combine the RNAS and the RFC. The new Royal Air Force (RAF), as it would be called, would maintain the two organizations' previous ground and naval support roles, but conspicuously Smuts specifically recommended adding an independent long-range bombing mission against German cities and industry. He argued that the new focus would turn the RAF into a force capable of winning the war through aerial bombardment.

Although many military leaders disagreed, Smuts had two aces in the hole. First, he had public pressure on his side to take revenge

against Germany for the Gotha raids, enabling political leaders to overcome resistance in the army and navy for creation of the new RAF.
Second, he found high-level backing for countering long-held fears
that launching a strategic bombing campaign would leave Britain too
short of aircraft to provide badly needed support for ground and naval
operations. Shortly after the Smuts report, Sir Weetman Pearson, the
1st Viscount of Cowdray, chairman of the Air Board, released a study
projecting that recent increases in aircraft production would result in
a large surplus of airplanes by the summer of 1918, wiping out the
shortages that had plagued the air services since the start of the war.

The shift in top policymakers' views on both issues was not lost
on the field commanders, who also were under pressure to respond in
kind to the German bombing attacks. On October 11, after receiving orders to begin bombing targets in Germany, Trenchard authorized the creation of 41 Wing under the command of Lt. Col. Cyril
Newall at Ochey, France, assigning it the primary mission of conducting bombing raids against German cities.[6]

Field Marshal Haig, commander of the British Expeditionary
Force, also felt increased pressure from the government to embark
on revenge-bombing strikes against German cities, addressing the
issue for the first time in his annual report on combat information.
"[T]he persistent raiding by hostile aeroplanes and airships of English
cities and towns have recently decided our own Government to adopt
counter-measures," he wrote. "In consequence of this decision a series
of bombing raids into Germany began in October 1917, and have
since been continued whenever weather conditions have permitted."[7]

Consistent with the new public and political pressure to bomb
German cities, 41 Wing began operations on October 17 with a raid
on the Burbach iron foundry near Saarbrucken. The British continued operations until the onset of winter weather limited flying in late
November.[8] Given such pressure for strategic bombing, it is understandable that the British services wanted one of their best officers
to be intimately involved in creating and coordinating any American
bombing campaign. As a result, they readily agreed with the assignment of Grey to the Strategical Aviation in the Zone of Advance staff,
to coordinate the Allied bombing efforts.

On December 22, when it became clear that the three major allies needed to coordinate their bombing plans to reap the biggest benefit, the British hosted an allied bombing conference. Major General Trenchard represented the British; General Maurice Duval, the commander of French Air Services, represented the French; and Gorrell represented the Americans.[9] The substantial differences in rank among the three representatives should have given the British and Gorrell their first indications that AEF leadership attitudes toward bombing were changing. Nevertheless, the conference proved useful in determining each nation's readiness to participate in a combined bomber offensive.

The British led the effort with a proposal for a strategic campaign against German industrial cities with a combined bomber force based in the Nancy area. The French did not support the British, believing that the plan was too difficult to achieve in 1918 without pulling resources away from the ground battles. The French also feared that Germany would retaliate, which they worried would cause more damage to their factories than the Allied bombing would to German industry. Finally, Gorrell asserted that American forces wanted to participate in the effort, but revealed his tenuous position by disclosing that he could not pledge U.S. support without first obtaining the approval of the AEF commander.[10]

Gorrell and Foulois followed up the conference with a visit to Trenchard's headquarters over Christmas. Trenchard proposed that American bomber forces join with his recently established 41 Wing in the Nancy area. His vision was to speed the Americans' training process by integrating them into British groups to learn from the more experienced English aviators. Once the Americans fielded enough squadrons to form their own group, Trenchard recommended, they should operate as an American bombing group under the British wing. Eventually, when the Americans came to provide the preponderance of bomber forces in a region, Trenchard indicated his desire to turn over command of that area to the American Air Service, with the remaining British forces coming under U.S. command.[11]

The plan offered many benefits for the growing AEF Air Service. First, there was the obvious learning value of flying under the tutelage of experienced British pilots. Locating the Americans and British on British bases would reduce the number of airfields that the Americans would need in the resource-constrained environment. Finally, joining with the British offered the Americans the opportunity to take advantage of their superior maintenance and supply systems. Since the U.S. supply system was struggling just to deploy and provision the Army, this promise of logistical support must have seemed ideal to Gorrell and Foulois.

Yet the plan met with stiff resistance within the AEF staff. The American generals viewed the subordination of U.S. forces, even air forces, to a British commander as problematic, as shown in a report that Foulois sent to the AEF chief of staff on December 23. After describing the British progression toward strategic bombing that fall, Foulois warned the staff that the British Air Ministry and the British War Cabinet were preparing a communication to be referred to the commander in chief of the AEF, recommending that the British, French, and American air services take the necessary steps to integrate into a combined strategic offensive against German industry. Maj. Gen. James W. McAndrew, the AEF chief of staff, responded to the memo, recommending that a three-member panel explore the issue, but cautioned that U.S. commanders would insist on meeting the needs for air support before exploring any cooperation with other Allied units in bombing campaigns.[12]

Gorrell's subordinate position at the conference and the AEF's reluctance to endorse the creation of a combined bomber force immediately posed a problem for American bombing advocates. Although Pershing had approved Gorrell's initial proposal, the general's staff began to worry about the independent nature of the bomber force. Just as Mitchell learned after he proffered his initial air strategy proposal, the AEF command staff simply would not accept an independent air force. The December conference entrenched this viewpoint, since it spoke not only of an independent bomber force but also of subordinating that force to a British-led effort. This dual affront prompted many staff officers to drop any support they may have had for strategic bombing.

Gorrell surely felt the sting of this attitude change. Despite his best efforts, he faced long delays in both policy decisions and aircraft deliveries. He even suggested that AEF staff officers deliberately had saddled him with additional duties expressly to keep him closely tied to their command structure.[13] Hoping to change the situation, Gorrell took a bold step: he wrote a memorandum to Foulois on January 2, 1918 arguing that the AEF command structure must coordinate with the Allies and take tangible steps to provide aircraft, pilots, and bases for the force to start operations.[14]

The memorandum likely ruffled feathers in the AEF headquarters. It not only included a critique of the staff's reception to the new proposal, but also asserted that bomber operations should be carried out independently and as part of a British-led campaign. Although this opinion likely won Gorrell favor with his British colleagues, it angered his American superiors. The anger seems to have caught Gorrell by surprise, and he rapidly took steps to modify his proposal to win back the support of the AEF staff.

Sometime between late December 1917 and the end of January 1918 Gorrell wrote a second proposal on strategic bombing entitled, "The Future Role of American Bombardment Aviation."[15] Once again he turned to the British, copying heavily from Trenchard's December 1917 report to the War Cabinet. Although Gorrell had lifted entire paragraphs from the Trenchard report, the memorandum contained more American ideas than his previous memorandum. In many ways it reflects Gorrell's attempt to update his November 28 recommendation to meet senior U.S. leadership concerns.

To accomplish this, Gorrell used a three-part approach. First, he tried to assuage concerns about independence. In the first paragraph, he paid homage to a single unified Army effort by claiming that "the Air Service is an integral part of a homogeneous team, no portion of which, working by itself, can alone decisively defeat the enemy."[16] He then continued the theme, often comparing airpower to a long-range gun and describing how strategic aviation could help sway the outcome of a battle.

Next, he omitted his earlier claim that aviation could win the war itself, suggesting only that strategic bombing would make the infantry's job on the battlefield easier. He challenged commanders to envision "what would happen if communications were destroyed, supplies of rations and [materiel] cut, and if reserve troops were subjected to the demoralizing effect of fire without defense?"[17] In this manner, he hoped to convince commanders that bombing factories would directly aid ground combat.

Finally, Gorrell added a new element: the morale effect of bombing. In his discussion of daylight versus nighttime bombing, Gorrell spelled out the trade-offs between the two. Daylight bombing caused more damage, but also meant more losses. Nighttime bombing reduced losses, but was not as accurate and resulted in less damage. He argued that this was not a trade-off that the U.S. Army had to make. Previewing future thinking, he contended that daylight missions flown in large formations with escorts would keep losses at acceptable levels. At the same time, bombing both in daylight hours and at night would have such a large adverse impact on enemy morale that it would offset the reduced physical damage that night bombing would bring.[18]

Arguing that the so-called morale effect might be more destructive than physical damage was perhaps the most interesting part of Gorrell's new recommendation. He had heard the claim before in correspondence with Tiverton and Caproni, but he had not included it in his own writing until now. Gorrell used two examples to support his argument. He cited British statistics on the losses in work hours that resulted from factory evacuations during the Gotha raids, along with French reports on the increased labor difficulties that followed German bombings near Pont-St.Vincent. Although the raids in France "have never interrupted the work for more than a few hours," he added, "it has become increasingly difficult to persuade the workmen to remain."[19]

Gorrell also modified his discussion of the core components of strategic bombing. He continued to stress the need for careful target selection and bomber force concentration. To mitigate Army fears, however, he toned down his call for making the Air Service independent. Finally, he added a psychological element by arguing that the morale effects of bombardment were as important as physical destruction. Although Gorrell cannot claim to have created any of these concepts, he does deserve credit for linking them in a formal policy proposal for a uniquely American vision of airpower.

Despite Gorrell's careful effort to meet American concerns, his second proposal fell on deaf ears. First, his earlier memorandum already had caused too much anger and resentment among senior AEF staff officers and they seemed unlikely to look favorably on any new strategic bombing proposal. Second, by early 1918 aircraft production shortages were readily apparent to the AEF staff, and Gorrell's new plan must have seemed like an extravagant use of limited bombing aircraft that ground commanders needed. Finally, Gorrell's widely known close ties to the British caused added consternation. Many senior Army officers likely saw his suggestions as a first step toward losing command of their bomber forces to a multinational independent bombing command led by the British.

Given this convergence of forces, it was obvious that Gorrell would be unable to create a strategic bombing force and use it in a major campaign. On January 21 a disappointed General Pershing removed him from command of Strategical Aviation in the Zone of Advance and assigned him to the AEF G-3 (operations) staff.[20] He still would work on long-range bombing policy, but his location outside the Air Service itself severely limited his influence on future operations. Gorrell eventually worked his way back into the Air Service as Patrick's chief of staff, but by then the Army's heightened need for direct air support during combat operations limited the appeal of his previous plans.

The removal of Gorrell—and the intensification of ground fighting in early 1918—effectively ended any prospect for mounting a strategic bombing campaign during that year. With resources limited, the Army and the Air Service turned their attention to operational planning and logistics systems. Nevertheless, the idea of strategic bombing did not completely die out and continued to simmer in the minds of many airpower leaders. When projections for 1919 finally showed a significant increase in the numbers of bomber aircraft available, AEF Air Service planners began to reconsider Gorrell's ideas. Yet, if anything, the challenges they faced had grown more numerous. In the intervening months competing plans for airpower had begun to gain favor with senior American military leaders. They not only threatened Gorrell's ideas, but also shaped an entirely new vision for strategic bombing in late 1918.

COMPETING PLANS FOR AIRPOWER

By February 1918 Gorrell had settled into his new job in the G–3 (operations) division of the AEF staff. Although he continued to work on strategic bombing, the realities of war soon intervened. In early 1918 the Germans realized they had to use their temporary numerical superiority for one last offensive in the west before the American military arrived on the battlefield. On March 21 they launched the Ludendorff Offensive, designed to break through the trench lines and isolate the British BEF. Although the still-training AEF was initially kept back from the fray, by June the Americans had entered combat at Château-Thierry and Belleau Wood. When the German assaults ended, in July, the Americans took a major role in the counteroffensive to push the Germans back and eventually win the war.

This new combat role for the AEF consumed the priorities, resources, and attention of its leadership. As the campaign continued through the summer and fall, the U.S. Army became more and more involved in ground combat. In this environment, aviation resources, already scarce, were almost totally allocated to ground support. Historian John Morrow sums up this change of events when he describes the U.S. optimism of 1917 waning in the face of the realities of 1918.[21]

The March 1918 German offensive took place at a critical time for the American military air component. The Air Service was just starting to deploy trained operational units, initially dispatched in April under the command of Billy Mitchell to the mostly quiet Toul sector of the front. The plan was for the new units to garner combat experience away from the major fighting to the north.

Besides the experience given the new pilots, the operations in the Toul sector also provided time for the new air commander to spell out his own vision for airpower. On April 30 Mitchell released a bulletin, "General Principles for American Aviation," to all squadrons under his command. Drafted by Parker, the publication contained a wealth of tactical principles to help squadrons develop their own standard operating procedures.[22]

The preface to this bulletin spelled out Mitchell's new vision of airpower. In only five paragraphs he laid out the core elements of his strategy. First, victory on the field of battle was the key to winning the war. Second, all branches of the Army had to work together for this victory to occur. Finally, the Air Service was one of the offensive arms of the Army. As with artillery or infantry it could not bring about a decision by itself, but by working with the other offensive elements it could help ensure victory.[23]

The preface suggested that Mitchell had come down on the opposite side of the doctrinal debate from Gorrell. Where Gorrell espoused a strategic war-winning role for airpower, Mitchell sided with the vision of Trenchard and Pershing that the primary mission of aviation should be to support ground action. Mitchell's view was curious, since both he and Gorrell had discussed aviation theory with many of the same British, French, and Italian bombing advocates. The two men even established a rapport during their shared time on the Air Service staff, where Mitchell read Gorrell's proposals. According to Patrick, their relationship did not sour until the summer of 1918, when Mitchell became angered after Gorrell coordinated surprise inspections of Mitchell's units while they were involved in combat operations.[24] Given this blowup, and the fact that Mitchell had been predisposed to the Trenchard-Pershing view, it is possible that Gorrell's failure in advocating a strategic mission encouraged Mitchell to return to the ground-centric doctrine. Either way, Mitchell's new strategy effectively avoided Gorrell's pitfalls of complete independence and claims of war-winning capabilities that had so agitated the senior AEF.

Even so, it would be a mistake to claim that Mitchell's decision was simply a vengeful reaction to the new Gorrell plan. Rather, it represented a fusion of the various concepts that he had learned in Europe during the past several months. For example, Mitchell appropriated elements of Trenchard's conception of airpower as an integral element in a ground-offensive-based strategy. Historian Alfred Hurley suggests that Mitchell attributed the close relationship that developed between Trenchard and Haig to their mutual conviction that the mission of military aviation should be to provide ground support.[25] It is possible that Colonel Mitchell saw supporting the Pershing plan as a way to forge a similar close relationship with Pershing. That is not the only possibility, however. Historian Thomas Wildenberg offers a different analysis. He suggests that "Mitchell took to Trenchard's ideas about airpower like a duck takes to water."[26] Indeed, Wildenberg paints Mitchell as a true believer in a ground-centric strategy. In any case, whether it was an attempt to gain favor with the AEF's senior leadership, to emulate the British model, or merely to acknowledge the need for ground support, Mitchell's strategy offered a different role for airpower than the one that Gorrell proposed.

In May 1918, Mitchell's vision received an unexpected boost when Pershing removed Foulois as the chief of the AEF Air Service and replaced him with Mason Patrick. Despite their early days as junior officers in the Mexican Expedition, there had long been a sour relationship between Foulois and Mitchell. Often considered rivals in the Air Service before its entry into World War I, the two men clashed when Foulois arrived in Europe more than six months after him and was placed in command of the AEF Air Service. The dislike intensified into standing hostility with the release of General Order No. 81 on May 29 installing Patrick as the AEF's chief.

Besides shifting the command of the AEF, the order also modified the command structure of the Air Service. Previously, the service had been divided into two major components—the Zone of the Interior and the Zone of Advance. The Zone of the Interior was responsible for pilot training, supply, and depot level maintenance of the service's aircraft. The Zone of Advance was the combat arm. It oversaw the operations of the pursuit, observation, and bombardment aircraft that were charged with supporting the ground forces and battling for air supremacy over the battlefield. By the spring of 1918 the two-part structure no longer satisfied the AEF's senior leadership. Although the Zone of the Interior remained a viable structure for supply, training, and administration duties, ground commanders began to complain that hewing to a special command for air combat was limiting the ground commander's control over aviation, and even hinted at providing an independent role for the Air Service. To meet those objections, General Order No. 81 disbanded the Zone of Advance command. Instead, the 1st, 2nd, and 3rd field armies would each have its own air units, commanded by a chief of the Air Service.[27]

Mitchell considered the order a demotion and a slap in the face. General Order No. 81 eliminated his position as commander of the

Zone of Advance and specified that Foulois was to become the chief of the Air Service for the 1st Army, with Mitchell as his subordinate in the position of chief of Air Operations for the 1st Corps.[28] As might be expected, the new commands, located near one another, only exacerbated the feud between the two men. Foulois documented one of the resulting exchanges in his memoirs, describing a strongheaded Mitchell who refused to release his staff, supplies, and equipment to Foulois when he arrived to take command of the 1st Army's Air Service. Ultimately, the 1st Army chief of staff had to order the two men to resolve the situation on their own.[29]

The problem dated back to the aviation rules that went in effect in 1909, which limited transfers into the then-fledgling air service to lieutenants who were under thirty. The adverse consequences of the policy, which had begun showing up during the Mexican Expedition, were becoming painfully visible during World War I. Patrick's biographer, Robert White, suggests that had there been qualified senior officers to take their places, Pershing might have removed both men from command.[30] Although this may be an analytical stretch, Pershing had few senior aviation officers with command, staff, and operational experience, and even if he had wanted to replace both men, there were no obviously qualified senior Air Service officers available.

Luckily for Mitchell, the third stage of the Ludendorff Offensive, which began in late May, provided some relief from that problem. For the first time in the war, Americans started to take a significant role in ground fighting with the 1st and 3rd divisions, fighting at Cantigny and Belleau Wood respectively. Mitchell's aviation units soon joined in to provide ground support.

Mitchell's personal flair and leadership style seemed tailor-made to inspire the young pilots, many of whom were still civilians at heart and chafed under the rigid regulations of Army life.[31] By July, Mitchell had become a celebrity in the AEF Air Service, successfully demonstrating his superior capability to motivate young men and organize them into formations that were capable of countering German airpower. Not just Pershing, but also Mitchell's old adversary Foulois noticed this superior leadership. In a stunning turnaround and a tribute to his professionalism, Foulois asked for reassignment to enable Mitchell to take over air operations for all of the 1st Army in late July.[32]

Mitchell's ascension greatly enhanced his ability to shape airpower doctrine. His operational focus on ground support left little room for thinking about or planning for strategic bombing operations. At the same time, logistical problems continued to slow the delivery of bomber aircraft to the front-line units. Although DH-4 daylight bombers were beginning to arrive, Mitchell's strategy meant that most were assigned to squadrons with a direct ground-support mission. The supply of night bombers was even worse. The delay in the production of Liberty engines slowed the delivery of British-produced Handley Page bombers to the American Air Service well into the summer of 1918. Production plans called for the delivery of fifty engines to the British factory in May 1918 for the production of long-range night bombers for the Americans; by August, however, only ten engines had arrived.[33] Even if the Air Service had the extra bombers, it did not have the aircrews to fly them. With a greater emphasis on ground support came greater losses of observation and bomber aircraft. Much as the British experienced over the Somme, the American Air Service discovered in the summer of 1918 that it also had a shortage of aircrews. All of these issues combined to drive strategic bombing to the background.

By July 1918 American strategic bombing advocates had reached a low point. During that month, the AEF staff decided to change the name of the Strategical Aviation in the Zone of Advance to the GHQ Air Service Reserve.[34] Although the name change was partly a response to the restructuring mandated by General Order No. 81, it was also likely designed to remove the appearance of an independent bomber command within the AEF. The step effectively brought home the realization that, at least for the time being, bombing would be used only in support of ground operations as directed by the AEF headquarters.

Although the name change signaled the end of Gorrell's dream of creating a large bomber command in 1918, it perfectly positioned Mitchell to develop a concept for offensive air operations to support the planned American counteroffensive. First at St. Mihiel and then later in the Meuse-Argonne Offensive, Mitchell masterfully integrated reconnaissance, bombardment, and pursuit aviation in support of ground forces. Ironically, given the AEF's disapproval of air service autonomy, perhaps the most interesting element of Mitchell's plan was the independent nature of his air forces. Mitchell successfully convinced senior ground commanders that his squadrons had to operate separately from division and corps commanders in order to gain initial aerial superiority over the front. He was far too experienced and politically savvy to push for a totally independent command. Instead, he maintained his links to ground commanders by ensuring that when the pursuit aircraft were accomplishing their mission, the air commander would simultaneously direct bombers to interdict the flow of reinforcements and supplies and provide intelligence through direct aerial observation missions.[35] In this way, Mitchell built a balanced air strategy that included a level of autonomy, but maintained the ground combat focus required to gain the support of senior American military leaders.

Nevertheless, Mitchell's plans were not the only potential course for airpower development. Although Gorrell's bombing proposal had been shelved, the British continued to work on their own plan. Although the strategy had become caught in the turmoil of creating the world's first independent air force, it still had an influence on American aviation strategy.

On April 1, 1918, the RFC and RNAS formally combined into the RAF. The new independent air force immediately faced stiff pressure from the public and the British government to conduct strategic attacks against German cities, both to avenge the Gotha strikes and to destroy German industry. In response, the Air Council recommended creating an independent bomber force within the RAF that would operate outside the control of the British Army with a primary mission of strategic bombing. As might be expected, the proposal would be hard to sell to the British Army leadership and difficult to organize and execute in a short time. The Air Council saw only one man for the job: Sir Hugh Trenchard. After a brief stint as the first chief of the Air Staff from January to April, Trenchard, who was by far Britain's most experienced air commander, had resigned his post in the face of conflicts over the role of the new RAF and was without a job when the Air Council started looking for someone to head the new bomber command. The government rapidly approved the Independent Force, as the bomber command was known, and cajoled Trenchard into accepting the appointment as its chief. On May 13 he officially took command.[36]

The debate shifted to defining the mission of the Independent Force. Under the guidance of Gen. Fredrick Sykes, the chief of the Air Staff, the group produced a paper for a mid-May meeting of the War Cabinet outlining a proposed strategy. Top priority for the new force was what he called "strategic interception," which he defined as "attacking the root industries and morale of the enemy nation." [37] He suggested two ways to accomplish that mission, both of which borrowed heavily from Tiverton's earlier recommendations. First, Sykes proposed bombing specific industrial systems to attack the enemy's means of war—critical industries such as weapons-assembly, coal productions, or iron manufacturing. That meant the bomber force would focus on critical industries such as weapons-assembly, coal production, and iron manufacturing. Second, Sykes recommended bombing densely populated industrial centers to disrupt work schedules and hurt morale.

At this point, Tiverton re-entered the strategic bombing discussion with a memorandum to Sykes dated May 22, 1918. In it, he pointed out that although Sykes' earlier paper had dealt generally with bombing policy, it fell far short of an actual plan. He warned that if Britain truly wanted to conduct a bombing campaign in 1918, it needed to develop a serious working plan quickly.[38]

Sykes agreed wholeheartedly with Tiverton, and asked him to prepare such a document, and Tiverton spent most of June working on it. The new proposal followed his previous ones by focusing on industrial targets and area bombardment around densely populated worker housing.

Tiverton's dream might finally have become a reality except for the actions of Brig. Gen. Cyril Newall, the 8th Brigade commander. On hearing of Tiverton's plan, Newall drafted his own study of the strategic problem for the chief of the Air Staff. In his report, entitled "The Scientific and Methodical Attack of Vital Industries," Newall concluded that the first priority for any air campaign must be to gain air superiority, without which bombers operating at long ranges over German cities would face unsustainable losses from air defenses. Only after British aircraft control of the air was assured could the bombers attack their targets freely. Next, Newall contended that Tiverton's target prioritization of industrial and city centers would waste limited airpower. Instead, he argued that if the enemy could not get their supplies and weapons to the front they would be of no use. Therefore, he proposed targeting rail and transportation networks as the first priority, with industrial factories as a distant third priority.[39]

Newall's ideas ignited a debate on the proper strategy for the new Independent Force. His ideas held much promise. The concept of winning air superiority first to enable pilots to pursue other missions was gaining rapid acceptance in all Asllied air forces, as evidenced by the previous discussion of Mitchell's strategy evolution. In addition, Newall's plan more closely matched Trenchard's own view of a ground-centric war. When it came time to decide on the actual strategy, the new Independent Force commander sided with Newall.

Historian Neville Jones suggests that a combination of French pressures to focus on operational bombing and Trenchard's own bias toward supporting Haig's vision of a ground war shaped Trenchard's decision.[40] Brig. Gen. Mason Patrick, the new AEF Air Service commander, reinforced this assessment in his postwar memoirs, where he recalled Trenchard's having told him that "he had fought for several years against the independent show, but that it had been forced on him."[41] In light of this attitude, it is likely that Trenchard continued to focus on supporting his old boss, General Haig, even in his new independent command.

The Independent Force became operational on June 5, 1918, when Trenchard took over command of the 8th Brigade. The unit comprised two flying wings: No. 41 Wing with three squadrons of daylight bombers; and No. 83 Wing, with two squadrons of night bombers.[42] Newall, the previous commander, became Trenchard's deputy commander.

The statistics of the force's operations indicate that Newall's and Trenchard's visions were the major forces behind its bombing operations. Throughout the summer and fall, the Independent Force struck industrial targets in only 20 percent of its missions; attacks on airfields, 30 percent; and railways, 50 percent.[43] Although these numbers may not follow those for a modern strategic operations force, they do make more sense when they are filtered through Trenchard's vision and the dominance of the ground war. Railway targets seemed to offer the best of both worlds, interrupting the flow of war materiel to the enemy's military forces while at the same time posting less-risky missions for the always-scarce bomber crews.

Interestingly, when Trenchard did focus on industrial targets, physical destruction was often a secondary objective. In late May, he sent a memorandum to the chief of the Air Ministry describing his strategy for a strategic bombing campaign in 1919. He wrote that "the aim of the Air Force is to break down the enemy's means to resist by attacks on objectives selected as the most likely to achieve this end."[44] Hidden within this statement was a sobering take on the morale effects of bombing. Under Trenchard's policy, using bombing to drive workers from their homes and factories was a legitimate military objective that was much easier to achieve than destroying a factory. Trenchard even computed a ratio for this idea, arguing that the psychological effect of bombing was about twenty times the level of physical destruction achieved.[45]

While the British turned to strategic bombing as a major element of warfighting in the summer and fall of 1918, the Americans also showed signs of renewed interest. The most dramatic change occurred in the long-range night bomber mission. Although Gorrell was on the AEF G-3 staff, he continued to work in the background to build the forces needed for a new strategic bombing campaign in 1919 after aircraft production had caught up to what had been called for in plans. On January 26, 1918, Gorrell helped negotiate the Rothermere-Foulois agreement, which detailed not only the British production of Handley Page bombers for the Americans, but also enabled the British to train American bomber crews. Although production delays slowed progress, by June 28 Patrick had established a Night Bombing Section to oversee the formation and basing of the new American long-range night bombardment squadrons along the front. The plans called for the establishment of the first two squadrons in November 1918, with a total of eighteen operational squadrons by the following April.[46] The new force became the backbone on which to build the proposed 1919 strategic bombing campaign.

The formation of daylight bombing forces proceeded at a more rapid pace. The first American daylight bombing squadron, the 96th Aero Squadron, began operations on June 12 with ten Breguet 14B-2 bombers.[47] Unlike the night bombers, the daylight aircraft had to contend with the continuing heavy demand for direct support of ground forces. As a result, the 96th lagged behind its British and French counterparts in the types of missions flown. During that summer, the squadron's single-engine Breguets seldom ventured more than sixty miles behind enemy lines, their pilots preferring relatively safe targets like railway stations and supply depots behind the front lines—this at a time when British bombers were conducting operations against industrial targets as far away as Cologne and Coblenz, 100 and 167 miles away respectively.

In September, the 11th and 20th Aero Squadrons joined with the 96th to form the 1st Day Bombardment Group. Although this might have offered hope that a day bombardment group might be tasked to support a new strategic campaign, the start of the Meuse-Argonne Offensive on September 26 meant the 1st Day Bombardment Group remained tied to attacking German troop concentrations and lines of communication. Still, the group did occasionally venture beyond the battlefront to attack more strategic targets such as important rail junctions along the German-French border.

The creation of the 1st and the plans for a night-bomber force were not lost on the British, who saw it as a potential strategic unit that could cooperate with their Independent Force in the long-discussed Allied strategic bombing campaign. By October 1918, the situation at the front was starting to change dramatically. With the Germans on the defensive and aircraft production finally catching up to predictions, American leadership showed a new openness to strategic bombing.[48]

There were differences among the Allies that had to be worked out before a combined bomber offensive could be planned, but these seemed within reach. The most important was the issue of independence. Earlier that summer, the AEF Air Service had completed a third proposal for a strategic bombing campaign during 1919. Pershing's new chief of staff, Major General McAndrew, immediately placed limits on this effort. In a memorandum dated June 18, 1918, he notified AEF Air Service Commander Patrick that although he approved of the planning for a future operation, he specifically precluded an independent air campaign or subordination under British leadership. His language left little room for doubt: "[I]t is therefore directed that these officers be warned against any idea of independence" and "selections of targets will depend solely upon their importance for our ground forces."[49] McAndrew's opinion had not changed by the fall, and the American Air Service found itself working under these same constraints.

Meantime, the issue of targeting also caused conflict among the Allies. The growing public pressure for revenge did not abate in England as the end of 1918 approached. In the British government, it intensified visibly. Air Minister Sir William Weir wrote to Trenchard in early November saying he "would very much like it if you could start a really big fire on one of the German towns."[50] It is likely that this letter struck a chord with Trenchard, since it meshed with his own view of the importance of the psychological effect of bombing.

The attitude caused consternation in the American command structure, however. U.S. commanders and political leaders alike feared that the British would inflict carnage on German cities in the name of revenge or destroying morale. In October 1918, Secretary of War Baker sent word to Pershing that the U.S. would not participate in any bombing plan that had as its objective "promiscuous bombing upon industry, commerce, or population."[51]

In many ways these two issues presaged later debates on strategic bombing strategy. Yet, in the end, World War I was over before any substantive actions could be taken to ameliorate the differences between the British and Americans. The unexpected timing of the armistice left many issues unresolved. Could strategic bombing itself be decisive? What would be the best way to accomplish a strategic bombing campaign? What type of force would be necessary to win a war through airpower alone? These questions were all left open to interpretation when the fighting ended on November 11, 1918.

TECHNOLOGICAL SHORTCOMINGS AND CONFLICTING LEADERSHIP

Perhaps a more useful question at this stage is why the Americans failed to accept strategic bombing on the same level as their British allies. Although some of the reasons have been discussed in the preceding text, two other important factors deserve further study. In their own particular ways, both technology and leadership also played a part in dooming prospects for an American strategic bombing campaign before the end of the war.

Technological limitations were a constant thorn in the side of American strategic bombing advocates. The key problem was the inability of America's aviation industry to produce large numbers of aircraft. From the beginning, the U.S. government and the Army in particular maintained policies that essentially discouraged the growth of a functional aviation industry. The attitude dated back to the Army's initial insistence that all airframes must be developed by the producer, with no financial support from the government.[52] This effectively limited the number of new companies, since few firms had the funds on hand to produce aircraft without outside support. The Army's continual resistance to buying the large numbers of aircraft required to spur the growth of an aviation industry exacerbated this initial policy. Even if an aircraft developer were to invest its own funds, there would be little chance of its making significant profits from the sale of large numbers of airplanes to the military. The effect was to limit both the size and production capabilities of the American aviation industry just when the United States needed aircraft the most.

As the United States entered World War I, the government finally addressed the issue of aviation funding. In July 1917, Congress appropriated $640 million for military aviation. Along with the money came a promise from industry experts the Army would be able to field 4,500 aircraft by May 1918.[53] Despite the promises of industrial representatives, congressional leaders, and the press, however, it was not until the war ended that the American aircraft industry was only just beginning to make good on its promised aircraft deliveries.

This was especially true for bombers. On May 29, 1917, the NANTB all but ensured a shortage of bomber aircraft when it determined a production ratio of 3:5:1 for pursuit, observation, and bomber aircraft.[54] When the American aviation industry fell behind schedule on aircraft deliveries, the manufacturers focused on the higher-priority pursuit and observation aircraft. Consequently, when Gorrell first took command of Strategical Aviation in the Zone of Advance, he had a plan for action but only a handful of aircraft to carry it out.

The statistics demonstrate the dire state of bomber production that Gorrell faced. The first American-built DH-4 daylight bomber was not shipped from Hoboken, New Jersey, until March 1918. By that time, Gorrell had already been relieved of his command and strategic bombing was fast fading from the AEF leadership's attention. In the end, only 196 American-made bombers ever made it to combat squadrons in France before the armistice was signed.[55]

This bomber shortage might not have been an issue were it not for simultaneous problems with British aircraft production. With the new push to produce a large bomber force, British industry had to retool to provide larger engines for the new aircraft. Unfortunately, the process often resulted in delays. A good example is the production of the Beardmore-Helford-Pulling engine for the DH-4 daylight bomber. In the fall of 1917, a problem with the engine's aluminum cylinders caused a six-month production delay, which was not completely resolved until April 1918.[56] Luckily, supplies of French Hispano-Suiza engines helped ameliorate the problem, but the delays in British DH-4 production meant American units did not receive their quotas of British-built aircraft until after Gorrell's plans had become overtaken by events on the ground.

A second factor disrupting bomber plans was the conflict among the visions of U.S. military leaders. Both at the AEF and the Air Service level, Gorrell had to contend with confusing and often inconsistent guidance. This surely was the case in December 1917, when Gorrell represented the Americans at Trenchard's inter-Allied bombing conference. Having just received Pershing's approval for his bombing proposal and a promotion to command the Air Service's strategic bombing forces, Gorrell must have expected Pershing to support the combined strategic bombing effort fully.

Yet, as Trenchard's deputy, Brig. Gen. Gerald Blaine, later pointed out, this was not the case. Shortly after the bombing conference, Trenchard called on Pershing to discuss the proposal to allow the AEF bombers to work with the British forces. In a memorandum dated January 13, 1918, Blaine described Pershing's response. He wrote, "I could see clearly and in fact he said no, that he was not at all desirous of putting American personnel under us."[57] This was an interesting turnaround, considering that Pershing had approved Gorrell's November 1917 bombing proposal, which was similar to the one that Trenchard advocated.

It is likely that two elements intervened to change Pershing's thinking. The first was the issue of independence. Pershing's staff contended that the Air Service's emphasis on conducting independent campaigns could hurt ground operations. The AEF chief of staff McAndrew's warning to Patrick that "it is therefore directed that these officers be warned against any idea of independence" demonstrates the pervasiveness of the concern in the general staff.[58]

The second issue on Pershing's mind was likely the realization that American ground forces were soon to enter combat. Given the delays in aircraft production, Pershing must have been concerned over the ability of the Air Service to support the ground offensive and a strategic campaign at the same time. He even alluded to this in his memoirs, referring to the double failure of the United States to produce aircraft and to send raw materiel to allies, resulting in only nine of the planned sixty squadrons being designated as combat-ready in February 1918.[59] In this light, Trenchard's proposal must have sounded as though it would be sapping U.S. airpower strength when it was needed most.

Historian Robert White suggests a potential third explanation for this strategic about-face—that Pershing was caught off guard by Trenchard's request, due to sloppy Air Service staff work. Simply put, Foulois never notified Pershing that Trenchard planned to ask him to provide U.S. bombers to the British effort. White demonstrates that Foulois knew of Trenchard's proposal for two weeks before the

Pershing-Trenchard meeting, but failed to brief his commander on the plan.[60] Given this information, it is possible Pershing simply reacted to being caught off guard by reverting to his staff's more conservative vision of American airpower.

Either way, Pershing and Trenchard resolved the issue through a series of letters. On February 6, 1918, Pershing wrote to Trenchard to announce that he would cooperate with his plan, although he would not place American forces fully under British command. Pershing ended the letter by promising that "you may be sure that I shall do everything in my power to make this cooperation as effective as possible."[61] Given the back-and-forth nature of Pershing's support for strategic bombing, it is understandable how Gorrell was caught in the middle. This helps explain why he worked so feverishly to modify his proposal in January 1918, when he perhaps should have been more focused on mounting bombing missions.

A similar leadership problem existed at the Air Service level. Rapid growth created a unique problem for the Air Service command staff, which lacked a robust pool of trained and experienced officers to man its critical planning functions. What few experienced personnel were available often left staff positions quickly to take command of important field operations. Although this was good for the overall Air Service, it hurt important planning and strategy functions.

By early 1918 senior AEF commanders could see the confusion and careless staff work emanating from the Air Service. Patrick alluded to it when informing his wife about his selection to command the AEF Air Service. He described Pershing's words to him as, "the fact is I am entirely dissatisfied with the way the aviation service is getting on and I want you at the head of it and have you bring order out of what is now chaos. There is bickering, they are running around in circles. There is need for a man to take hold of it and whip it into shape. I want you to do this for me."[62]

Pershing's words describe a problem that also dated back to the origins of the Air Service. When House Resolution 5304 codified the long-standing Army policy of only allowing unmarried lieutenants under the age of thirty to join the service, it meant Pershing had to deal with a large number of young and inexperienced officers in his

wartime air service.[63] This youthful command structure often resulted
in clashes of individual egos that more experienced officers would
likely have been able to resolve. A good example of this is the rivalry
between Foulois and Mitchell. If such a fight had broken out between
two ground commanders, Pershing might have replaced them both
with other experienced officers. Yet, in the case of the Air Service,
there simply were no other men with the pedigrees to replace either
commander. Pershing had no choice other than to bring in outsiders
and had to keep a lid on the conflicts as best he could.

Given this staff environment, it is understandable how Gorrell had
difficulty turning his vision for strategic bombing into reality. Problems
with production numbers were only exacerbated by staff confusion
that limited the availability of the aircraft on hand. Competing egos
often drew attention from strategy discussions. It is likely that Gorrell
never fully knew if he had staff support or not. Given these issues, it is
understandable how the already complex job of planning and executing a strategic bombing campaign became an almost impossible task.

CONCLUSION

If 1917 was a period of growth for strategic bombing theory, 1918 was
the year that the hard realities of war once again focused military leaders on ground campaigns. This was especially true of the Americans.
Lacking the political pressure to respond to German bombings of the
European homeland, American military leaders refocused their attention on ground combat. The focus only intensified as the Army started
taking a larger role in combat operations toward the fall of 1918.

Gorrell provides a personal illustration of the fate of American
strategic bombing theory during the final year of the war. As 1918
started, he rode a wave of British pressure, American openness, and
great expectations to what seemed to be the threshold of a bombing
campaign. Unfortunately for him, reality did not quite square with his
hopes. Even before the year began, signs of AEF staff animosity toward
Gorrell's strategy became visible. The first sign was the U.S. reluctance to accept the British proposal for a combined bomber offensive in December 1917. A lack of staff support during Gorrell's short
tenure as commander of Strategical Aviation in the Zone of Advance

further limited bombing. Finally, the resource requirements to support American ground forces in their growing combat roles spelled the end of any potential strategic campaigns in 1918.

Instead, a more balanced aviation strategy based on the traditional view of airpower as a supporting element of ground forces came to dominate. Mitchell utilized this strategy to win a double battle. First, he successfully wrested control of the air from the hard-pressed German air forces. Then, he won a perhaps more difficult battle. Mitchell convinced the majority of ground commanders that his vision of a semi-independent air service supporting a ground-centric war was the proper air strategy to use.

Interestingly this did not spell the end of strategic bombing as an option in the U.S. military. Continued pressure from the British helped keep the idea alive within elements of the AEF and the Air Service. By late 1918, facing diminishing resistance and expecting a surplus of aircraft in 1919, the AEF leadership once again seemed open to the concept of conducting strategic campaigns. Gorrell had been working behind the scenes to secure the production of long-range bombers and the training of their aircrews. Although there was still a hesitancy to conduct any campaign outside American-approved lines, it seemed that 1919 might be the year when strategic bombing would once and for all prove itself in combat. The end of the war stopped this effort, leaving the lingering question of whether strategic bombing could have worked. Future airmen would have to answer it.

CHAPTER 5

Solidifying Doctrine through History

The successes of military aviation in World War I revolution-
ized the way that battles would be fought, but for proponents
of strategic bombing the war's end brought a new challenge:
how to codify what they had experienced and learned so that it could
be passed along to future generations.

There was little time to lose in recording these lessons and using
them to put together a doctrine that would guide the expansion of
long-range bombing. Many of the young men who fought in the
skies over Europe quickly returned to civilian life when the hostilities
ended, and with their departure the military lost a treasure trove of
operational experience. Each year, the ideas and understandings that
had been hammered out and burnished during the war faded and
were replaced. The officers who had been part of the AEF Air Service
wanted to create a legacy that would ensure that bombers and crews
were ready the next time fighting broke out.

The question was how to accomplish the task. History offered a
variety of models illustrating how the Army had handled such challenges over the years. In some cases, lessons-learned repositories had
been re-worked into standard operating procedures for squadrons to
incorporate into their training curricula. In others, the material was
reorganized into operations manuals that described problems and set
forth the doctrine needed to help deal with them, eventually becoming the reference point for Army thinking in the early twentieth
century. Indeed, in this case, issuing a new manual for the Air Service
seemed like an ideal way to disseminate the principles and techniques
that had been learned in combat during the Great War. Yet, there were

problems with this approach. Manuals were notoriously focused on daily operations, too often giving short shrift to the wealth of background information that explained why a particular tactic, policy, or course of action might be the best choice.

To help avoid such shortcomings, Maj. Gen. Mason Patrick, the Air Service chief, opted for a less frequently used choice: he decided to put together a history of the AEF Air Service, at least as a starting point. Shortly after the war ended, he set up the machinery to collect the material, and invited all officers to contribute.[1] At the time, the notion of compiling such a tome must have seemed like an unwieldy way to develop a military doctrine. Simple operational manuals were much smaller and would have been easier to use in everyday training. There was little chance that the typical pilot or aviation unit would be eager to absorb thousands of pages of historical research.

Yet, Patrick made a second decision that all but guaranteed that the effort would be successful. He placed newly promoted Col. Edgar Gorrell, his determined chief of staff, in charge of the project. As Patrick no doubt expected, Gorrell went well beyond merely writing a history of what happened in the air. He also ensured that the volume captured the theoretical debates, strategy arguments, and tactical decisions affecting military aviation in World War I. More important for the future of strategic bombing, he also wrote a history of the Strategical Section of the Zone of Advance and embellished it with a copy of the American bombing survey that had been conducted at the end of the war. Taken together, these steps ensured that future generations would have access not only to his ideas, but also to a wealth of statistical data.

In this way, perhaps without truly realizing the full implications of what he had set in motion, Gorrell effectively compiled an official history that would shape future doctrinal debates. When the next generation of aviators turned its attention to the possibilities of strategic bombing, they would have a ready-made handbook containing insights into the origins of the concept and offering supporting data that would help convince skeptics in ACTS and the general staff.

OPERATIONAL MANUALS

In their attempt to codify the lessons from World War I, many Air Service leaders turned to the methods that they had learned as young officers. For most Army branches and field offices, the operations manual was literally "the book" in the old saying, "I want it done by the book." It imparted the leadership-approved methods for solving various military problems. It had served a similar purpose in the era before the appearance of formal doctrine documents.

Even Billy Mitchell employed the technique. On November 15, 1918, the war's most famous aviator assumed command of the Air Service for the U.S. 3rd Army, which constituted America's contribution to the occupation force that was monitoring German compliance during the Treaty of Versailles negotiations.[2] For Mitchell, the assignment represented a unique opportunity. After the frenetic pace of leading large air offensives, he finally had time to focus on non-combat activities. He immediately ordered his staff to begin working on an operational Air Service manual for the Third Army, based on his experience during the war.

Mitchell's staff completed the final draft of *Provisional Manual of Operations of Air Service Units* on December 23, 1918.[3] In what today would be called a standard operating procedure, Mitchell documented the daily processes used by aviation units under his command during the battles of St. Mihiel and the Meuse-Argonne. Although the manual covered all aspects of aviation, two sections are especially important here.

The first, entitled "The Routine of a Day Bombardment Group," laid out Mitchell's overall vision for bombing. Just like his earlier operational plans, which had been drafted during the summer and fall of 1918, this one continued to cite bombing as primarily a direct ground-support mission. The document left little room for debate when it specified that daylight bombers must be used in conjunction with ground operations. It added that "all target selection should occur at the G-3 [operations] level to ensure [that] targets match with the ground commander's objectives."[4] Finally, it extended the direct ground-support theme to its discussion of tactics, implying that any potential daylight-bombing target would be close to the front lines and therefore defended by Army units equipped with machine guns and light antiaircraft artillery. Accordingly, all tactical discussions revolved around the need to overcome threats associated with the forward edge of the battle area; almost none dealt with issues involving long-range flights, such as navigation or defense against enemy aircraft.

Night bombing, outlined in the second section of the document, should have contained a significant role for strategic bombing, as demonstrated from the use of nighttime missions that targeted urban areas toward the end of World War I. But Mitchell all but ignored that innovation, suggesting that the only future role for nighttime missions was in harassing enemy troops. With just a single short paragraph, he dismissed night bombing as only potentially useful in avoiding aerial combat and in disrupting enemy operations through harassment.[5]

This brings up an interesting question: was this really a sign that Mitchell did not support strategic bombing, or was it simply a lack of knowledge resulting from the fact that the 3rd Army's Air Service had no long-range bombing aircraft of its own? It is true that, dating back to the April 1918 *General Principles for American Aviation Bulletin*, Mitchell had been calling for the placement of aviation units as semi-independent components, tied directly to the ground war, with little or no strategic mission.[6] Still, this marked a conspicuous change from his earlier advocacy of long-range bombing in the early summer of 1917, when he had asserted that "with this class of aviation the United States may aid in the greatest way and which, it is believed if properly applied will have a greater influence on the ultimate decision of the war than any other one arm."[7] Whether Mitchell's opinions truly had evolved or, as some historians suggest, he automatically favored any policy that he thought would bolster his own professional standing, remains open to debate. What is known is that Mitchell's 1919 operations manual effectively turned bombing into just another tool to use in defeating an enemy army.

Although Mitchell's provisional manual had limited impact in stimulating new thinking about strategic air power, it set a precedent for codifying and sharing new ideas. When the AEF issued the manual as an Air Service Bulletin on December 24, 1918, it immediately set the standard for transforming operational experience into doctrine.[8] Given the nature and origins of the document, it articulated the conventional Army vision of aviation as merely one element working in conjunction with others to achieve the defeat of the enemy's army.

Despite Mitchell's prominence, there was one important short-coming in his approach that doomed its long-term influence. The Army had intended for its manuals to be superseded as new technology and operational theories proved themselves. So although Mitchell's manual began as the gold standard, it could not remain such for long. Ironically, when the manual was sent out as an Air Service Bulletin to all aviators, it whetted their interest in keeping the document current and spurred more of them to submit their own proposals for changes.

Even as Mitchell's manual was gaining attention in the AEF Air Service headquarters, another senior leader attempted to codify his ideas into doctrine. Now–Lt. Col. William C. Sherman was the chief of staff for the 1st Army's Air Service—a post that enabled him to oversee all aviation-related operational, administrative, and planning elements in that unit's sector of the front. Much like Mitchell, Sherman understood the need to codify the 1st Army's airpower lessons into a formal document. In early 1919, his own contribution, *A Tentative Manual for the Employment of Air Services*, made its appearance.

Sherman's manual expanded on Mitchell's initial concept. Where Mitchell had documented daily procedures, Sherman created a true Air Service manual on a par with the infantry's counterpart, Field Service Regulation.[9] Moreover, its impact was much greater; it proved a success on both sides of the Atlantic. On April 11 the AEF leadership cabled the manual to Washington, where it was widely read by many Air Service officers. One reason that it attracted so much attention was that Sherman had created a comprehensive document covering airpower theory, planning, and operations. Accordingly, it was regarded as one of the first doctrine documents in the U.S. Air Service.

What is more, Sherman's manual contained a detailed discussion of strategic bombing. He expanded on Mitchell's direct ground-support role to add as a mission "the destruction of the materiel, personnel, and morale of the enemy" as objectives for the Air Service.[10] Although Sherman's wording was not a ringing endorsement of strategic bombing, he clearly acknowledged that bombing could play a significant role in destroying enemy materiel and morale far behind the front lines. It was an important start.

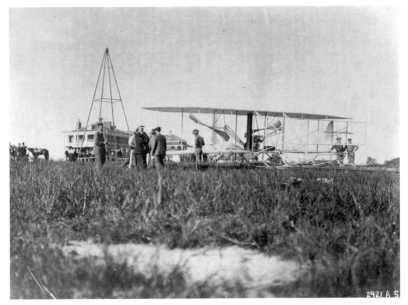

While the Wright Brothers first flew on December 17, 1903, the Army did not buy a machine until after the Wrights completed two trial flights and received approval from a specially convened Board of Officers in 1909. (Air Force Historical Research Agency)

Despite the ongoing war in Europe, limited government funding meant that the U.S. Army Air Service grew very slowly in the United States. (USAFA Special Collections)

The 1st Aero Squadron's Curtiss JN-3 aircraft proved underpowered for operations in Mexico, but the pilots' experience started them thinking about how best to use military airpower. (USAFA Special Collections)

Brig. Gen. Benjamin Foulois played an active role in shaping early American airpower doctrine through his command of the 1st Aero Squadron, his clashes with Billy Mitchell, and his time as Chief of the Air Corps in the 1930s. (USAFA Special Collections)

Lt. Edgar Gorrell combined his experiences in Mexico with the 1st Aero Squadron with a network of European advisers to draft in November 1917 the first American proposal for a sustained strategic bombing campaign. (Air Force Historical Research Agency)

While working from his headquarters at 45 Avenue Montaigne near the Arc de Triomphe, Edgar Gorrell started a friendship with Lord Hardinge Goulborn Goffard Tiverton of the Royal Naval Air Service, a leading proponent of strategic bombing in Britain. (USAFA Special Collections)

William "Billy" Mitchell and his wife examining tiger skins. While best known for his attempts to create a separate independent Air Service, Mitchell contributed several operational manuals discussing bombing, including his *Provisional Manual for Air Service Units* in 1918. (USAFA Special Collections)

While the sinking of the *Ostfriesland* failed to warrant an independent Air
Force, it did create a new mission to justify the purchase of long-range
bombers during the Great Depression: coastal defense of the United States.
(U.S. Navy and Marine Corps Museum/Naval Aviation Museum)

During the tight budgets of the 1920s, the Air Service sometimes turned to dropping different types of "bombs"—like when it recruited Babe Ruth to catch a baseball from an aircraft on July 22, 1926, at Mitchell Field in Garden City, Long Island. (USAFA Special Collections)

The center for aerial doctrine development in the 1930s was the Air Corps Tactical School (ACTS) at Maxwell AFB, Ala., where the doctrine of High Altitude Daylight Precision Bombing was developed. (Air Force Historical Research Agency)

Like many other members of the "Bomber Mafia" at ACTS in the 1930s, Ira Eaker and Carl "Toohey" Spaatz went on to become aerial leaders in World War II when they attempted to put their doctrine ideas into practice. (Air Force Historical Research Agency)

The 4-engine long-range B-17 proved the ideal technology to turn the dream of strategic bombing into a reality during World War II. (Library of Congress)

Even with its popularity and acceptance, however, Sherman's manual suffered from the same shortcoming as Mitchell's—that is, like many other Army manuals, it required regular updates. Whenever a change was published, the obsolete version of the manual was either relegated to the scrap heap or hidden away in Army archives, where only intrepid historians were likely to see them again. By the time a new generation of aviators sought to look through them, these manuals were no longer within easy reach. Luckily for strategic bombing theorists, the Army began producing a different type of document after the war that contained a greater number of ideas and displayed them in a format that would ensure that they would be available for generations. It was called an official history.

THE OFFICIAL HISTORY

As the war's end neared, Gorrell once again returned to the Air Service command staff after his tour with the AEF G-3 (operations) section. On October 28, 1918, Patrick selected him as the service's new chief of staff—an appointment that made Gorrell, then age twenty-seven, the youngest colonel in the Army. The position fit Gorrell's strengths perfectly. Since his arrival in France in June 1917, Gorrell had excelled at administrative staff work. As a member of the Bolling Commission, he had written detailed descriptions of European aviation technology and had crafted well-reasoned arguments for buying aircraft from the British and French. Next, he worked tirelessly to draft and gain approval for a strategic bombing plan that would enable the Americans to coordinate their missions with the growing British and French campaigns in late 1917. Although that effort failed, he kept his reputation as a steadfast planner and staff officer. As the air planner for the AEF operations staff, Gorrell turned his attention from strategic bombing to coordination of the tactical bombing, observation, and pursuit requirements that Mitchell needed for his successful campaigns of the summer and fall of 1918. These experiences had made him the perfect candidate for Patrick's staff. In just the few weeks before the war ended, Gorrell impressed Patrick with his organizational skills and his ability to encourage others to accomplish difficult tasks and complete them on time.[11]

Gorrell's skills meshed well with Patrick's plan to develop a single comprehensive history of the AEF Air Service in World War I. As early as February 1918, General Pershing recognized the need to start gathering data for an official history of the American armed forces in World War I. On February 16, his headquarters issued General Order no. 31, tasking all subordinate elements of the AEF to establish historical sections to oversee the collection of documents and unit war diaries for a grand history of the war. On May 11 Patrick designated the Information Section to fulfill this role for the AEF Air Service.[12]

The Information Section worked mostly behind the scenes during the last few months of the war to collect important orders and staff paperwork, but when the war ended it was clear that authorities would soon be making a major effort to compile an official history of the Air Service and its role in the AEF. Always a step ahead, on November 19 Gorrell sent telegrams to all Air Service components asking them to prepare such a document for their own units and submit it to the Information Section.[13]

Gorrell's insight proved accurate. On December 4 Patrick ordered him to assemble a staff and personally oversee the preparations of an AEF Air Service history. Patrick's vision went beyond just compiling the histories of individual units. He also asked for written contributions from every unit commander and aviator. And he warned that no officer would be released to return to the United States until Gorrell had personally accepted and approved his submission.[14] The result was a document entitled, *Final Report to the Chief of the Air Service, AEF.* Over time it has become better known as the Gorrell history.

Besides displaying his administrative talents, overseeing the project also offered Gorrell a chance to instill his own priorities into the official history. Gorrell envisioned his study as a book that each Air Service officer would own and consult in developing his own thinking on airpower doctrine.[15] As a result, he took a special interest in the history well beyond that ordered by Patrick. Gorrell personally wrote several sections of the final product, including two that later proved critical for the way future generations theorized about strategic bombing.

The first of these was the history of the American Liaison Office in Paris. This portion chronicled the Bolling Commission's travels, the early theoretical debates, and the interactions with the French and British aviation missions. Gorrell was perfectly situated to write this, since he had been a central player in all of these early coordination efforts. He even included several of his own conversations with the British and French concerning the evolving thoughts on strategic bombardment that otherwise would have been lost.

Gorrell described the strong ties between these first American aviators in Europe and their French and British contemporaries—relationships that were not surprising, since the young Americans often looked to the more experienced Europeans for help in interpreting the evolving air war. What was remarkable, however, was how Gorrell played down the Italian influences on the Americans. Despite his previous acknowledgment of Caproni's advice in his earlier reports and policy recommendations, Gorrell did not include any references to Caproni or Italian bombing in this section.[16] The reason for the omission is not clear even to this day. Gorrell may have been reluctant to bring to light his failed attempts to convince Air Service leadership to buy large numbers of Caproni aircraft; or he may have believed that Capt. Fiorello La Guardia, who had been the liaison to Italian authorities on behalf of the Joint Army-Navy Aircraft Committee in Paris, would cover the issue in his own submission; or perhaps it merely reflected the fact that the Americans moved closer to the British and French as the U.S. forces began combat operations. The record remains muddy, but Gorrell's failure to credit Caproni properly may help explain why many historians overlook the Italian influence on early U.S. airpower theory and technology. Despite this omission, the Paris office history was important because it preserved most of Gorrell's theoretical influences and it documented the early debates and decisions concerning strategic bombing in the fledgling AEF Air Service.

The second section of the Air Service history that Gorrell wrote was the one concerning night bombardment, which recounted the early efforts to create American bombing squadrons and develop a strategic bombing campaign. Although a large portion of the section describes Gorrell's actions as commander of Strategical Aviation in the Zone of Advance, his inclusion of his November 28, 1917, proposal for a bombing campaign probably had a longer lasting effect. Had he not made it part of the book, Gorrell's strategy may have become just another staff proposal lost to history. Instead, it maintained a prominent place in one of the few sections of the official history that discussed long-range or strategic bombing, and it was readily accessible and easy for future researchers to find.

Gorrell did not stop with the November proposal. He also high-lighted the reasons that he believed that the senior AEF leadership had failed to support strategic bombing. Gorrell placed the majority of blame on himself when he wrote that "the Air Service failed to secure the approval of the General Staff and consequently suffered from the fact that its plans for the use of the Strategical Air Service were not synchronized properly, especially from the mental point of view of its employment, with the ideas of the [GHQ]."[17] He even admitted that this failure was due to his own inexperience, which had led him to believe that gaining Pershing's approval would be enough to ensure the cooperation of the senior AEF staffers—a serious mistake for a young staff officer.

It was yet another reminder of the consequences that would plague the Army for its earlier rules limiting transfer into the Air Service that had limited officers' entry into the Air Service to lieutenants who were under thirty. Gorrell himself was a perfect example. Only twenty-six when he took over the Strategical Aviation section, he had had limited general staff duty, had not attend the Army Staff College, and had little experience working with senior officers. Would a more seasoned officer have been able to bring strategic bombing to fruition during those years? Given the reticence of many senior Army officers during those years, it is doubtful. Still, Gorrell's inexperience did not serve him well in this staff battle.

Besides poor coordination, Gorrell also cited technological short-comings as a reason that strategic bombing failed to gain the Army's acceptance during the war. He succinctly spelled out the problem when he wrote that "entirely too much optimism was felt for the American Production Program," which resulted in a shortage of bomber aircraft in the AEF Air Service. Gorrell was unforgiving on this point, arguing that "it was only the cold matter of fact experience which proved to the world that money and men could not make an air program over night and that the time to prepare for war was not after war had been declared."[18] In modern parlance, Gorrell might have said that if promises sound too good to be true, they most likely are. As such, he not only castigated the Army and Air Service for believing the rosy aircraft production predictions, but he also highlighted the need for realistic industrial planning at home before hostilities broke out.

Besides these two sections, one other portion of the history contained especially valuable insights for future strategic bombing theorists. In writing their contributions, many officers included their personal critiques and recommendations as well. Gorrell decided to incorporate the best of these in a separate section entitled "Lessons and Recommendations." Although they generally focused on tactical or logistical issues, they also contained several references to bombing.

The Lessons and Recommendations section was comprehensive. At the end of the war, Patrick ordered that no one could depart for America until he "furnished in writing to Colonel Gorrell any information of value which he possess and which he has acquired while in the American Air Service."[19] Predictably, a flood of submissions came in from the field. Many were hastily written memorandums of little value, designed to get the author released for return to the United States as quickly as possible. Others, however, were well-developed, thoughtful examinations of individual experiences and how they might be applied to military aviation in the future. Three examples deserve special attention.

The first was a submission by Col. Thomas DeWitt Milling, the chief of the Air Service for the 1st Army. Milling had a distinguished career in the AEF Air Service, serving as the chief of Air Service training in Europe before replacing Billy Mitchell at the 1st Army.[20] Milling's greatest contribution was his discussion of bombing tactics and technological issues. On tactics, he recommended that all long-distance bombing missions include pursuit aircraft whose mission would be to protect the bombers. He pointed out that following heavy losses of aircraft and personnel in the early fall of 1918, the 1st Army Air Service decided to add a pursuit group to all bombing raids beyond the front lines, and it had yielded important benefits.[21] Not only were fewer American bombers lost to enemy fighters, he reported, but the U.S. pursuit aircraft also were able to shoot down German fighters that previously had been free to target American bombers. The bombers proceeded to their targets unmolested.[22]

Milling also brought up some specific technological problems—particularly a design flaw in the De Havilland DH-4 daylight bomber that became a major morale problem in the latter stages of the war. Unprotected gasoline tanks on the DH-4 often ignited into raging fires when struck by antiaircraft artillery shells or machine-gun bullets, usually resulting in fiery deaths for the aircrews. Milling pointed out that both the French and British had developed protected fuel systems that almost always averted such fires. He questioned why the United States had not either developed its own fuel protection technology or adopted the British and French models.[23]

His example highlighted one of the major technological problems faced by the American Air Service in World War I: the lack of an accepted system for assessing needs and ideas from the field, translating them into workable new technologies, and then manufacturing them efficiently. Even more tragic for the American aviators, their European allies seemed to have instituted such a system already. In his classic study of technological innovation in World War I, *The War of Invention: Science in the Great War: 1914–1918*, historian Guy Hartcup described how both the British and French developed government-run networks of educational and scientific institutions working to develop new technologies to meet requirements identified at the front. Coming late to the war and lacking any experience with a military-industrial system, the Americans had their hands full just trying to build the needed aircraft. Making technological changes on an industrial scale was simply beyond their ability in 1918. Fittingly, Milling's specific example of DH-4 fuel tanks echoed Gorrell's call to build an industrial system capable of supporting military operations during peacetime, not just when war demanded immediate action.

Another contributor, Maj. George E. A. Reinburg, commander of the 2nd Day Bombardment Group, straddled the fence between strategy and technology. On the strategy side, he paralleled Gorrell's earlier vision, writing that "observation and bombing are the principal roles of the Air Service, while pursuit is to protect those roles."[24] Like

Gorrell, he challenged the fundamental understanding of why an air force existed. When America entered the war, the emphasis on the use of aircraft for observation and to achieve air superiority had led to a production ratio of 3:5:1 for pursuit-to-observation-to-bomber aircraft. Reinburg challenged this ratio, arguing that bombing was a core mission of the Air Service and should be assigned the same priority as observation.

Although Reinburg's point about strategy was important, it paled compared to his technology recommendations. He began by explaining that expected results for bombing, especially in the press and public, were unreasonable given the state of aviation technology at the time, so the Air Service needed to develop a plan that addressed the issue from both ends.[25] It was not enough to develop new technologies that would increase accuracy and destructive force; the military also needed to work with the public to educate and excite citizens about realistic airpower capabilities.

At the same time, Reinburg also identified a major gap in the relationship among intelligence, targeting, and air operations. He lauded the AEF for having integrated its intelligence gathering with the industrial analysis and targeting systems of its British and French counterparts, but then called for even greater effort to coordinate intelligence with the Allies' air missions. He called for creating an intelligence office under the Air Service's command to conduct immediate assessment of operational results so that planners could consider them in revising the air campaign before the next mission.[26] He predicted that tightening the coordination between intelligence and operations could reduce redundancy and bring more pressure to bear on the enemy's industrial system in a shorter amount of time.

The third major contribution was that of Capt. N. W. Owens, the Air Service adjutant and onetime night bombardment staff officer, and it concerned the industrial problems involved in building a large bomber force. Although most aviators viewed the Liberty engine as a triumph of the American industrial effort, Owens reminded his fellow officers that it wasn't always hailed as a success. He described how problems with the engines in the Handley Page bomber program demonstrated that there were still significant failures even in this highly touted success story. The original plan called for the delivery of fifty Liberty engines to the Handley Page factory in May 1918, another one hundred in June, and one hundred sixty more by the end of July. Later, the goal was revised to call for a steady forty engines a week. But reality was quite different from the plan; Liberty was able to deliver only ten engines by the end of August, and they were incomplete. By October 1918, the factory had to request the shipment of parts alone, since most engines arrived missing major components and were not usable.[27] Owens used this example to recommend the establishment of an aviation industrial core during peacetime to avoid these types of problems during future rapid military buildups.

As Gorrell had predicted, the official history contained a wealth of information for those seeking background information on bombing in World War I. His own two sections provided the context of his proposals and demonstrated the theories behind strategic bombing. Milling, Reinburg, and Owens added to the information with their descriptions of strategic and technical, and production problems faced during the actual bombing campaigns. From their works, future bombing advocates would gain an understanding that building and supporting a bombing force was just as critical as using it in combat. Finally, tactical hints by Milling and Reinburg provided guidance for future theorists in determining how to use bombers in combat.

THE WORLD WAR I BOMBING SURVEY

The only major item missing in Gorrell's history was what actually happened during the bombing campaigns of World War I. The unit histories and individual recommendations seldom discussed the actual missions, their results, or how they affected the larger war. This also must have struck Gorrell, since he had convinced Patrick of the need for such a study of the effects of bombing in the European war. This resulted in the analysis officially entitled, *Results of Air Service Efforts as Determined by Investigation of Damage Done in Occupied Territories*, commonly called the World War I Bombing Survey. Gorrell then made sure to include the report as a companion to the official history so its data would not be lost.

With the full support of Patrick, Gorrell began the process by asking the Air Intelligence Section to conduct a detailed assessment of the bombing effort. Section leaders quickly realized this was beyond their capability and sent a formal request for such a study to the AEF G-2 (intelligence) section, which approved it on February 19 and tasked the First Army G-2 to accomplish the mission. From March 1 to May 20, teams of 1st Army intelligence officers examined bombing sites in an area bounded by the Rhine River and the line running through Dusseldorf, Duren, and Meziers.[28] The area covered all U.S. strategical bombing missions, along with most strategic targets of the RAF Independent Force and some French units. The 1st Army G-2 did consider expanding the area to include more targets, but it ran into difficulties in gaining access to cities east of the Rhine.

The survey, a remarkable analysis for its time, investigated one hundred forty cities based on planned bombing missions by the western Allies. The survey combined information from three sources— physical observation, a review of records; and interviews. It also included the results of attempts to corroborate interview data with city records and diary accounts. The high standards improved the level of intelligence that the analysts were able to compile, but it also limited the pool cities In the end, this high level of information requirements limited the pool of cities that they had the time to visit to eighty instead of one hundred forty. The authors reported that it was impossible to obtain data from the other sixty cities because records had been either destroyed or shipped to Germany before the Allies had arrived.[29]

The report had four sections. Section one contained a general narrative on the effects of Allied bombing. In what today would be called an executive summary, it provided an overview of the document's findings, including an analysis of the bombing results and recommendations for future campaigns. Section two contained the meat of the data in detailed reports on the bombing effects in sixty-seven cities, along with data to back up the conclusions and recommendations contained in the general narrative. Finally, sections three and four of the survey provided supporting data in the form of maps and photographs.

The general narrative was the most widely read portion of the survey. Its primary importance was in providing estimates of the damage caused by Allied bombing. The survey began by identifying an estimated 35 million marks' worth of physical damage to German cities and industry. Although this number may seem high for the limited number of missions and the rudimentary bombing technologies utilized, it was an accurate calculation of the damage either observed by American investigators or gained through German damage reports. Yet, when adjusted to today's dollars, it is only $324 million.[30] Considering that the Federal Emergency Management Agency estimated that Hurricane Katrina caused more than $80 billion in physical damage in 2005, this estimate seems appropriate for the limited long-range bombing campaigns conducted during World War I.

The narrative then attempted to expand beyond the physical destruction to estimate the cost of the less-tangible effects of bombing. First, it calculated the expense of lost production to the enemy's economy. The investigators found twenty-two cities that kept records of lost work hours resulting from the bombing. From these records, they estimated that the Germans lost more than 71 million marks' worth due to factory disruptions, extra cost of transportation, and worker absenteeism.[31] In terms of today's U.S. dollars, that was the equivalent of a little more than $5 billion.

The authors must have understood that this number seemed high, as they included a large amount of supporting data to buttress their assertions. The section had relied heavily on official reports and interviews for objective data. For instance, the authors quoted the manager of the Burbach-Esch-Dudelange Iron Works in Easch as asserting that "it took about 30 minutes after a raid or alert before all personnel were back at work."[32] Based on interviews like this, the survey calculated the loss of seventy minutes per raid or alert as the workers went to shelters, waiting out the bombing, then returned to their work stations. At the same time, the authors pointed out that a single raid might trigger multiple alerts, since the bombers penetrated enemy airspace and threatened several cities before their intended targets became clear. Therefore, a single raid might result in production losses many times higher than the actual physical destruction accomplished by the bombs.

Next, the survey examined the impact of bombing on civilian morale. Through a series of interviews, the investigators attempted to determine how bombing created such confusion and fear that it might paralyze a population. Although this portion of the general narrative was the least scientific, it made a strong argument that bombing instilled fear in the local population that disrupted their daily lives and work habits. Again, the authors included specific examples to extrapolate economic costs from their subjective analysis. Items such as official records reporting three people dying of fright after a raid on Ehrange on August 23, 1918, seemed to corroborate that bombing had a chilling effect on civilian populations. An interview with a railroad official in Thionville, who claimed that he was forced to increase the numbers of workmen after each raid because his workers were too shaken up to accomplish tasks without extra help, supported the survey's conclusions about the loss of production from fear. Finally, even military reports often recognized a so-called morale cost to bombing. One reported that the German military had closed its troop rest facility at Bouley because the frequent bombings had kept soldiers from getting enough sleep.[33]

Based on these factors, the report ended with a final estimate of the cost of bombing to the German economy. Although the document included the 641 killed and 1,263 wounded in bombing attacks, it concluded that the most sweeping results of bombing were economic. The study estimated that bombing cost the German war effort 204 million marks, including an estimated 133 million marks in direct cost from physical damage and loss of production and another 71 million marks in indirect cost from civil defenses, morale loss, and air defense.[34] To put that in today's U.S. dollar value, it equaled approximately $15 billion in economic damage. At the same time, the survey reiterated that its estimate was based on only sixty-six out of one hundred forty cities targeted in the study area where U.S. officials could find verifiable data.[35] It suggested that if the trends found in these sixty-six cities held true for the others bombed by French, English, and American aircraft, the real economic impact of the bombing raids could have been three to four times higher.

Because this tantalizing possibility must have seemed far-fetched to many Army leaders, the report's authors sought to pre-empt any criticism based solely on numbers. On page seven of the report, they fully acknowledged that their cost estimates were just that—only estimates and not hard figures. Still, the survey pointed out that even if the totals turned out to have been overstated, they reflected the damage from a relatively small number of broadly targeted missions—not from a dedicated campaign that specifically targeted critical industries. The authors invited future readers to speculate on what might have been accomplished if the Air Service had focused on strategic bombing and not on ground support.

After discussing the likely economic costs and the impact of the bombing raids on morale, the report offered recommendations for future bombing operations. It began by acknowledging the primary mission of airpower in supporting ground forces, but then quickly hinted that a new role beckoned for the nation's Air Service. An example of this occurred on page eight, where the survey acknowledged that there was almost no support within the Army for a separate or independent bombing force, but then quickly went on to attack this deeply held belief in a discussion of target selection. It recommended reversing the long-standing priorities—which placed enemy troops first, railroad facilities next, and industrial targets third—arguing that there was more value in targeting industry than hitting either troop concentrations or transportation systems. Since destroying the enemy's ability to produce weapons was more valuable than disrupting their arrival or using them at the front, industrial targeting should be the first priority for future air forces, it concluded.[36]

The end-of-the-book summary went even further, spelling out specific recommendations that later became the key theoretical debates of the 1930s. On the issue of targeting, the Americans refuted the British use of city bombing to break the enemy's morale, arguing instead that precision targeting of industrial facilities brought about the same economic and manufacturing damage without the moral questions involved in hitting civilians directly. "Bombing for morale effects alone such as took place over Cologne, Frankfurt, Bonn, and Wiesbaden is not a productive means of bombing," it asserted. "The effect is legitimate and just as considerable when attained indirectly through the bombing of a factory."[37]

Although it was largely hidden in the later portion of Gorrell's official history, the Bombing Survey contained a wealth of information and assessments for future visionaries. Since Gorrell's history remained on the shelves in many important U.S. Army Air Service (and later Air Corps) libraries throughout the 1930s, the survey proved accessible. Together with Gorrell's history of the Paris liaison office and the Strategical Section, it provided a vision for strategic bombing to help stimulate the thoughts of young theorists and the statistical evidence to apply strategic bombing in the next great war.

TURNING A CORNER

Gorrell's influence on aviation did not stop with his history. Even before he departed from Europe, Gorrell began to expand his aviation resume. His successful war record, degree in aeronautical engineering, and reputation for superior administrative capabilities drew him into important roles in shaping aviation's future. At the same time, he frequently showed dissatisfaction with working within the stiff confines of a bureaucracy that often did not agree with his positions. Eventually, this led him to abandon the Air Service for new adventures, but it never removed his love for aviation.

Nevertheless, in 1919 Gorrell was fully committed to shaping the future of the Air Service, in whatever way he could. He worked within the system as the chief of staff of the AEF Air Service to improve day-to-day operations. He also exerted a tremendous effort in collecting as many historical lessons and critiques of the Air Service's experience in World War I as possible in his postwar official history. Finally, Gorrell's experience and capabilities led to his selection to work for President Woodrow Wilson during the Paris Peace Conference.

Wilson arrived in Europe on December 13, 1918, to prepare for the peace negotiations. Once he arrived in Paris, the president gathered a team of advisers to help prepare the American positions on the several different aspects of the proposed treaty. One of these elements concerned the future of international aviation and flying in Germany, to be addressed by a subcommission called the Aeronautical

Commission of the Peace Conference. When Wilson inquired about a qualified officer to advise him on the subcommission's activities, General Patrick proffered Gorrell, and Wilson appointed the young colonel as the president's adviser on international aviation concerns for the remainder of the Paris Peace Conference.[38] Most likely, that started Gorrell along his future path as an expert in civil aviation.

The Aeronautical Commission did not start its formal work until March 1919, when it set about creating a set of rules for international aviation. The panel worked through a series of conventions where representatives from twenty-seven countries gathered to reach agreements. Their work concluded with the *Convention Relating to the Regulation of Aerial Navigation* on October 13, 1919. In the treaty all twenty-seven countries agreed to adhere to international flight standards and methodologies to coordinate aviation issues that crossed international borders.[39] The commission eventually came within the fold of the League of Nations and became the forerunner of the International Civil Aeronautics Organization.

Gorrell continued to work closely with the commission and advising the president and his successors after Wilson returned to the United States in mid-February. He himself returned to America in July 1919. In both cases, the experience opened Gorrell's eyes to the potential for civilian aviation in the postwar world. More important, it likely kindled a commitment to civil aviation that became an important part of his later life and career.

While Gorrell was busy working on international aviation, his old boss, Mason Patrick, continued to coordinate the activities of the AEF Air Service, overseeing the large drawdown of American aviation in Europe, and dreaming of retirement. Like Gorrell, Patrick also had worked on issues related to the peace treaty negotiations. He spent much of January and February coordinating what type of air activity Germany would be allowed to maintain after the war. Patrick reflected in his later memoirs that this was a disappointing time for him, since the closed minds of his French and British counterparts limited any debate on the issue.[40]

Then in May, Patrick turned his attention back to shaping the future of the U.S. Air Service. On April 19, 1919, General Pershing convened the Dickman Board in Paris to review the performance of each branch of the AEF and make suggestions for improving tactics and organization. Patrick tasked Benjamin Foulois to draft the Air Service's response, which was fairly conservative and mirrored much of Mitchell's previous recommendations. One of the important differences was in the area of bombing. Foulois argued that the primary mission of an air service was the collection and transmission of information for use by the Army, followed by direct support to Army units. He almost completely dismissed bombing, labeling the bombardment of distant targets a luxury.[41]

Interestingly, this is one of only two areas where Patrick felt the need to disagree with Foulois in writing. He attached a dissent, explaining that "once it is possible to place a bombing force in the field, its size should be limited only by the nation's ability to provide it and by the numbers and importance of the enemy activities which are to be attacked."[42] Although Patrick's response was not an endorsement of strategic bombing, it represented an openness to the concept that would continue until his return to command of the U.S. Air Service in the 1920s.

The conclusion of the Dickman Board coincided with the arrival of Assistant Secretary of War Benedict Crowell in May 1919. Secretary of War Newton D. Baker had appointed Crowell to lead the American Aviation Mission, with orders to tour Italy, France, and Britain to observe and report on aviation developments. Baker even included a direct order to Crowell to "limit himself to fact-finding and submit no conclusions as to air policy."[43] Yet, one vocal member of the mission especially concerned both Patrick and Pershing. Howard E. Coffin had long been associated with calls to consolidate all of American aviation into one department or service.

As might be expected, Coffin's stance soured both Patrick and Pershing on the whole mission. Nevertheless, Patrick was still a military man, and he followed orders when Crowell asked that he provide a recommendation for the future structure of the postwar Air Service. Patrick gave Crowell the standard Army vision of an Air Service as a separate combat branch, operating within the Army, with observation, pursuit, and ground attack as its three missions. Crowell reacted to the recommendation with near-contempt and continued to search for officers who might be willing to support Coffin's vision of an independent air service. Patrick's attitude toward Crowell and Coffin came through in his personal reflections. His diary entry for June 21, 1919 provided a perfect example: "I have seen little of the said Assistant Secretary," he wrote. "I fancy Coffin has told him he need pay no attention to me."[44]

Although neither Patrick nor Crowell was advocating changing the direction of the Air Service, the differences between them accurately reflected the changing attitudes toward military aviation that were beginning to drive theoretical debates at home. With the war over, political and economic pressures once again became part of the doctrinal and organizational discussions. It was no longer solely a question over what the mission of airpower should be, but also how that mission fit in with political and economic priorities in the rapidly changing domestic and international situation. Much like the arguments about airpower and governmental policies of the early 1900s, the postwar vision of airpower once again was going to be seen through a civilian prism.

On July 13, 1919 the Crowell team and Patrick and Gorrell boarded the passenger liner *Aquitania*, separately, for the return trip to the United States, and according to the two Army officers each side kept to itself throughout the voyage across the Atlantic. For his part, Gorrell agreed to function as Patrick's aide, and the two men built a life-long friendship as they discussed the potential for airpower in future wars and the long road ahead for military aviation.[45] Thus, the voyage was emblematic of the churning forces that would influence aviation in the early 1920s, pitting political goals, economic realities, personality conflicts, and military desires against each other in a drawn-out debate over the role of military aviation, in the process sidelining further talk about strategic bombing.

Gorrell arrived in Washington in July 1919 and was immediately assigned to the operations section of the general staff. His primary duty was to represent the Air Service during a congressional investigation into U.S. aviation performance during World War I, headed by the Wisconsin Republican James A. Frear. Over the next several weeks, the committee conducted a long series of interviews with military offi-cers, industrial leaders, and aviation critics and finally issued a report that was highly critical of the Air Service. The panel castigated the Air Service for deficiencies in procurement, training, and operations, especially during the buildup of forces in late 1917. Gorrell helped write the minority opinion for the committee, arguing in dissent that aviation performed better than should have been expected. He main-tained that despite the sizable budget allocations, there had been no foundation on which to build a large aviation industry, train thousands of pilots, and conduct massive aerial campaigns—particularly in such a short time.[46] Instead, he asserted, under those circumstances Congress should praise the Air Service for achieving as much as it did.

Despite Gorrell's eloquent defense of airpower, he became frus-trated with the political process. Seeking a new challenge, he resigned from the military in March 1920 to pursue a career in the auto industry, eventually rising to become president of the Stutz Motor Company.[47] Still, the onetime career airman could never truly leave aviation behind. After a long furlough, he once again returned to avia-tion in the 1930s, just in time to influence a new generation of air power theorists.

CONCLUSION

When it was published, Gorrell's history was exactly what propo-nents of strategic bombing needed. The breadth and depth of his study guaranteed that it would remain a powerful reference work for American aviation for decades to come. Although the work drifted into obscurity during the 1920s, when the nation was riveted to polit-ical debates about airpower and when more exciting aviation person-alities commanded the public's attention, the history was rediscovered in the 1930s. As students at facilities such as the Air Corps Tactical School began to search the history files to help them form their own ideas on airpower, Gorrell's vision of bombing once again found a theoretical and intellectual home.

Farsighted beyond his years, Gorrell created a document that, unlike the manuals of Mitchell or Sherman, survived the test of time to inform the next generation of aviation thinkers. It contained not only the historical documentation of what actually happened, but also gave readers a firm understanding of the theories that underlined the visions of long-range bombing of German industrial targets outlined by Tiverton, Grey, and Gorrell himself. Just as important, Gorrell was smart enough to include the World War I bombing survey as a component of his history. As a result, when members of the new generation of theorists began to create its own vision of strategic bombing, they had a wealth of statistical data on which to base their assumptions and to convince others of the possibilities of the new offensive weapon.

CHAPTER 6

Strategic Bombing to the Periphery

By 1920 the debate over strategic bombing had become lost in the political and social upheaval that had enveloped the nation after the end of World War I. Edgar Gorrell, the foremost American proponent of long-range bombing raids during the conflict, was now firmly ensconced in his new job as president of the Stutz Motor Company. At the same time, two important developments at home temporarily blocked any prospect of reviving the issue: first, U.S. foreign policy took a more isolationist turn from President Wilson's more-activist wartime posture, quelling what had been the driving force for the development of a comprehensive airpower doctrine. Second, the Army took advantage of the new political environment to clamp down on what it viewed as heretical thinking inside the Air Service—the long-festering proposal to create an independent military aviation component.

The combination effectively removed both the ends and the means that bombing advocates had employed earlier to support their cause. With no major foreign adversary threatening to wage war in the immediate future, there seemed little need for a strategy designed to break the industrial might of an enemy combatant. If there were no imminent threats, then there was no need for a large, expensive standing army. The resulting demobilization, budget cutting, and return to prewar doctrine enabled the Army's leadership to reassert its dominance over Air Service commanders, who had been pushing during the war to embrace strategic bombing and eventual independence from ground-force commanders. The postwar shift to the "normalcy" promised by President Warren G. Harding diverted attention from strategic bombing and sidelined it to the periphery of Army doctrine.

Still, military aviation had powerful advocates in both the Congress and the press. A new breed of Air Service officer, the politically connected advocate, used such connections to fight for continued expansion of airpower, new missions, and greater autonomy. The goal was to reshape the Air Service based on a new defense-oriented national security strategy. Long-range bombers no longer would be sent solely to strike at the enemy's factories. What made more sense politically—and from a budgetary standpoint as well—was to build a force in which tactical and operational offensive aircraft would work together to find, attack, and destroy what was now the most likely short-term threat to America—in this case ostensibly a naval incursion by a foreign power.

With that in mind, strategic bombing was put on a back shelf while its advocates explored a new role for aviation in defense of the American coasts, a mission that held out the promise of prestige, funding, and possibly even some measure of autonomy. Yet much like Gorrell himself, the bombing theorists did not intend to remain idle. For his part, Gorrell maintained his influence through frequent correspondence with leading military aviation figures. To be sure, strategic bombing proponents kept their heads down during the public debates about aviation that were taking place in Washington. Behind the scenes, however, in small, private strategy sessions, airpower proponents slowly and subtly refashioned the concepts that they had developed during the war.

SHAPING FORCES

The most important of these political shifts began even before the war formally ended. Six days ahead of the Armistice the mid-term congressional elections brought the Republican opposition to power, signaling that trouble lay ahead for President Wilson. Where Wilson had tried to use the election as a referendum on his plans for the postwar world, the Republicans argued that his globalist policies had made America too big a player in the international system, much to its own detriment. His "Fourteen Points" plan for peace and the restructuring of Europe, which would have committed the United States to playing a major role in the newly created League of Nations, only seemed to confirm the Republican criticism. Former President Theodore Roosevelt summed up the feeling of many Americans toward Wilson's new vision when he said, "To substitute internationalism for nationalism means to do away with patriotism."[1]

The death knell for Wilson's internationalist strategy came when the Senate refused to approve the Treaty of Paris and allow the United States to join the League of Nations. Instead of becoming a major participant in the new international system, the United States ended up returning to its traditionally isolationist posture. With that, there no longer was any need for Washington to maintain a large, extremely costly wartime military.

The swift demobilization that followed brought sharp cuts in military spending on personnel and equipment and predictions of shortages of both manpower and aircraft. As expected, the massive reductions hit the Air Service hard. Of the twenty thousand officers on duty at the end of the war, only a little more than two hundred remained in the aviation component at the start of 1920. To make matters worse, all of these officers were "on detail" from other branches of the Army and would have to return to their regular branches. The Air Service still was not a recognized corps within the Army, but merely a subdivision of the Signal Corps.[2]

The Air Service faced other, less immediately apparent effects that would squeeze its personnel even further. Hemmed in by the 1909 restriction that allowed only junior officers to become pilots, the service had had to promote them rapidly to fill its wartime staff and command billets. Now, with demobilization, most would be forced to return to their permanent prewar ranks—the bulk of those no higher than first lieutenant. As a result, Air Service officers experienced jaw-dropping demotions, in sharp contrast to their counterparts in artillery or infantry billets. Foulois, the onetime chief of the AEF Air Service, recalled the sheer shock he experienced while disembarking from his troopship as a brigadier general and becoming a captain the moment he stepped onto the pier.[3]

As a result, the Air Service of the early 1920s faced a serious shortage of field-grade officers, limiting its ability to select qualified squadron commanders. That left the Army with two options: it could permit junior officers to fill command positions that traditionally called for more senior rank, or it could transfer non-flying officers of the appropriate rank to command aviation squadrons. As might be expected, neither choice was pleasing to Air Service leaders.

The personnel shortages highlighted a larger problem for the Air Service. Although wartime needs had shaped the overall structure within which the Air Service had evolved, the Army underwent changes during the postwar years that effectively steered doctrine away from strategic bombing. First, the demobilization and sharply reduced budgets emboldened traditional Army leaders to reassert control over their often-rebellious aviation arm. Second, a series of technology shortcomings made it impossible to expand airpower doctrine to fulfill Gorrell's vision of developing a strategic bombing force that would be capable of winning wars. Finally, the overwhelming challenges that Air Service leaders faced in maintaining personnel, supply chains, and training diverted their attention from theoretical debates on how to use airpower in combat.

The most constricting of these internal pressures was the return of tight Army control. Although the final year of the war had convinced senior Army leaders of the value of airpower, many of them balked at the airmen's talk of a "war-winning" role for aviation or the concept of an independent air force. They preferred to find a way to alleviate aviation's budgetary, personnel, and command concerns while still hewing steadfastly to the Army's long-standing view that ground forces were the key to victory.

The loss of support for establishing strategic bombing as a primary mission also reduced enthusiasm for an autonomous, or even independent, air force. Despite some congressional interest in the example of the British Royal Air Force, the Army strongly opposed any autonomy for the Air Service, especially if the new service were assigned strategic bombing as a primary mission. Secretary of War Baker dismissed the opposition in his 1919 annual report to Congress, not only rejecting strategic bombing as too expensive, but also posing a counterargument—that heavy bombing campaigns would only stiffen an enemy's will to resist and would prove a detriment to any war effort.[4]

In this atmosphere, strategic bombing theory became a drag on the Air Service's push for adequate funding and autonomy.

The return of the Air Service as a support element for ground operations was underscored in January 1919, when a two-star artillery officer, Maj. Gen. Charles T. Menoher, became the chief of the Air Service. Menoher had commanded the 42nd Division and the VI Army Group during the war, but he had no practical experience in aviation. More troubling than his lack of aviation experience was his publicly stated view that the Air Service belonged to the Army and its sole purpose in combat was to provide direct support of the foot soldier.[5] Not only did this dash hopes for strategic bombing advocates, but it essentially doomed the possibility of achieving autonomy for the Air Service. In Menoher's mind, strategic bombing was a theoretical waste of time, and talk of independence was tantamount to heresy.

Menoher's views became Army policy on August 8, 1919, when Secretary Baker named him to head a board of four general officers to review the status of the Air Service and determine its proper size, structure, and mission in the postwar Army. The composition of the Menoher Board left little doubt about its direction. The other three panel members, all major generals, were from the field artillery. When the Menoher Board released its final report on October 27, it was a major blow to the Air Service.

The panel's principal conclusions seemed to close off any expansion of the Air Service. The board acknowledged that aviation would probably play a larger role in future wars, but asserted that no nation could afford to maintain a large combat-ready air fleet in peacetime. Instead, it recommended that America focus on developing a commercial aviation industry that would be able to help in mobilizing military aviation in any future war.[6] It also cautioned that creating a separate air force would be counterproductive, for two reasons: it would cost too much and it would undermine the time-honored principle of unity of command in wartime. These two core arguments would serve as the cornerstones of Army resistance to Air Service independence for the next two decades.

Still, the board's report was not all negative for the Air Service. Menoher understood that airpower would be an important element of future wars. His report pointed out that the United States lacked a technological and industrial system that could provide the kind of aviation research, aircraft production, and pilot training that the nation would need to maintain long-term preparedness. To overcome these deficiencies, the board recommended that Congress increase funding for military aviation and establish a single government agency to oversee research and development in both military and civil aviation.[7]

These last recommendations would have tremendous payoffs for the future Air Service. By broadening the discussion to include technological research, production capabilities, military power, and the proper role and structure of an air force, the Menoher Board started America down the path to building a civil military industrial program that would see it through the next war.

This was only a vision in 1919. Although it had only been a year since World War I had come to an end, technological development in military aviation had come to a halt. Eager to speed demobilization the slash-spending Congress (and the Army) turned to using war surplus aircraft rather than buying new, more advanced models. The policy hit bomber units especially hard. Hemmed in during the war by bomber-limiting production ratios and recurring manufacturing problems, the Air Service's end-of-war inventory contained far more surplus pursuit, observation, and attack aircraft than bombers.[8] Bomber squadrons quickly wore out their leftover aircraft; they found few opportunities to replace them.

Recognition of the technological standstill permeated the thinking of Air Service theorists. In his book, *Air Warfare*, airpower doctrine pioneer William Sherman acknowledged that as late as the 1920s the predominant view of bombers was that although they were critical for exercising airpower, they were technologically inferior and the United States would have to achieve air superiority in the entire theater of operations before they could be used in sufficient numbers to play a major role.[9]

Col. Edwin E. Aldrin, chief of the Military Aeronautics Division, was also a critic, asserting that American aviation production had little ability to design aircraft or engines and what capabilities had been acquired during the war quickly had atrophied with the end of the wartime budgets.[10]

Even at this early stage, however, changes were in the offing. In February 1919 Aldrin's division was assigned the mission to fix the problem. Just a year later the Air Service established its own air engineering school at McCook Army Air Field near Dayton, Ohio. Although the engineering school focused on identifying aerodynamic principles and not building aircraft, it had a major impact in persuading civilian aircraft-manufacturing companies to pursue technological advances that first would be useful to the military and later could be used in civilian aircraft—a staple of military-industrial relations today.[11]

The military's influence on technology development by civilian companies would prove especially important in the push toward strategic bombing. In one example, Billy Mitchell, then chief of the Air Service Training and Observation Group, asked Aldrin to work toward developing high-altitude aircraft. The resulting research led to the development of high-powered air-cooled engines, propeller innovations, and high-altitude cooling systems, all of which were critical in the design of larger higher-flying aircraft.[12] These advances eventually made their way to the civilian aircraft industry and contributed to the development of a new class of airliners and cargo planes that offered greater lift, range, and speed capabilities.

For the Air Service, Mitchell's push for more advanced technology also marked the start of the transition from a pursuit-plane-based force to one that was built around the long-range heavy bomber. The advances that Aldrin described, combined with the need to acquire new bombers in World War II, produced a series of new designs for long-range aircraft each more capable than the previous one. Meanwhile, the ample supply of war-surplus fighters and observation planes sharply reduced the military's demand for pursuit aircraft—and limited the ability of the Military Aeronautics Division to influence technological changes for lighter planes.

The last of the internal forces shaping the Air Service in the years after World War I involved manpower. In the rapid demobilization, the Air Service lost hundreds of experienced aviators to both civilian airlines and state National Guard units. The fact that many pilots had to revert to their prewar (junior) ranks only compounded the problem. To cap it off, the Army adopted a promotion policy that entailed grouping officers from all branches and corps into a single pool and then basing promotion primarily on seniority.[13] The result was that Air Service officers were placed behind their counterparts in the infantry and artillery, even though many of the aviators had held more senior ranks and commands during the war. Expectedly, many pilots became disgruntled over their plight, which they saw as fraught with sharply reduced budgets, outmoded aircraft, and an unfair system of promotions, and that now was curtailing the independence they had enjoyed during the war.

The attitude seems to have penetrated the psyche of Air Service personnel throughout the Army. Only a month after returning to command the Air Service in 1921, Mason Patrick received a letter of congratulations from an old friend, Maj. Gen. Francis J. Kernan, then chief of the Philippines Department, in which Kernan expressed his concern over the plight of Air Service personnel.[14] Patrick's response tersely described the discipline problem that the Air Service faced as it entered the 1920s. "[I]t is the youth and inexperience of its officers whom it is necessary to place in responsible positions that are largely the cause of the trouble," he wrote Kernan. "I mean to impress upon them as firmly as may be necessary the fact that their duty must be performed properly, that the constituted authorities must exercise efficient supervision over them, and that they must learn the essentials of discipline."[15]

Kernan's remarks reflected still another consequence of the 1909 personnel policy that had limited the entry into military aviation to junior officers under age thirty. When combined with the freedom from traditional Army discipline that many of them had experienced during World War I, it created an eager group of maverick airmen who were ready to rebel against any reassertion of Army dominance over the structure, budgets, and doctrinal thinking of the Air Service. This not only created a morale problem for Patrick, but it resulted in a group of avid supporters for Mitchell's fight for Air Service independence.

The influences of these shaping forces were evident in the National Defense Act of 1920, often called the Kahn Act, after its sponsor, Representative Julius Kahn, a Republican from California. Signed into law on June 4, the measure established the size of the current Air Service, but it also identified possibilities for the expansion of airpower in the future. Two elements of the law were important for the Air Service. First, the legislation reorganized the Army into three components—the active Army, the National Guard, and the Army Reserve. In doing so, the Kahn Act significantly reduced the size of the active-duty Army to just 280,000 soldiers, which again was lowered to 191,000 in February 1921. For the Air Service this meant a permanent strength of only 1,514 officers and 16,000 men.[16] Although future funding difficulties would ensure that the Air Service would never reach its authorized strength of 17,514, the certainty of having permanent ceilings enacted into law provided a level of long-term stability for planning purposes.

More important than size was the role of the legislation in freeing the Air Service from its position as a part of the Army Signal Corps. In doing so, the statute designated the Air Service as a separate branch within the Army, provided for a major general as its commander and, finally, required that only aviation officers be placed in command of air squadrons—a step that had become a major thorn in the side of the airmen.[17] Although the law did not address other personnel issues, the provisions gave the Air Service a degree of autonomy that enabled it to develop an airpower doctrine without quite as much oversight by the Army leadership.

In retrospect, the Army Reorganization Act worked more to the benefit of the Air Service than to its detriment. Although the law reduced the service to seven aviation commands, only one of which involved long-range heavy bombing, its establishment of the Air Service as a separate command element would yield significant benefits over the next several years. A memorandum dated July 6, 1921 from Maj. Gen. William G. Haan, director of the War Plans Division, to General Pershing detailing the effects of the Army reorganization on all branches demonstrated that the separate status of the Air Service had helped it fare better in the drawdown than most branches of the Army. Most branches suffered personnel reductions of approximately 50 percent during this era. Even the infantry took a 47 percent cut, falling to just 58,000 men by the end of the year, from 110,000 before.

At the same time, the Air Service suffered only a 36 percent loss, downsizing to 10,300 men, from 16,000 before.[18]

The result was to establish the parameters within which airpower advocates would operate during the next decade. Although the changing political environment meant less money and less equipment, the formal designation of the Air Service as a branch provided just enough autonomy for airpower theorists to continue their work. The pent-up frustrations of military aviators encouraged further change.

AIR SERVICE REACTION

Aviation leaders did not take the setbacks of the immediate postwar era sitting by. Key leaders cultivated relationships with political figures and the press to push for broadening the missions of the Air Service, gaining more autonomy and turning it into a separate service.[19] Yet, pursuing these relationships contained the risk that they might backfire. In the aviators' eyes, their campaign was dedicated to the betterment of military aviation; winning support from Congress and the public would be a valuable asset in trying to achieve their goals. At the same time, they were still Army officers and were obligated to follow the orders of their superiors.

Not only did these officers risk provoking the wrath of senior Army leaders, but they also faced an uncertain reception from the nation's new president. In 1920, the Republicans regained the White House with the election of Warren G. Harding. Harding had a tough fiscal outlook, promising to run the government as a business, with a tight budget and a skepticism about new spending programs. As such, he supported the Budget and Accounting Act of 1921. Today the law is most remembered for having established a formal budgeting process, overseen by a new Bureau of the Budget, which reported to the president. A lesser-known part of the bill, however, directly affected the Air Service. Apprehensive about individual elements of the executive branch seeking funds directly from Congress, Harding had backed a provision that prohibited federal agencies from pressuring Congress directly for additional funding.[20] As a result, Air Service officers who attempted to secure congressional backing for higher budgets not only faced internal disciplinary action within the Army, but they also might run afoul of the president.

As historian Tami Davis Biddle points out, this led to a contradiction for Air Service officers. Publicly senior aviation officers had to appear to hew to Army policy on the question of service independence, yet inside the military they continued to press for a broadening of their missions and increased autonomy.[21] The dilemma was how to do both at once.

In the next several years, Air Service leaders split into three factions. One group favored outright rebellion, another sought to seek independence by working within the system; and a third borrowed tactics from the other two. Each of these groups shared a vision for an independent Air Service, but differed on two important aspects: why it was needed and how to achieve it. Contained within these differences were the seeds that grew into the airpower strategy of the new Army Air Service.

The first faction comprised those Air Service officers who favored the outspoken campaign led by Billy Mitchell. In January 1919 Mitchell returned from Europe as a man with a mission: he was determined to create a new, fully independent air force, most likely with himself as its first leader. As early as April 3, he argued at a meeting of the Navy's General Board that the new ability of airplanes to sink naval vessels required a full rethinking of national defense policy, complete with structural changes in the services designed to enable them to use military aviation to its best advantage. To do this, he proposed creating a new Department of Defense that would oversee the Army, Navy, and an independent Air Force and ensure that their funding, equipment, and doctrine worked in concert with one another.[22]

Mitchell's speech became the first salvo in a battle to create a separate air force within the national defense structure. Mitchell's rise and fall in working toward that goal has been well documented, but there are three elements of Mitchell's saga that provide insight into the evolution of strategic bombing.

The first is the rationale that he unfailingly gave for creating an independent air force—that there was a separate national defense mission to consider and that only airpower could accomplish it. The mission was twofold—first, to protect America from strategic attack, and second, to enable it to conduct strategic campaigns against its enemies.[23] Mitchell argued that it was a mission that neither the Army nor the Navy was prepared to carry out.

This overall strategic view led to Mitchell's second contribution to the advancement of strategic bombing. When Mitchell returned from Europe, General Menoher appointed him chief of the Air Service's Training and Operations Group. One of its central missions was to formulate a new strategy and doctrine for the postwar Air Service. Mitchell pulled together a staff of experienced aviators and airpower advocates—including Thomas Milling, William Sherman, Leslie MacDill, and Lewis Brereton—and imbued them with his own vision. Many would go on to play an important role in developing airpower doctrine even after they left the group.

Although Mitchell instilled his own ideas about airpower in members of the staff, he also gave them the freedom to explore other visions of airpower and to weigh them in preparing the group's recommendations. The concept they embraced was that for the Air Service to become independent it had to offer a war-winning mission and strategy that no other service could provide—an idea that would eventually prove central to the creation of the modern U.S. Air Force.

Mitchell's leadership drew a devoted following throughout the Air Service. "Billy Mitchell was the idol of every pilot," Maj. Gen. James P. Hodges recalled later, ". . . [a]nd I suppose 99 and $^9/_{10}$ths percent of them were influenced by his vision and strategies he advocated."[24]

The third way that Mitchell influenced the advancement of strategic bombing was in developing a formal doctrine for it—a role that often has been obscured in historians' focus on his later well-publicized struggles with government officials and military leaders. In the 1920s, he played an integral role in drafting the early tactical manuals that formed the basis of aviation doctrine and supervised the creation of a series of new postwar manuals. With no formal doctrine-writing unit within the new Army Air Service, these publications became the de facto doctrine for operational squadrons.

The next phase in the dissemination of his doctrinal thinking came in a new *Tactical Application of Military Aeronautics Manual,* published in January 1920. In that one, he described the principal mission of the Air Service as one that sought "to destroy the aeronautical forces of the enemy, and, after this, to attack his formations both tactical and strategical"—a phrase tied directly to his vision of promoting a new airpower mission that could not be carried out by ground or naval forces.[25] More important for strategic bombing, the manual went one step further in outlining the role of bombing, arguing that it offered "probably the greatest value in hitting an enemy's nerve center" such as a headquarters complex or a communications node.[26] In those two sentences, Mitchell succinctly laid out his rationale for creating a fully independent air force. Its defining element would be shaping a strategic role for airpower. Long-range heavy bombers would be its principal weapon.

Although Mitchell's official role in doctrine development ended in June 1920, when he left the Training and Operations Group, his later works continued to emphasize the link between defining a strategic mission as a rationale for creating an independent Air Service and advocating the use of large-scale bombing as a means for accomplishing that mission. In his 1921 book, *Our Air Force,* he argued that the first battle of any future war would occur in the air and would enable the winner to use airpower to attack enemy cities without fear of retaliation.[27] The vision continued to influence doctrinal thinking for years to come.

While Mitchell epitomized the Air Service officers who wanted to rebel against the Army and Navy, Mason Patrick exemplified those who wanted to avoid conflict. Patrick saw military aviation at a crossroads. "[T]here are enthusiasts, on the one hand, who believe that the coming into being of aircraft have practically scrapped all other combat agencies; and on the other hand, conservatives who consider aircraft mere auxiliaries to previously existing combat branches," he wrote in 1920. "The truth, of course, lies between the two views."[28] As a result, Patrick favored working within the system to bring about a change in thinking that would eventually lead to a new structure.

Patrick shared Mitchell's perspective on why the military's aviation component should be designated an independent service.[29] The two men differed only over how to achieve that goal. Whether it was Patrick's own experience in having had to deal with the pugnacious Mitchell or a sign of his maturity and his years of experience in the regular army, he firmly believed that working within the system offered the best chance for success. A small, but determined group of fellow officers agreed.

The third faction pressing for airpower independence, which favored using elements of both men's playbooks, was typified by Benjamin Foulois. Foulois mostly worked within the Army structure, but he was not averse to taking a poke at the Army when the chance arose. In contrast to Mitchell and Patrick, who argued that none of the existing services could take on the new mission, Foulois contended that the Army could do the job if it were forced to expand its air arm to include strategic bombing as a primary mission. In testimony before Congress on October 16, 1919, he complained that the Army's leadership was "only interested in the defensive side of airpower and had neglected the fighting side of military aviation since the end of the war."[30]

Despite his attack on the Army's leaders, Foulois was more pragmatic than Mitchell. He understood that full independence for the air component would come only incrementally, in a series of steps rather than all at once. At the same time, he favored using whatever political influence was necessary to push for rapid change, rather than quietly working within the system. In truth, however, his approach saw little success. Unlike Mitchell, he was not a vibrant visionary who could draw young officers, the press, and the public to his side. His direct attacks on senior Army leaders limited his ability to persuade senior officers to support the aviators' cause, and in time they came to see him as an outsider and a threat.[31] As a result, Foulois had little effect on the airpower debate during the early 1920s, although his experiences shaped his actions in the early 1930s, when he once again emerged as the chief of the Army Air Corps.

Each of these factions had a role in shaping both the future of the Air Service and the thinking about strategic bombing. Mitchell's confrontational posture drew plenty of attention and helped guide a legion of young officers in the early 1920s. Nevertheless, when Mitchell's approach proved detrimental to both himself and his cause the younger officers began to seek a new tactic and Patrick's long-term incremental approach won more converts. Even so, Mitchell's concepts of a distinct national security mission that included both strategic defense and heavy bomber attacks continued intact as Patrick became the movement's leader.

DOCTRINE DEVELOPMENT IN THE SHADOWS

The internal debate on how to achieve independence played a major role in shaping the development of airpower doctrine in the early 1920s. Historian Tami Davis Biddle cited a key turning point that occurred during those years as airpower theorists struggled to portray long-range heavy bombing—which previously had been considered purely an offensive weapon—as part of Harding's new postwar defensive national security policy.[32] Mitchell again led the effort, arguing that the reason that airpower was the key to the strategic defense of the United States was because it was so capable of destroying naval vessels. Such mental acrobatics not only helped keep airpower relevant in the public mind, but they also helped airpower proponents make the transition from the offensive perspective that had spawned strategic bombing during the war years to the new defensive security mindset that replaced it when peace was signed.

Biddle's narrow focus does not shed sufficient light on the highly nuanced evolution in airpower thinking that was occurring among many mid-level Air Service officers; indeed, too often historians have concentrated on the role of coastal defense and the fight for Air Service independence as the drivers of airpower doctrine. Yet, inside the important think tanks of the early Army Air Service, coastal defense was just one of the many potential missions—some of them clearly secondary—that fell under the rubric of strategic bombing.

The first document to discuss long-range bombing in any detail came from Mitchell's Air Service Training and Operations Division. The group's *Tactical Application of Military Aeronautics Manual* contained the three core elements of airpower thinking in the early 1920s: the need to gain air superiority at the start of any conflict, the traditional airpower mission of supporting ground forces, and the benefits of creating an independent strategic mission. As might be expected, the manual drew the attention of many senior Army officers—and their ire as well. Even so, the leadership's single-minded focus on Mitchell's manual also had an unintended positive effect: it ceded a measure of autonomy to the mid-level officers who developed operational and tactical guidance.

The relative independence permitted the young officers to expand strategic thought in their lower-level manuals and training texts without the direct threat of oversight. A good example was the *Aerial Bombardment Manual* produced in 1920 by the Training and Observation Group. Drafted by Thomas Milling and William Sherman, the manual was an early effort to shift long-range bombing theory from *strategical to strategic*. In it the authors described bombardment aviation as "becoming an important part of the Air Service," adding that "it is believed by many that with sufficient numbers it will win a war."[33] Although this statement may have seemed similar to the ideas advocated by Gorrell and the British during World War I, it represented a key step forward in the post–World War I Air Service. Not only did it show that the concept of strategic bombing still percolated in the minds of airmen, but it also demonstrated that they could keep it alive in their doctrinal manuals even after the Army had reasserted tighter control over the Air Service.

Still, despite the seemingly greater freedom that Air Service manual-writers thought they enjoyed, the fact was that the service's senior staff was housed so close to senior Army leaders, the reins were still tight, and even seemingly routine manuals often received a critical eye. What many thought the Air Service needed was a doctrine command that was located away from Washington. In the summer of 1920, the airpower advocates got their wish. The Army established a new Air Service Tactical School (ASTS) and based it at Langley Field in Hampton, Virginia. The school traced its origins to the Army Reorganization Act of 1920, when the newly created U.S. Army Air Service began to think about how to restructure itself. Traditional Army branches such as the infantry and artillery had employed similar schools for training their young officers and later provided mid-career education on command and staff functions. Now a full-fledged branch, the Air Service realized that it also would need a mid-career school to prepare young field-grade officers for higher-level posts.

The ASTS acquired a new doctrine-writing mission in September 1921, when the War Department ordered each of the Army's combat branches to republish all of their training material as a series of formal training regulations. Partly to meet this requirement, Mason Patrick restructured the Training and Observation Group, calling it the Training and War Plans Division. The new division lacked the manpower to revise the Air Service's training materials, so it tapped the newly created ASTS to develop the documents.[34] The ASTS now had a new double mission, where it both trained mid-level aviators for new command and staff duties and took the lead in developing airpower doctrine.

For its part, the ASTS responded immediately. Where the school had spent most of 1920 training its first class of students and participating in Mitchell's bombing experiments, it branched out in 1921 to preparing strategy, tactics, and doctrine. Maj. Thomas Milling, its first commander, took a unique approach. Instead of detailing a few instructors to write doctrine, he integrated the task into the school's courses by encouraging students and staff alike to debate airpower theories and develop new doctrinal concepts as part of their education.[35]

As part of this process, in May 1921, William Sherman, Milling's assistant, drafted *The Fundamental Doctrine of the Air Service* as a precursor to a new manual entitled "Training Regulation 440–15." The new publication drew heavily from Gorrell's June 1919 *Manual for Air Service Operations*, which Sherman had helped draft while working on Gorrell's staff.[36] In the new manual Sherman identified two core functions for airpower—ground support and strategic bombing operations. He also recommended specific proportions for the missions, assigning 80 percent to strategic operations and 20 percent to ground support. The ratio was difficult for many Army leaders to accept, which may explain why the school's first training regulation remained in draft format until January 1926, while several boards of officers reviewed the draft and recommended changes in the intervening years.

Despite the Army's foot dragging, the ASTS's slow assault on the parent service's view of airpower continued in 1922. In the final draft of Air Service Training Regulation 440–15, Milling avoided Sherman's controversial recommendations for mission ratios, but he again listed the two broad mission categories—direct ground support and independent offensive actions.[37] Although the language stopped short of openly advocating strategic bombardment, it provided a justification for categorizing long-range bombing as a primary mission in an official publication that later become the core document of the early Air Service.

By 1924, these concepts were starting to spread from budding think tanks at Langley Field to the mainstream of Air Service thinking. On March 27 Patrick expanded the idea in a lecture to the Army's general staff officer training school at Fort Leavenworth, Kansas, entitled "Fundamental Conceptions of the Air Service." He began by reassuring the officers that the service still saw its primary mission as "[assisting] ground forces to gain strategical and tactical success." Then came a caveat: this did not mean air forces would be "under the immediate control of local commanders." Rather, Patrick insisted, ground commanders must understand that for airpower to be successful it had to "operate independently and sometimes far afield of the current ground operations."[38]

Although Patrick's remarks focused solely on the role of airpower in relation to ground forces, strategic bombing theory continued to evolve as well. The job of determining the best way to use bombers in war often fell to mid-level officers at the ASTS who were operating outside direct Army oversight. Their new vision of strategic bombing began to come to life in updates to the Bombardment Course textbook used to teach students the art of long-range bombing. The 1924 edition was especially important in the development of strategic bombing theory. It began by critiquing the World War I bombing campaigns. Using Gorrell's own World War I Bombing Survey for statistical support, the document argued that strategic bombing during the war had been too haphazard to succeed. Instead, it reasserted Gorrell's and Tiverton's earlier argument that target selection and concentration of aircraft were critical for success.[39] The result was that for the first time since the end of World War I, a manual had addressed the critical issue of target selection in strategic bombing.

Given the Army's close oversight of Air Service doctrine, it would have been difficult to put thoughts such as that into the major doctrinal manuals. Therefore, many Air Service members took to advocating their beliefs in books that were outside the editorial purview of Army leaders. In 1926 Sherman took such an approach with his *Air Warfare*, in which he indicated that "from the very nature of the weapon, bombardment aviation is used for strategic purposes rather than tactical."[40] He then pushed the idea further, describing four categories of bombardment—attacks on large population centers, destroying enemy supply lines, neutralizing fortifications, and, in a reflection of the times, the destruction of warships in coastal defense.

Even more important was Sherman's discussion of what a future strategic bombing campaign might look like. He pointed out that in modern warfare the mobilization of the military was inevitably accompanied by the companion mobilization of war-related industries. Although it was impossible to destroy all of an enemy's factories, Sherman argued that a carefully targeted bombing campaign could cripple the whole system by destroying specific components of an adversary's industrial network, which he labeled as "key" plants.[41] Sherman's vision of a strategic bombing campaign can be viewed as a precursor to Maj. Donald Wilson's more famous Industrial Web Theory, made popular at the just-renamed Air Corps Tactical School in 1933, which contended that a nation's military industrial complex was an interconnected system. If an air force could destroy the critical links and nodes of that system, the enemy's entire warfighting effort could be hobbled.

Sherman's book skillfully depicts the evolution of strategic bombing theory from 1920 to 1926. Despite the focus on shaping airpower to meet the demands of senior Army commanders (who insisted on a primary mission of providing ground support) and members of Congress (who wanted it to include the politically popular defense of coastal installations), the concept of strategic bombing always remained foremost in the minds of key mid-level Air Service officers. Often working through smaller tactical manuals that attracted little attention even within the Army, these strategists continued the slow evolution of bombardment theory. Out-of-the-way places such as Langley effectively became the think tanks, not only for the study of airpower in general, but also for developing doctrine to provide guidance for the use of its major elements—observation, pursuit, attack, and bombardment. In taking on such tasks, the ASTS sparked a new round of thought that would lead to major changes in the soon-to-be-designated Army Air Corps.

BRINGING THE ELEMENTS TOGETHER

The theoretical groundwork laid by the Air Service would have meant little if its leadership had not made simultaneous structural changes that enabled their officers to put it into place. From the start, the doctrinal debates had taken form against the backdrop of political sparring over the very future of the Air Service. Although the political debate did have some influence on the direction of airpower thinking in the early 1920s, its true importance was in creating an Air Service organization that would be capable of carrying out the concepts that were developed in the late 1920s and early 1930s.

The first of these structural debates occurred with the creation of the Lassiter Board in December 1922. Throughout that year, Air Service Chief Mason Patrick had been forwarding complaints about the status and structure of the service to John W. Weeks, the secretary of war. The letters largely involved the limited availability of aircraft and the question of whether non-aviators should command flying squadrons. On December 18, Weeks responded by asking Patrick to provide him with proposed recommendations on what the proper structure and size of the Air Service should be and what should be done to correct its deficiencies.

Patrick based his proposals on Sherman's draft of Training Regulation 440–15, which was now widely accepted within the Air Service. The draft called for dividing the Air Service into two major components—one consisting of observation aircraft assigned to division and corps commanders for direct support of ground operations; and a second, dedicated to an offensive force, that would comprise bombers, fighters, and attack aircraft, all under the command of General HQ

Reserve headed by the senior Air Service officer. Sherman again used his 20 percent to 80 percent ratio to apportion forces, recommending corps commanders get the smaller fraction for observation duties, while the GHQ Reserve contained the bulk of offensive airpower for independent offensive operations.[42] Patrick believed that this plan offered enough airpower to meet the daily needs of ground commanders and still maintain the ability to concentrate the bulk of the combat aircraft at the proper time and place to achieve strategic objectives.

In early 1923, with Patrick's plan as a basis, Weeks appointed a board of officers under Maj. Gen. James Lassiter to review the Air Service plan and make formal recommendations. It wasn't smooth sailing. From the start, Patrick's plan faced stiff opposition from Maj. Gen. Hugh Drum of the War Department's General Staff. In a counter-proposal to Patrick's, he asserted that the proper way to determine Air Service requirements was to figure out what aviation support the divisions and corps needed and then form the remaining airpower into a highly controlled GHQ Reserve to meet limited long-range bombing or reconnaissance needs.[43]

Lassiter largely sided with Drum, overruling Patrick's proposals to locate only observation planes at corps and division levels and to place strategic bombing forces under the GHQ Reserve.[44] In the end, the Lassiter Board rejected the Army Air Service plan and recommended the placement of multifunction air force elements in each Army corps. In doing so, it reaffirmed the Army's long-held position that airpower was similar to other support forces and that its assets should be dispersed among different levels of command. Division commanders would control observation squadrons, and each corps commander would have pursuit and attack squadrons assigned to distribute as he saw fit. This left only a small core of bombardment squadrons, along with some pursuit aircraft, available for strategic missions in a GHQ Reserve force.

Even with this setback, there were still some positive recommendations for the Air Service in the Lassiter Board's final report. The most important was an acknowledgment of the deterioration of the military's airpower capabilities since the end of the war. "[A]ir power has come to play an increasing role in warfare since World War I, but our nation has not kept step with the evolution," Lassiter wrote.[45] To rectify the situation, he recommended that Congress increase the number of aircraft in the Air Service to 1,655, with 1,003 stationed in the United States and the remaining 652 placed with overseas garrisons.

Adamant about holding down military spending in the wake of the war, Congress never approved funding for the board's recommendations, but the process still was useful in two respects. First, it set out a marker for the size, structure, and mission of the Air Service, which now was re-set at approximately 1,600 aircraft, largely assigned to corps commanders for use in direct ground support. More important, the document set the stage for future political battles, because it underscored the differences between the Army and its Air Service component, and motivated airmen to continue the fight.

A three-pronged war waged during 1923 and 1924 over the status of airpower and the Army Air Service. First, Billy Mitchell led a highly publicized fight against the Army and Navy in his quest for the creation of an independent air force. Second, the Army and the executive branch fought a battle to keep Congress from determining the national defense structure. Finally, Air Service moderates fought on a smaller scale to revise the Lassiter Board's findings and provide more autonomy and a more workable structure for the Air Service.

In late 1924 these battles boiled over. The push for an independent air force culminated in two formal investigations, one in the House by a Select Committee of Inquiry into the Operations of the U.S. Air Service, and a second, called the President's Air Board, set in motion by newly elected President Calvin Coolidge. The results of these inquiries would be codified in legislation that shaped the future of U.S. aviation to the start of World War II.

The first probe, which began in October 1924, explored the status, role, size, and structure of the Air Service, and the select committee, chaired by Rep. Florian Lampert, a Republican from Wisconsin, spent eleven months hearing testimony from one hundred fifty witnesses. Although Mitchell's star power dominated the sessions, which were widely covered in the press, more moderate airmen such as Mason

Patrick also testified. As the probe continued, panel members focused on four problem areas for the Air Service—its structural position in the Army, the overlapping of its responsibilities with the Navy, inadequate funding, and the deterioration of the civilian aviation industry.[46] From the panel members' statements and questions, many observers expected that the committee's final report would side with the Army Air Service and recommend the creation of an independent air force under a new Department of National Defense that would have jurisdiction over all three services—the Army, Navy, and Air Force.

The prospect of a restructuring of the national security system and an independent air force was too much for Coolidge. In September 1925, he decided to try to pre-empt the Lampert Committee by appointing his own investigative panel, to be called the President's Aircraft Board. Its chairman would be Dwight Morrow, a Coolidge friend who had been a college classmate. As an outside businessman, Morrow had seemed independent, but in reality he was a man with a mission—to pre-empt the Lampert Committee's report and make it irrelevant.

Just as the Army's Lassiter Board had done, Morrow began by declaring Patrick's plan for the Air Service as a starting point for debate—a move that effectively limited any talk of a fully independent air force or a new national security structure, since Patrick's proposals had focused merely on autonomy for the service within the Army. A bevy of senior army officers testified that the Patrick plan conflicted with unity of command and simply would cost too much to put into effect.[47]

After rushing through its hearings, the Morrow Board issued its final report on December 2, 1925, a full two weeks before the Lampert Committee released its findings supporting the formation of an independent Air Force and the establishment of a Department of National Defense—enabling the president to take the wind out of the congressional panel's sails. Moreover, far from advocating independence for the Air Service, the Morrow Board refused even to recommend autonomy for the Air Service within the Army, citing unity-of-command issues and declaring that "air power has not demonstrated its value for independent operations to justify such a reorganization."[48] Instead, the panel recommended a name change, from the U.S. Army Air Service to the U.S. Army Air Corps, and the creation of a new assistant secretary of war for air to help deal with the funding and policy questions that continued to plague the Air Service.[49]

In the end, the two-week head start—along with Coolidge's personal support—left the Morrow Board the victor; the Lampert Committee's recommendations were largely ignored. Congress approved the Air Corps Act of 1926, which contained the bulk of the Morrow Board's recommendations, and on July 2, the president signed it into law. Besides the change of name, to the U.S. Army Air Corps, the law did little to provide the Air Service with more autonomy or to strengthen military aviation as an offensive striking arm rather than an auxiliary support service.[50] Still, the legislation did have important benefits for the future of airpower. It established a new post of assistant secretary of war for air that would pay dividends in future budgetary and strategy fights. It also helped resolve long-standing personnel problems by creating two billets for brigadier generals. Most important, it authorized a five-year funding program to expand the size of the Air Corps to the 1,650 officers and 15,000 enlisted men originally set by the Kahn Act and to increase the number of available aircraft to 1,800.[51]

As a result, a series of congressional and Army studies shaped the structure of the Air Service during the early 1920s. Although many view the establishment of the Air Corps in 1926 as the first step to air component autonomy, it was not designed that way by its instigators. What made the new Air Corps structure the first step in independence was how the young airmen in positions on the Air Corps staff, at the newly redesigned Air Corps Tactical School, and at other outlying stations used the new structure to continue the fight for autonomy and their vision for airpower doctrine.

CONCLUSION

Historians and military professionals alike often overlook strategic bombing development in the early 1920s. They view this era as the age of Mitchell and the fight for independence, not as an important step toward the bomber fleets that would rule the skies over

Europe in the late stages of World War II. There is plenty to justify their viewpoint. The combination of geopolitical and internal forces did conspire to thwart the ascension of strategic bombing theory at the end of World War I. This was followed by a new defensive national security strategy and a return to isolationist sentiment, which resulted in a large demobilization and tight budgets. Finally, strategic bombing got lost in the more glamorous fight for Air Service independence conducted by highly public figures such as Billy Mitchell. In the end, these forces combined to push strategic bombing to the periphery of military aviation.

Yet, the evolution of strategic bombing did not come to a halt during this period. Instead, it continued in the shadows, often in directions that shaped both the future of the Air Service and America's national defense policy. The new focus on coastal defense spurred long-range bombing technology in ways that would one day make the vision of men such as Gorrell a reality. Additionally, mid-level airmen on the Air Service staff and at ASTS began to lay the foundations for concepts such as precision - and high-altitude bombing, and the Industrial Web theory. Finally, the political debates on airpower brought structural changes that set the stage for the procurement and organization of heavy bombers.

The end of World War I lulled America into a sense of security behind its protective oceans. Yes, there was the remote threat of a coastal attack from a foreign naval fleet, but dealing with it would not require major strategy changes. The debate was only over which service would be best able to meet the challenge. In just one short year, however, that picture began to change. When Charles Lindbergh succeeded in flying across the Atlantic Ocean, it hinted at major changes in aviation. To many analysts, it also served as a warning that American military planners needed to start thinking about how to defend U.S. forces against aerial threats—and how the United States might use its own airpower as an offensive weapon.

CHAPTER 7

Marrying Technology and Doctrine

The Air Corps Act of 1926 marked a turning point in the evolution of strategic bombing. Although the sponsors of the law had intended it to restrain the freewheeling behavior of the the Army's aviation component, it had the opposite effect. Rather than dampening independent thinking, the measure actually spurred greater efforts within the aviation cadre to develop a new, broader airpower doctrine. It also encouraged the leadership of the newly created U.S. Army Air Corps to update that doctrine continually to incorporate the improved aircraft capabilities that rapid technological advances were producing.

Yet, there still were many factors that conspired to limit the acceptance of strategic bombing, both within the Army Air Corps itself and in the broader defense establishment. The long-standing fight between the Air Corps and the Army leadership was in no way resolved; senior Army generals still saw aviation as only a support element for the infantry and artillery. New funding for added personnel and new aircraft still was scarce, especially in the wake of the steep spending cuts that were ordered in the midst of the Great Depression. Finally, although the Air Corps had attained some limited autonomy, it still faced problems involving personnel levels, organizational structure, and technology development that diverted its leadership from strategy issues. As a result, the years between 1926 and 1934 saw another transition period for military aviators, not the accelerated takeoff that airpower proponents had hoped.

Three of these factors played the largest roles in shaping this phase of the airpower evolution. The first clearly was money. Both the spending cuts themselves and the War Department's propensity for siphoning off funds from the Air Corps budget to meet other Army needs severely limited the amount available for developing new aviation technology and conducting large-scale exercises to test doctrine-related proposals. The second was the new postwar national defense policy. The fact that it was designed to maintain a defense-oriented posture made it difficult to justify the creation of a strategic bombing force, whose mission would be to attack targets on an enemy's home turf. Finally, the fast pace of technology advancement raised the risk that new aircraft ordered would become obsolete before they became operational, further complicating the acquisition issue. With so few dollars to invest in new aircraft, should the Air Corps buy new planes when they were ready for purchase or wait on promised new technology that itself might soon be overtaken by still more-advanced innovations?

At research institutions such as the Air Corps Tactical School and the Air Corps Material Division, theorists and engineers explored how airpower might be used in the future without the constraints of budget ceilings, political opposition, or limitations on technology. By theoretically throwing off the shackles of current reality, these innovators shaped the future of airpower in their own visions, with the assumption that policy and technology eventually would catch up. Although there still would be many political and budgetary battles ahead, the advances of the late 1920s and early 1930s set the stage for the advent of the age of strategic bombing.

AMERICA CATCHES THE AVIATION BUG, 1926–28

In the late 1920s there were clear signs that the momentum had begun to build. In early 1926, the newly renamed Air Corps Tactical School issued an updated version of the *Employment of Combined Air Forces Manual*, the basic strategy document for the Air Corps, which set out the emerging vision of airpower. Although the new manual retained the Army leadership's policy of classifying bombing raids as missions in direct support of ground troops, it also put forward the suggestion that airpower could perform that mission more effectively by launching indirect attacks on command headquarters, supply depots, transportation routes, and industrial targets.[1] In doing so, Maj. Oscar

Westover, the school's commander, had worked out a new approach for developers of airpower doctrine. Doctrine writers already had recognized that they would have to give lip service to the ground-support mission in order to win approval of senior Army leaders, who had insisted on making this the first priority. Rather than challenge this, Westover deftly redefined "direct ground support" to include the use of strategic bombing to destroy the enemy's war resources and erode its will to fight.

Westover's new manual marked the beginning of a shift in doctrinal thinking back to the bomber as the primary weapon in the airpower arsenal. Under the new rationale, the bomber would offer the greatest support to ground forces, in both a direct and indirect role. The shift quickly became evident in other manuals issued by ACTS that year. Even the 1926 textbook for pilots of pursuit aircraft acknowledged the growing importance of bombing in the school's thinking. To bolster the contention that advances in technology worked to make bombers more formidable, the text argued that recent improvements in defensive armament had made it significantly more difficult for enemy fighters to carry out strikes against bomber formations and that "attacks by individual pursuit planes in daylight would be largely limited to harassing fire."[2] Although this was not a ringing endorsement for strategic bombing, it demonstrated that bomber technology and strategy were starting to gain force. Even courses designed for pilots of pursuit aircraft had to consider the difficulties of challenging bombers.

As a result of these developments American airpower doctrine was primed for change. Unfortunately, none of the aircraft in the current inventory was suitable for a strategic bombing campaign. The primary long-range bomber of the early 1920s, the twin-engine Martin B-2 biplane, lacked the range, lifting power, and accuracy to provide anything beyond direct ground support or harassing raids.[3] Needed was a catalyst to meld the latest advances in aircraft technology with the rapidly developing evolution in the ideas of airpower theories.

The catalyst emerged on May 20–21 of 1927, when Charles Lindbergh, a little-known aviator from Minnesota, made the first trans-Atlantic flight in history, capturing the public's imagination and creating aviation enthusiasts throughout the United States. Before Lindbergh's

eye-popping achievement, most Americans had thought of aviation as
the realm of stunt pilots and barn-dusters or as the setting for a military
feud between the Army and a scrappy general named Billy Mitchell.
Lindbergh's flight forever changed America's attitude toward aeronautics, setting in motion a fast-growing public support for aviation that
would soon be reflected in congressional actions.[4]

Lindbergh's success also helped bolster civil aviation in the
United States. Before his solo flight to Paris, the closest thing to a
civilian aviation market in the United States was the twelve contracts
the federal government awarded under the Air Mail Act of 1925.[5]
With the twenties roaring and America awash in money, good times,
and self-confidence, the time was right for the emergence of a civil
aviation industry.

In shaping the future of civil aviation, Lindbergh served as a
spokesman for the fledgling airlines and a good will ambassador.[6] With
such support, civil aviation grew at an exponential rate. In 1927, the
nation's airlines carried only 8,679 passengers. By 1928 that number
quadrupled to 48,312. Two years later, more than 380,000 Americans
had taken to the skies on civilian airliners—an impressive increase by
any measure, but only the start.[7]

With this kind of growth, airlines could no longer rely on the old
World War I technology. They needed new and more capable aircraft.
As passenger traffic increased and routes got longer, civilian airlines
began demanding much the same performance characteristics and
equipment for passenger aircraft as the Air Corps desired for bombers—
longer range, great lift capability, and more reliability. Before long,
the technological requirements of military and civilian buyers essentially had merged.

The relationship between military and civilian aviation grew closer
with two significant changes in Air Corps leadership. The first took
place on July 16, 1926, with the appointment of F. Trubee Davison as
the assistant secretary of war for air. The second came on December
14, 1927, when Maj. Gen. James E. Fechet replaced Mason Patrick
as the new chief of the Air Corps. Both men helped increase the
Air Corps' budgets, revamp the organization's culture, and develop a
comprehensive airpower doctrine.

Of the two men, Fechet made the larger impression. Although Fechet himself had little operational flying experience, he had spent several years on the Air Service staff. where he became thoroughly familiar with major airpower issues and the internal workings of Washington.[8] Still, his biggest contribution was the fresh perspective that he brought to the Air Service. Most notably, he saw the 1926 Air Corps Act as a positive document for airpower, interpreting it as granting the Army's aviation component a relatively high level of autonomy—meaning the Air Corps could now focus on how to use airpower in warfighting instead of having to struggle to gain independence or to divert its attention to the coastal defense mission. At the same time, realizing that creating doctrine was beyond the capability of his small Washington staff, he delegated the strategy and doctrine-development tasks to ACTS.[9]

That left him dealing with the other side of the problem: how to build an Air Corps that would be capable of meeting the new doctrines that were coming out of ACTS. To Fechet, the answer centered on using the five-year aircraft inventory expansion authorized by the Air Corps Act to buy newer and more capable bombers. Although the law contained a provision increasing the number of Army aircraft to 1,800 by 1932—from 1,254 before—it did not specify what types of airplanes these should be.[10]

Given the political and budgetary pressures to reduce costs, Air Corps leaders favored buying both observation and attack aircraft, which would align the service more closely with the Army-assigned ground-support mission. When Army authorities did broach the subject of bombers, they urged the Air Corps to develop an all-purpose aircraft to help hold costs in line.[11]

As might be expected this flew in the face of the Air Corps' long-time hope of moving toward a long-range strategic bombing force. Maj. Hugh J. Knerr, commander of the 2nd Bombardment Group, protested that the Army recommendation would "stifle the most powerful military weapon in the Army and increase the incorrect employment of airpower."[12]

Davison's appointment in 1926 gave the aviators an ace in the hole in the budget battles. When he became assistant secretary of war for air, the Air Corps had a political appointee on the secretary's staff, a privilege that no other Army organization had been granted. Historian Ronald Rice points out that having this civilian, not liable to military rules or general orders, as its representative provided the Air Corps with a senior advocate who could work within the system to alleviate budget cuts and acquire more resources during the lean years from 1928 to 1932. It paid off. During that period, while the overall Army budget plunged by 37 percent, funding for the Air Corps declined only 12 percent.[13] Although this was not entirely Davison's doing, his intercessions with the secretary of war and Congress undoubtedly played a large role in holding the cuts in the aviation budget to a minimum.

Even with its new, enhanced political power, the Air Corps had daunting technological problems to overcome. Bomber designs advanced slowly, constrained by both a lack of adequate funding and inattention by the Air Corps' leadership. Despite Davison's best efforts, there was no progress on bomber acquisitions or research funding between 1926 and 1928.

There were three reasons for the stagnation in bomber design. The first was the crisis in the Army. After almost a decade of drawdowns and cutbacks, mainline Army units such as infantry and artillery sorely needed modernizing. Many Army leaders favored limiting bomber research in order to pay for updating these traditional combat branches. At the same time aviation was not the only part of the military that was seeking research and development funds to finance new technology. In December 1927, for example, the Army created its first experimental mechanized unit to explore how to integrate tanks into its combat plans.[14] The combination of the need to refurbish the oldline combat units and to test tanks and other new technology drew money away from the aviation budget.

The second reason for the stagnation centered on a political issue that was outside the control of the military. Since the demobilization after World War I, there had been little public attention to military budgets. Airpower was a notable exception. The Billy Mitchell trials had helped keep people interested in aviation, leading to a willingness on the part of Congress to be more generous to the Air Corps than to other components of the Army. Yet the strong tide of isolationism and antiwar fever that gripped the American public in the late 1920s threatened to change that dynamic. On August 27, 1928, fifteen countries, including the United States, signed the Kellogg-Briand Pact in Paris agreeing not to use war to settle international disputes. By the end of the year, sixty-four countries were members of the treaty.[15] One effect of the treaty in the United States was to reinvigorate the antiwar movement and put pressure on the government to limit military spending further. After all, why should America invest heavily in its military if it had joined with its potential adversaries in pledging not to use military action as a tool of statecraft? Both politicians and military leaders had sensed this shift. In Fechet's year-end report to the secretary of war, he warned that a rise in antimilitarism had created a difficult political climate that limited the ability to buy new bombers, which clearly were offensive weapons.[16]

The third reason for holding back on bomber development was the continuation of the larger fight with the Navy over airpower missions. Many historians focus on the five-year expansion program contained in the Air Corps Act and forget that the Navy had begun a similar effort under the Naval Aircraft Expansion Act of 1926, which called for a naval air force of more than 1,600 airplanes.[17] Not only did the Navy's program compete for research and acquisition funds, but it also had an operational side effect that threatened long-range bomber production for the Army. The Navy reignited the simmering hostilities after Mitchell's resignation, announcing that it would once again look into basing its aviation units on shore to help with naval support and coast defense.[18] The move undercut the Air Corps' five-year expansion program, which had relied on the Army's coastal defense plan to justify the development and purchase of long-range bombers.

The continuing spat with the Navy made the already hesitant Army leadership even more skittish. Why should it seek funds for extremely expensive long-range bomber research, which was only a small portion of the Air Corps portfolio, if the coastal defense mission might be better-suited for naval aircraft? The Navy's success in buying fifty-four planes to protect Pearl Harbor and the Panama Canal only reinforced this attitude in the Army General Staff.[19] Even bomber advocate Maj. Gen. James P. Hodges conceded that the competition over missions and budgets was not between fighter and bomber advocates, but rather between the Air Corps and the Army and Navy.[20]

The combination of these factors severely limited the budgets for bomber research and acquisition. To make matters worse, even when the Army won congressional approval for acquisition, it did not always result in more aircraft. Historian Jean Dubuque found that the Army had become proficient at diverting such monies to other priorities. From 1926 to 1931, he reported, Congress approved $182.8 million for aviation spending, yet only $126.2 million of that actually went to the Air Corps. The remaining $56.6 million was transferred to other Army programs.[21]

A CHANGING VISION OF AIRPOWER, 1928–30

The newly created Air Corps spent its first few years finding its place in the military structure and fighting for money for research and acquisition. The last two years of the decade was a period of significant progress in the evolution of strategic bombing. With the battle over autonomy settled for the moment, aviators had more time to consider the question of how airpower should be used in war. In many ways, the deliberations marked a return to the lessons that pilots had learned in the final year of World War I.

In this environment, the role of the bomber once again dominated strategy discussions. Although Westover's 1926 manual had begun the shift to the bomber as the primary weapon of the Air Corps, the strategy revision issued by ACTS in 1928 initiated the process of hammering that thinking into doctrine. That year, Lt. Col. Clarence C. Culver became the new commander of ACTS. Culver realized that the school needed a structured curriculum based on a centralized doctrine, but no such document existed. Instead, the Air Corps relied on a series of disjointed strategy and tactics manuals. Culver decided to develop a baseline doctrine to guide the development of subordinate texts on pursuit, bombing, observation, and other missions.[22]

Culver summarized his new vision in a memo entitled "The Doctrine of the Air Force," which he circulated among key Air Corps staff officers on August 30. Where the Army remained wedded to the view that a country must first defeat an enemy's army or navy before it could impose its will, Culver brought in the new concepts espoused by military thinkers such as J. F. C. Fuller and B. H. Liddell Hart that it was no longer necessary to defeat an enemy's army or navy to win a war. Instead, all that was required was to break the enemy's will to fight.[23]

Fechet's response to Culver on September 9 was encouraging. If this new theory of warfare were taken to its logical end, he said, it would mean that if "the proper means were furnished to subdue the enemy's will . . . the objective of war could be obtained with less destruction."[24] What went unsaid, but was well understood by both men, was that only one weapon offered a means to break an enemy's will to resist without requiring the defeat of its army or navy first—airpower.

ACTS built on this new postulate in a major curriculum revision in 1928. Besides embracing the new theory about warfare, the school also decided to switch its methodology completely. Before 1928 instructors examined what actually had happened in World War I as a guide to how airpower should be used. From now on ACTS would take a more theoretical approach that focused on how airpower might have been used more effectively in various situations. With this entirely new approach, the school was no longer just studying historical precedent; it became an academic institution concentrating on the theoretical use of airpower—an incubator for new ideas, logically testing them, and finally integrating them into airpower doctrine. Robert Finney, the foremost historian of ACTS, described the lasting effect of this transition as turning the school into a "cerebral testing ground for ideas, where innovative young officers could envision air power without the restraints of reality."[25] As a result the curriculum change opened the door to a series of airpower dreamers, who in turn shaped not only doctrine but also the technology needed to carry out their hopes. The results of this shift were best seen in a new capstone course entitled "The Air Force," added to ACTS for the 1929 academic year, which consolidated the ideas from individual strategy courses into a single integrated plan for the employment of pursuit, observation, attack, and bombardment aviation into one aerial battle plan.[26]

Two training exercises that year underscored the value of these academic changes. The first involved naval exercises being conducted near the Panama Canal in which the Navy deployed the USS *Saratoga* to help simulate a hostile fleet that was using carrier-based aircraft to attack the Canal Zone. To Air Corps leaders, the presence of the carrier was a graphic confirmation of what they had been arguing for months—that the nation needed a force of long-range heavy bombers to intercept any such carrier-based task group one thousand miles out at sea in time to ward off what could have been a devastating naval air attack.[27]

The second involved an Army training exercise—the annual V Corps area maneuvers in Ohio that May. As part of the demonstration, formations of Air Corps twin-engine Martin B-2 bombers blunted a simulated invasion force by smashing its supply, communications, and command systems. The bombardment was so effective, at both avoiding engagements and destroying ground targets that the lead aerial referee, Maj. Walter Frank, concluded that "a well planned air force attack is going to be successful most of the time."[28]

The lessons of both exercises were clear even to the ACTS students. Capt. Charles W. Walton of the class of 1929 wrote in a paper that "we can see the seeds of decisive military action, especially when aviation can operate without restrictions imposed by superior commanders."[29]

The new course structure at ACTS encouraged junior instructors to explore ideas more deeply and to come up with their own concepts to improve airpower. In 1930, two instructors in the bombardment course, Capt. Robert Olds and 1st Lt. Kenneth Walker, suggested making Major Frank's point even more strongly: "[A] well organized, well planned, and well flown air force attack will constitute an offensive that cannot be stopped."[30] Within a few months, the Air Corps had shortened it to what became almost a motto for strategic bombing proponents: "The bomber will always get through."

The speedup in the evolution of airpower theory during the late 1920s was accompanied by a parallel surge in technological innovations in civilian aeronautics that promised to pay dividends for military aviation. The development of closed-cockpit, high-altitude, reliable long-distance airliners and cargo planes capable of carrying significant loads dovetailed with the Air Corps' requirements for the design of a heavy bomber, leading to close cooperation between the industry and the military. Although the civilian companies bore most of the burden, the Air Corps Material Division at Wright Field in Dayton contributed research and development for high-altitude engines, flight controls, and pressurization—innovations that were incorporated into both airliners and bombers.[31]

These advances removed any doubts about whether long-range bombing would be technologically feasible, but they also heightened the urgency for the Air Corps to decide what types of bombers it wanted and how it would use them. Major Knerr, commander of the 2nd Bombardment Group, suggested that the Air Corps needed two types of bombers—fast medium bombers and slower, long-range heavy bombers—and proposed that it split research and acquisition dollars between them.[32] Although that seemed to make sense, given the state of technology and the budget pressures at the time, it troubled Air Force leaders for the rest of the 1930s. Long-range bombers would be heavier and more capable, but medium bombers were more flexible and less expensive, enabling the service to buy more of them to meet its inventory targets. The debate would influence the development of both the technology and the strategy for the coming decade.

For the moment, Knerr's position was widely accepted at ACTS. In early 1930, the school conducted a study of air force combat requirements and agreed with Knerr's recommendations. From then on, Air Corps research budgets were split between medium twin-engine bombers needed for ground support and long-range, four-engine bombers that would be required for strategic attack missions.[33]

The onset of the Great Depression disrupted those plans. Responding to the nationwide economic collapse, Congress voted to cut federal spending sharply. President Hoover, convinced that any new military conflict would most likely evolve from a minor maritime or trade dispute, ordered the armed forces to slash all programs that were not deemed essential—especially expensive offensive weapons such as bombers.[34] The Army General Staff agreed.

Compounding the issue was the long lead time needed to put a new bomber in active service. With no other complications, it took up to five years to design, test, build, and deploy a bomber.[35] There also were delays in congressional funding. With the current rate of technological advance, by the time these new bombers entered the Air Corps inventory they were obsolete—a factor that further limited bomber acquisition. As a result, the Air Corps ended the 1920s with only fifty-one bombers in its inventory, all of them medium-range.

A RETURN TO THINKING ABOUT WAR, 1930–31

The onset of the Great Depression in 1929 dealt a severe blow to the Air Corps' push to create a strategic bomber force. The collapse of the U.S. economy and the resulting change of administration in Washington led to retrenchments in military and civil aviation alike. Newly elected President Franklin D. Roosevelt sought a 51 percent cut in military spending and slashed government payrolls, in the process eliminating the post of Assistant Secretary of War for Air that had proven so beneficial in helping the Air Corps withstand budget cuts in the past.[36] The cutbacks further reduced bomber inventories and dashed hopes of testing any new designs anytime soon.

The financial collapse that spread around the globe caught political leaders, businessmen, and ordinary citizens by surprise and brought economic devastation to the United States and much of the world. It also unexpectedly led to a new way of thinking about the use of strategic bombing.[37] Observing how vulnerable national economies were to disruptions in key sectors and how interlinked those sectors were to one another, airpower theorists began thinking about how carefully planned bombing campaigns could devaste an enemy's economy—by destroying critical infrastructure and key industrial targets. Studied targeting of key railroad junctions, utilities, factories, and fuel depots could cripple a nation's economy and even bring it to a standstill. Over the next few years, the concept would be developed and refined and used extensively in World War II, and would come to be called "The Industrial Web."[38]

Despite these stunning setbacks three important internal changes in the Air Corps helped push the effort ahead. The first was the movement of ACTS from Langley Field to Maxwell Field, Alabama. In 1928 the Air Corps had realized that Langley was too hectic for professional military education and doctrine development. Because operational requirements constantly pulled instructors and students away from their studies, the service needed a quiet location away from the turmoil. In early 1929 it found just such a site at Maxwell, which offered an out-of-the way venue where students could focus on academic work without the interruptions that came with an operational flying base that was relatively close to Washington.[39] The only limitation was that Maxwell was undeveloped. There were only a few buildings on the field, and there was nothing that could serve as a modern school. The construction delayed ACTS' move until July 15, 1931.

With the new location came a new commander. Far removed from Washington and Army oversight, Lt. Col. John Curry, the new commander, changed the school's approach. Curry had had a long career in military aviation. He had flown with the 1st Aero Squadron in Mexico, seen combat over France, and supervised the purchase of Ford Island, Pearl Harbor, Hawaii, for Army aviation.[40] Under his tenure, ACTS would become a clearinghouse for ideas, where new concepts could be rigorously tested and doctrine created.[41] The assistant commandant at the time, Maj. Hume Peabody, recalled Curry's telling the instructors that each was free to teach as he saw fit in order to stimulate debate, and "then with the ideas we get from the students, we are going to hit a happy medium."[42]

As part of that effort the institution established a modern library system to support the academic work. From 1931 to 1934 Maxwell Field set up a formal book department that maintained a library and bought thousands of new books.[43] The library included an impressive collection of archival material from World War I, including Edgar Gorrell's *Air Service History of World War I* and his Bombing Survey, which became central documents used by future strategic bombing theorists. Most notably Maj. Donald Wilson's 1933 Bombardment Course cited Gorrell's works on several occasions, which most likely drew students' attention to these documents.[44] The use of the two volumes indicated that Gorrell's ideas, and especially his supporting statistical data, were fresh in the minds of the bomber advocates at ACTS as they adapted the old World War I doctrine for the new era.

With a new attitude and a library in place, all that remained to realize Curry's vision was a central concept on which to base the new doctrine. In late 1932 Walker spelled out the central tenets of the core doctrine in a memorandum to the ACTS commander critiquing a new Air Corps field manual. In it he proposed that all future Air Corps doctrine be guided by three principles: first, that bombardment was the basic arm of the air force; second, that for bombing to be effective would require precision-targeting capability, which would necessitate limiting bombing raids to daylight; and finally, that airpower was too costly to waste, so bombing raids must be focused only on targets that are vital to the enemy's economy.[45] Although much work would be required, Walker's memorandum was a crucial document that laid the groundwork for strategic bombing doctrine.

The second event of 1931 that helped open the way for the rise of strategic bombing was the end of the bitter dispute between the Army and Navy over which service should be assigned the mission of wielding airpower in defense of the nation's coastal areas—a rivalry that had drained energy and resources from both. In a January 9 accord hammered out between Gen. Douglas MacArthur, the Army chief of staff, and Adm. William V. Pratt, the chief of naval operations, the two agreed to a simple solution: they would limit the Army's role to deploying shore-based aircraft to defend the homeland and its possessions while the Navy would use only carrier-based planes whose mission would be to protect the fleet at sea.[46] The pact left the air components of both services free to expand within the confines of those missions. For the Air Corps, the agreement marked a giant leap forward. As Air Force historian Maurer Maurer pointed out later, it temporarily settled a long-standing dispute and "sanctioned a justifiable reason for developing long-range bombers for coastal defense."[47]

Finally, 1931 saw two important technological advances that helped secure the success of strategic bombing doctrine. The first of these was the Martin B-10, the first all-metal monoplane bomber that the Air Corps acquired. Although still only a twin-engine medium bomber, the B-10 contained innovations that promised that advancing technology would soon make heavy bombers a reality. It had a top speed of 213 miles per hour, a 24,000-foot service ceiling, and a range of 1,000 miles.[48]

The B-10 lacked only one important capability—a precision bombsight—to meet ACTS' requirements for strategic bombing, but another breakthrough was on the horizon. As fate would have it, another invention in late 1931 appeared to offer the accuracy necessary for a long-range heavy bomber. A Dutch engineer named Carl L. Norden had just invented a new bombsight that Air Corps officers believed could finally make high-altitude strategic bombing possible, and they recommended buying it immediately.[49]

The Air Corps faced a dual challenge in acquiring the Norden bombsight. First, it had to overcome Army reluctance to purchase a new technology that was designed to support high-altitude strategic bombing, when Army leaders themselves preferred to buy medium bombers that would help stay within budget restrictions and keep the Air Corps focused on its ground-support role. Second, the Norden bombsight was already under contract with the Navy. With the bad blood between the two services it was highly unlikely that the Navy would give the Air Corps the right to order its own version of the bombsight. This was especially important, considering that the Air Corps wanted to use the bombsights in carrying out its new long-range coastal defense mission, although naval air still saw it as a Navy role. In the end, the two reached an agreement under which the Air Corps could buy Norden bombsights from the Navy, but this became unnecessary after the U.S. entry into World War II forced the two services to work together.[50]

Although the new command structure may not seem like much of an advance in the evolution of strategic bombing, it was indeed a significant leap forward. Before the establishment of the GHQ Air Force, strategic bombing had been no more than an idea that had shown promise; the Air Corps had lacked the organizational structure needed to train pilots, fly bombing missions, and command bomber groups anytime soon. With the change put into effect by the Drum Board, however, there was now a command structure that could take the concepts honed by ACTS, along with the technological innovations nurtured by the Materiel Division and turn them into actual operational doctrine. Biographer John Shiner considers the development of the GHQ Air Force structure as Foulois' greatest achievement as chief of the Air Corps.

CREATING AN ORGANIZATION, 1932–34

When Maj. Gen. Benjamin Foulois became Chief of the Army Air Corps in December 1931 he brought a wealth of knowledge with him. The most experienced aviator in the Air Corps, he had been the founding pilot in the new Air Service in 1909. He commanded the 1st Aero Squadron during the Mexican Expedition and then the AEF Air Service in the early days of America's involvement in World War I. Perhaps his most important preparation for the job of chief of the Air Corps, however, was a three-year tour in the 1920s as U.S. military attaché in Berlin. Foulois' work with the Germans convinced him that they would once again rise to threaten Europe, this time using airpower as their primary weapon for conquering the continent.[51] With that in mind, he took charge of the Air Corps determined to boost funding for heavy bombers as a counterweight to the threat of a resurgent Germany.

Foulois soon began pressing for more aircraft, greater autonomy, and a change of mission to focus on strategic attack. In February 1933 he sent a memorandum to Brig. Gen. Charles E. Killbourne, the assistant chief of staff of the Army, recalling a discussion the two had had with General MacArthur the previous December, which had identified a structural problem in the current system that limited the effectiveness of airpower in war. Although most observation squadrons and some pursuit units were under the command of corps commanders or district commanders, the vast majority of the Air Corps' combat power was controlled by the GHQ Reserve Commander. Foulois argued that this system was flawed because there was no centralized structure to train, support, and command these air forces in a time of emergency or war.[52]

Foulois did not stop at merely complaining. He laid out recommendations for a new tactical structure for the Air Corps. The centerpiece would be a new combat command called the "GHQ Air Force," which would control *all* offensive airpower—including bombers—in

both peacetime and war, and would operate directly under the supervision of the overall ground-force commander.[53] Although Army
corps commanders would retain some observation planes and pursuit
aircraft for support operations, the GHQ Air Force commander would
plan, coordinate, and execute aerial attacks against enemy forces. To
top it off, Foulois recommended that the new command be placed
under the authority of the chief of the Air Corps or at a minimum
should be directly commanded by an airman.

. The proposal had an impact on MacArthur. On August 11 he
convinced Secretary of War George H. Dern to appoint a board of
officers led by Maj. Gen. Hugh Drum to review and revise the Air
Corps' structure and war plans. The Drum Board report was not a
complete victory for Foulois, but it did significantly enhance the
Air Corps' position on strategic bombing. The panel recommended
maintaining the Army's traditional control over aviation, cautioning:
"Whether operating in close conjunction with the Army or Navy, or
at a distance therefrom, all of these agencies must operate in accor-
dance with one general plan of national defense."[54] Still, there was
much in the report to hearten the Air Corps. Most notably, its conclusion that "a properly constituted GHQ Air Force, a unit heretofore
lacking, could detect the approach of an enemy force, attack it before
it reached shore, oppose a landing, and support ground operations
against an invader."[55]

The GHQ Air Force would not become operational until 1935,
but work on the Drum Board report's recommendations for its structure and doctrine got under way quickly. MacArthur approved its
doctrine on October 17, 1934. Like the Drum Board report the
doctrine manual was a mixed bag. On one hand, it clearly stated that
"the idea that aviation can replace any of the other elements of our
armed forces is found to be erroneous"—effectively rejecting any
further talk of Air Corps independence.[56] At the same time, the document provided enough autonomy for the Air Corps to pursue strategic bombing, making clear that "the GHQ Air Force will operate
as a homogenous unit, capable of operations in close cooperation
with ground forces or independent thereof, coming under the direct
control of the commander in chief during war."[57]

Although the new command structure may not seem to have been a big step in the evolution of strategic bombing, it was a momentous leap forward. Before the establishment of the GHQ Air Force, strategic bombing was always an idea that showed promise but had no avenue for converting the concept into doctrine inside the Army or even the Air Corps. With the change put into effect by the Drum Board, there was now a command structure that could take the ideas of ACTS and the technological developments of the Material Division and turn them into actual operations. Biographer John Shiner concluded that Foulois' greatest achievement as chief of the Air Corps was to provide the GHQ Air Force organizational structure for command and control of the strategic mission.[58]

CONCLUSION

The era of 1926 to 1934 saw the continuation of the organizational, technological, and budgetary limitations of the early 1920s. The world situation and America's view of what its role should be in that world had not changed significantly. If anything, the advent of the Depression in the late 1920s and early 1930s exacerbated America's tendency toward isolationism and antimilitarism, creating mounting political, economic, and social forces that influenced the direction of airpower thinking. These forces centered on three key issues: money, defense policy, and the state of aviation technology. All were found wanting in one way or another in the late 1920s.

Still, the elements of change were present to aid in the evolution of airpower doctrine and technology toward the strategic bomber. The growing popular support for aviation after Charles Lindbergh's famous flight helped spur excitement for civil aviation that led to the rapid advancement of airliner technology. These advances eventually spilled over into military bomber technology, resulting in increases in range, payload, and speed, and making the bomber as capable as most American fighters of the time.

Advocates at ACTS quickly seized on the new capabilities to proclaim that the bomber was becoming an unstoppable force. This meshed neatly with the new emphasis on developing airpower theory, not constrained by the current budgetary, technological, or political restraints. In the minds of the bomber advocates at ACTS advances such as the Martin B-10 bomber became stepping-stones to creating doctrine about how to use the next generation of four-engine bombers. This openness to new ideas spread like wildfire throughout the Air Corps and helped move strategic bombing theory to the early stages of what would become an accepted doctrine.

As might be expected, the theoretical focus, while helping aviators overcome many limitations, also created potential problems. Yet, in the end, the work done between 1926 and 1934 proved of critical importance in the evolution of the bomber as a weapon and of strategic bombing as a doctrine. As Billy Mitchell and Edgar Gorrell had laid the foundations for bombing in World War I and its aftermath, the new generation of airpower thinkers at ACTS, the Material Division, and the Air Corps staff created the skeleton that would hold the flesh of strategic bombing doctrine leading up to World War II.

CHAPTER 8

The Triumph of the Bomber Advocates

By the beginning of 1934 American military aviation once again appeared ripe for change. The rise of Hitler in Europe and the growing threat from Japan in the Far East dampened some of the antiwar sentiment that had developed after World War I. The creation of the new GHQ AF suggested that senior Army leaders had begun to recognize the value of placing long-range bomber activity under a separate command. Finally, technology had evolved to the point where it not only provided what bomber crews required at the time, but it was capable of going even further. It seemed as though strategic bombing was about to become a reality.

The underlying situation was far less encouraging, however. Strategic bombing was still largely a theoretical exercise, taking place almost entirely in the classrooms at Maxwell AFB; the Air Corps had only a handful of heavy bombers to use in testing and proving strategic bomber theory. Nor was bombing theory fully accepted inside the Air Corps; some officers still argued that the best airpower strategy would center on using pursuit aircraft to attack enemy planes.

Perhaps most troubling, the steady advances in military aviation only intensified the objections from artillery and infantry officers, who opposed giving the air component more independence. They saw any aviation mission that justified greater autonomy as a direct threat to the Army's traditional role as a ground force. Resentful and wary of the gains made by strategic bombing proponents—and emboldened by a new senior leadership in the Army—the traditionalists decided they had to act immediately. They joined with the pursuit strategy advocates in taking aim at discrediting the very concept that had led to the creation of the Air Corps—the military value of the long-range heavy bomber. The result was a fight for the future of American military aviation strategy.

The clash of these forces might have sealed the fate of strategic bombing except for one critical event—the start of World War II in the late 1930s. The war changed everything for strategic bombing advocates. It quelled opposition in the Army, intensified the political and budgetary support, and finally forced the Air Corps to draft a formal doctrine in the shape of an initial war plan.

POLITICAL, STRUCTURAL, AND TECHNOLOGICAL CHANGE, 1934–36

The greatest of the three forces affecting the development of strategic bombing between 1934 and 1936 was political change. Franklin D. Roosevelt's inauguration as president in March 1933 and Hitler's ascendancy as chancellor of Germany three months earlier set off a series of events that dramatically shaped American airpower. By early 1934, Hitler had begun building a 500,000-man army, while a militaristic Japan was well on its way to asserting its might in the Far East. Although the world situation did not yet call for drastic measures, many American politicians realized they no longer could afford to keep the military at low speed. The shift was neither immediate nor dramatic at first, but it marked the start of a gradual reversal of years of neglect. In 1935 Roosevelt asked for and received the largest appropriation for military spending since 1921.[1]

Other, less dramatic episodes increased the pressure for improving the capability of the military. For strategic bombing, the most important was the suspension of airmail in February 1934. After discovering potential illegalities in the awarding of mail routes, Roosevelt decided to cancel all domestic airmail contracts. No one knew how long the stoppage would last, but in the interim the president needed to keep the mail routes open. He ordered the Air Corps to take over airmail deliveries.

Between February 19 and June 1, in what the press dubbed the "Air Mail Fiasco," the Air Corps lost twelve pilots in fifty-seven accidents.[2]

The widely reported difficulties caused an uproar in both the public and Congress, which quickly questioned whether the track record boded well for more-difficult operations. "If [the Army] is not equal to carrying the mail, I would like to know what it would do in carrying bombs," railed House Speaker Henry T. Rainey, a Democrat from Illinois.[3] In the end, the comparison was too much to ignore. America had spent a disproportionate amount of its military budget on growing airpower; had that money been wisely spent?

Once again scandal sparked the appointment of a board of professionals to review the Air Corps. Headed by former Secretary of War Baker, the eleven-member panel convened on April 17 with a slate of civilian aviation experts and senior military officers. The civilians included luminaries such as Karl Compton, Clarence Chamberlin, James Doolittle, Edgar Gorrell, and George Lewis; the military appointees were Major Generals Hugh Drum, Benjamin Foulois, and George Simonds; and Brigadier Generals Charles Kilbourne and John Gulick.[4] It was the most experienced group of aviation experts ever to study the Air Corps' mission, resources, and performance.

At its first meeting the board decided on the scope of its deliberations—to consider how the Air Corps Act of 1926 had shaped military aviation and to recommend how to overcome any shortcomings. It broke down the workload into three major areas of inquiry: did the Air Corps have the best technology available, was its training sufficient, and was its effectiveness limited by structural deficiencies?[5] With this in mind, the panel conducted more than twenty-five hearings and heard testimony from 105 witnesses. It issued its report on July 18.

As with similar panels before, the Baker Board's conclusions were mixed. On one hand, they seemed likely to make the job of building support for strategic bombing more difficult. They closed the door on further talk of autonomy, declaring that "The idea that aviation can replace any other element of our armed force is found, on analysis, to be erroneous." They also recommended that any future expansion of aviation should take place only as part of a comprehensive Army augmentation program.[6]

Yet the report also contained findings that benefited the Air Corps and, in the long run, the bomber advocates as well. One of the most

important structural problems uncovered was the lack of any repre-
sentation of aviation on the Army General Staff, which it speculated "may account for some of the misunderstanding and erroneous
impressions concerning airpower." It also criticized the absence of
an adequate operational command-and-control structure to organize,
train, and coordinate airpower during a military crisis—a shortcoming that it said hindered the effectiveness of airpower.[7] As a result it
strongly supported the establishment of the new GHQ AF to fill the
command and control gap.

Finally, the Baker Board decried the state of Air Corps technology. It cited the strong advances in civilian aviation as a model for
the Army. It even recommended supporting linkages between the Air
Corps and the aviation industry. In a section influenced by the veteran
bombing advocate Edgar Gorrell, the board recommended that "officers should be developed who were especially qualified in engineering and for dealing with industry."[8] Along these lines, Foulois asked
the Air Corps Material Division to create a personnel development
program that would offer aviators an opportunity to gain tactical experience, academic training, and practical experience.[9] The board itself
helped create a group of Air Corps officers who would be able to work
directly with industry to design the next generation of military aircraft.

In sum, the Air Mail Fiasco turned out to be a long-term boost
for the Air Corps. By bringing the poor state of aviation technology
and training to the forefront, the board spurred investment and structural change. It would be years before the recommendations would
be carried out; as in the case of the previous investigative panels, the
Baker Board's prescriptions did not contain authorizations for additional funds. But the document did provide political support that
helped the Air Corps in its budgetary and organizational battles over
the next several years.

The board's recommendations for structural changes were also
crucial to the success of strategic bombing. It was only with the
consolidation of command and control over airpower that Air Corps
finally would be able to turn theory into doctrine and then into practice. The first of these changes took place on December 31, when the
War Department formally created the GHQ AF.

To test the GHQ AF as an organizational concept the Air Corps ordered the 2nd Bombardment Wing to conduct an exercise in the first week of April 1935 that combined bombers, attack aircraft, pursuit planes, and observation aircraft as a self-contained force operating from a single location. Although senior leaders had considered this a workable model, the exercise uncovered severe logistical problems resulting from having based multiple types of aircraft together. The after-action review by Col. John Curry, the wing commander, minced few words, suggesting that the Air Corps' previous concepts of continually moving aircraft forward and building giant multi-aircraft bases were grossly outdated. Instead he pointed out that new advances in flight ranges and communications would enable aircraft to operate from many bases well behind the lines and still consolidate to achieve mass over critical targets.[10]

As a result of the exercise the Army reorganized the GHQ AF structure to make it more compatible with conducting long-range bombing raids. Large mixed-aircraft units directly tied to Army corps commanders had proven unwieldy. The reorganization would create new wings built around a single aircraft type and synchronized from a central command component. That in turn would simplify logistics, improve coordination, and increase the ability of both the bombers and other aircraft to mass at a decisive time and place. This was exactly what strategic bombing advocates needed—a command structure that used up-to-date technology to enable long-range bombers to rely on protection from escort fighters while the bombers were conducting an independent campaign.

There still was one major point before strategic bombing could be considered combat-ready. Until now, the most important advances in proposed doctrine had been through student papers, instructor-led discussions, and tactics manuals. For bombing to make the leap from discussion topic to fully accepted doctrine it needed a formal process. Unfortunately, the Air Corps lacked both a procedure and an organization for creating doctrine. When ACTS moved from Langley Field to Maxwell Field, the previous doctrine-related organization—the Air Board—ceased to function.

By 1933 this situation had become unacceptable. In calling for a new Air Board, the Plans Division pointed out that the Air Corps was still relying on the 1922 Training Regulation 440–15 for its officially approved airpower doctrine. Reacting to the need, the Air Corps reestablished the Air Board at Maxwell on August 17, 1933 with the same mission, members, and linkages to ACTS as the old Langley board.[11] Once instituted, the board revised its mission, just as ACTS had been transformed from a tactical school at Langley into a theoretical strategy development organization at Maxwell. In August 1934, the board members convinced the Air Corps to change the name of the board to the Air Corps Board and add to its portfolio the development of uniform doctrines.[12]

The establishment of the Air Corps Board also intensified ACTS' own emphasis on doctrine development. Amid a rapidly increasing student body, the school restructured its entire curriculum. By the 1935 academic year, more than 50 percent of the course load was related to air tactics and doctrine.[13] ACTS also changed the structure of its courses, shifting the format for most classes to a twenty-minute lecture followed by fifty minutes of student discussion.[14] The shift provided time for faculty members and students to bring up new concepts, test them in open discussion, and pursue specific ideas in additional research. Where particular sets of ideas attracted sufficient support, the Air Corps Board often turned them into formal studies.

What strategic bombing proponents still lacked was the bomber designs and advanced technology to carry out the new doctrines. The tremendous technological changes in the mid-1930s set the stage for the advent of strategic bombing. The Air Corps' earlier decision to follow Maj. Hugh Knerr's recommendation to split development funds between medium- and long-range bombers led in 1933 to dual specifications for new bomber designs—one for a medium bomber that could carry a 2,000-pound bombload for 1,000 miles at 200 miles an hour and a second for a long-range heavy bomber capable of carrying similar loads for 5,000 miles at 200 miles an hour.[15]

Two of the aircraft designs submitted by civilian manufacturers piqued the interest of senior officers. The Army General Staff favored the twin-engine B-18, a medium bomber produced by the Douglas Aircraft Company that met all the applicable specifications and had an initial price tag of only $58,500. Strategic bombing enthusiasts in the Air Corps regarded the four-engine Boeing B-17 as the perfect heavy bomber. With an initial range of 2,600 miles and a top speed of 250 miles an hour, it offered what Gen. Henry H. Arnold called "airpower you could put your hands on."[16]

Indeed, the Air Corps was so enthusiastic about the B-17 that it requested sixty-five of them in place of some one hundred eighty other airplanes previously authorized for fiscal year 1936. The Air Corps may even have succeeded in winning approval for the bombers had the B-17 prototype not crashed before the Army could conduct official trials. Although the crash was caused by the failure of the test crew to unlike rudder and elevator controls, and not by inherent design problems, the delay gave the opponents of heavy bombers time to mount a challenge.[17]

The result was an internal debate about the choice of aircraft to meet the Air Corps' combat mission. The Air Corps pointed out that the B-17 could carry large payloads at speeds greater than many pursuit aircraft could fly. It also argued that in addition to strategic bombing, it also could serve as a cost-effective weapon for defending America's coastlines or supporting ground troops. The Army General Staff countered with three arguments in favor of the B-18. First, it cost about half as much as a B-17, so the military could buy twice as many aircraft with the same money. Second, buying the medium bomber would keep the Air Corps focused on what the Army thought should be its proper role—providing combat air support for ground troops. Finally, the service argued, the heavy bomber was an offensive weapon and as such ran counter to America's defense-oriented national security policy.[18]

Unexpectedly, the Air Corps found an ally in Gen. Douglas MacArthur, the Army chief of staff, who wanted to increase the entire bomber inventory, in the belief that bombers could disrupt an enemy's rear operations more effectively than any other weapon.[19] Although this was not a ringing endorsement of strategic bombing, it provided sufficient backing for the Air Corps to continue buying heavy bombers and researching new technology. Despite MacArthur's support, opposition to the heavy bomber program remained entrenched in the General Staff, which pressed MacArthur to forgo the B-17 in favor of the B-18.

In the end, the untimely crash of the B-17 prototype and continued opposition from the General Staff prompted the Air Corps to try an end run in an effort to keep the B-17 program alive. In November 1936, using his authority under Section 10(K) of the Air Corps Act, Westover, the chief of the Air Corps, bought thirteen of the Boeing bombers for experimental service testing.[20]

As the disputes over airpower policy continued at higher levels, the Air Corps Tactical School continued to make small, but important changes in its strategic thinking. With the growing attention given heavy bombers, Maj. Donald Wilson developed a new, more sophisticated approach to bombing strategy that drew on Gorrell's earlier discussion on targeting industrial systems.[21] He argued that air tacticians did not have to destroy all of an enemy's factories for a bombing campaign to be successful. Because the industrial components of larger countries typically were interdependent, merely attacking key elements—such as specific production facilities, transportation arteries, or utilities—would be sufficient to disrupt the entire economy.[22] The idea was not new. Colonel Bares, Lord Tiverton, and Gorrell all had raised similar points in their World War I–era writings. What was different on this round was that Wilson had time to convert that principle into a practical plan.

Wilson started with an experiment. Reasoning that most major cities would have similar weak points, he and one of his students, Capt. Robert M. Webster, gathered information on water, gas, electric power, transportation, and public safety systems in New York; selected those whose destruction would have the greatest impact; and compiled a list of targets for fictional bomber squadrons within range of the city. Later to become known as the "Industrial Web Theory," it was the first concrete example of how strategic bombing could cripple an enemy city.[23]

In June 1936, Maj. Gen. Oscar Westover, ordered the Air Corps Board to create a formal doctrine in order to help justify future budget requests—a document that would include the industrial targeting system that Wilson had just developed. Learning from the still-raging fight with the General Staff, Westover proposed assigning the Air Corps a threefold mission that encompassed coastal defense, combat air support for ground troops, and strategic bombing operations that he argued would enhance the prospects of the Air Corps' acquiring heavy bombers.[24]

Although Westover's latest plan had little chance of being approved by the General Staff, it did serve as the Air Corps' starting point in the next fight over roles and missions—this one a contest among the Army General Staff, the Air Corps, and the Navy. The General Staff and the Navy sought to limit one or more of the proposed missions, while the Air Corps, which perceived the dispute as a life-or-death struggle, fought to maintain all three. In the end, defining the battleground helped move toward an eventual resolution of the dispute.

THE GREAT BOMBER FIGHT, 1936–39

The next phase of the airpower struggle took place primarily outside the political limelight, in the staffs of the various services and in the military budget-making process. The first round began on October 2, 1935, when Gen. Malin Craig replaced MacArthur as chief of staff of the Army. Where MacArthur had been open to the idea of assigning a major role to heavy bombers, his successor was decidedly against it. Instead, Craig wanted to rebuild the Army's traditional combat components, which left little room for strategic bombing. Partly to accomplish this he pressured the entire Army to limit spending on research and development and buy readily available weapons instead.[25] He also turned down Westover's request for two groups of operational B-17s, replacing it with an order for less-expensive medium bombers.

The General Staff had intensified its opposition even before Craig took over as chief of staff. On June 25, 1936, Brig. Gen. George R. Spalding released a study that declared that the bomber met no current or future Army mission requirements and as a result should be defunded.[26] The study permitted the purchase of a few experimental bombers, but it effectively precluded buying new ones for operational use. Spalding's document served as a major roadblock for strategy developers at ACTS, since the Air Corps would have no heavy bomber units with which to test its theories in actual exercises.[27]

The Air Corps' leadership quickly returned the fire. Avoiding any mention of strategic bombing, Brigadier General Andrews, the GHQ AF's first commander, defended the request for heavy bombers as necessary to carry out the Air Corps' already approved missions. He argued that having a fleet of long-range heavy bombers would help the Air Corps defend the U.S. coastline by being able to "stop hostile air expeditions at their source." He contended that bombers would be the most adaptable weapon for finding and destroying enemy aircraft carriers. Most important, he cautioned that if the Army did not approve the purchase of B-17s now, it would not have a long-range strike capability when America entered its next war.[28] In effect he warned that the defense establishment would not feel the impact of Craig's decisions until the next crisis, when it would be too late to fix them.

Even after the Craig-era controversy Andrews remained the most vocal critic of the Army's bomber-limiting policies. In a series of speeches at the Army War College—whose faculty strongly supported the General Staff's opposition to strategic bombing—he asserted that "bombardment aviation is and always will be the principal striking force in air operations." To limit heavy bombers was to throw away the weapon with the most potential of inflicting losses on an enemy, he declared.[29]

Although the Air Corps' campaign wasn't changing many minds, either in the Army hierarchy or among the nation's political leaders, a new factor appeared that focused public attention on the need for strategic weapons: the world situation was changing rapidly, with the outlook growing bleaker by the month. By 1937 Germany, Italy, and Japan had created a worrisome alliance that posed what aviation historian Thomas Greer described as "no longer a direct threat of invasion, but concern over Axis subversion and incursions into Central and South America."[30]

Proponents of strategic bombing seized on this new anxiety as a justification for buying long-range heavy bombers, arguing that they would be the most effective way for the United States to enforce the Monroe Doctrine, which had claimed Central and South America as part of America's sphere of influence. The Air Corps Board produced a study that concluded that defending the hemisphere could be best accomplished by airpower without the need for large fleets or massive ground-force deployments.[31] ACTS followed up with its own analysis, basing the purchase of large numbers of heavy bombers on the need to protect the Western Hemisphere. It said to carry out this mission the Air Corps would need twenty squadrons of long-range heavy bombers with bases in Panama, Puerto Rico, and possibly Brazil.[32]

The Air Corps' third line of attack was to let the technology speak for itself. In May 1937, GHQ AF sent seven of its experimental B-17s to take part in joint Army-Navy exercises off the Pacific Coast. The B-17s easily outperformed the older B-10 bombers, using the new Norden bombsight to hit the battleship USS *Utah* with as little as five seconds run-in time.[33] The performance was so stunning that it led the GHQ AF chief of staff, Col. Hugh J. Knerr, to declare that the B-17 was "the best bombardment aircraft in existence."[34] Although Knerr may have overreached, most Air Corps officers supported his assertion that the B-17 was truly a remarkable airplane that offered a larger payload, greater accuracy, and a longer range than any other aircraft or other bomber available.

Members of the General Staff argued that the B-17 was the wrong aircraft at the wrong time. They argued that the cost—about $280,000 a plane, compared to only about $120,000 for a B-18—would prevent Craig from rebuilding the ground forces, in the process creating a lopsided Army, which they knew would cut deeply into Craig's hope of rebalancing the force structure.[35]

They also sought to discredit the B-17's spectacular achievements in the recent exercises—by citing attaché reports from the early use of aircraft in the Spanish Civil War and the Italian invasion of Ethiopia, which claimed that high-altitude bombing was largely ineffective. The assessments had prompted the Army War College to conclude that worldwide military operations supported the conclusion that the best method to employ airpower was in support of ground forces.[36]

Craig added fuel to the fire when he restricted over-the-water flights to 100 miles or less—a move that seemed to play into the hands of the Navy, which had modified the Joint Action Agreement in November 1938 to permit that service to develop naval air bases and to purchase long-range aircraft. The suspicion that Navy leaders had been involved in convincing Craig to restrict over-the-water flights raised tensions between the Air Corps and the Navy, providing more impetus for the General Staff to reduce funding for heavy bombers. General Arnold later shed light on the Air Corps' belief when he speculated that the Navy had been embarrassed when the Air Corps proved that it could find the Italian passenger liner *Rex*, 725 miles east of New York City, based on limited information during an exercise conducted the previous May.[37]

As the issue festered into 1938, Brigadier General Spalding tried a new tactic: he asked the Army Chief of Staff to convene a joint Army-Navy board to review the Air Corps' missions and requirements. His hope was that the General Staff officers and naval officers on the panel would once and for all decide the heavy bomber debate in his favor. On June 29 the board issued a report declaring that there was no likely military requirement for aircraft larger than B-17s, and recommended that the Army limit its purchases of the plane and reduce spending on research and development. In response Spalding revised the Air Corps acquisition budget for fiscal year 1940 to transfer all funding for four-engine bombers to the two-engine bomber program.[38]

That finally persuaded the chief of the Air Corps Maj. Gen. Westover to enter the fray. A strict advocate of working within the staffing process, Westover had largely avoided the fight over heavy bombers until now. In a memorandum to Craig, Westover complained that Spalding had gone beyond the far-reaching Joint Board study by removing all funding for heavy bomber programs, not just those larger than B-17s. He warned that the cutback would be irreversible if it were put into effect.[39]

The intra-military turmoil, which pitted the Army, the Navy, and the Air Corps against one another, was potentially the greatest barrier that proponents faced in attempting to establish a strategic bombing force. In the end, however, world events soon overtook the infighting.

THE ONSET OF WORLD WAR II AND
THE TRIUMPH OF STRATEGIC BOMBING

The Munich Agreement of 1938 and the onset of World War II breathed new life into the push for a strategic bombing component. It generated strong support for the use of long-range heavy bombers. And it forced the Air Corps to develop a formal doctrine for strategic bombing. With war looming, America finally had to come to grips with its national security policy.

The Air Corps was better-equipped for the task than it had been in earlier days. A large portion of its best aviators had spent much of the 1930s as either students or faculty members at ACTS, where they had absorbed the concepts of strategic bombing and had worked through the theoretical problems that it faced. By 1939, they had moved into Air Corps staff billets, where they were positioned to put those teachings into effect.

Well before the war began, American military leaders were starting to revise their view of the nation's airpower needs. With mounting concerns over the rise of German military power, Craig reversed himself in June 1938 and asked the secretary of war to add eleven B-17s and thirty-two B-18s to the already approved 1939 acquisition program. Perhaps more impressive, his change of heart occurred despite the General Staff's warning to the Air Corps not to request any more four-engine bombers that year.[40]

On July 11 Hugh Wilson, the U. S. ambassador to Germany, cabled Roosevelt with an alarming assessment of Nazi Germany's military prowess that proved to be a turning point for American airpower. He contended that Germany's air force was more than just a weapon of destruction; it also was effective as a tool of political blackmail.[41] Merely the threat of possible German air attacks had been a major contributing factor in European countries' reluctance to challenge Hitler's expansionist demands, Wilson reported. He warned that only a credible American air presence could provide a deterrent that Hitler would heed.

The Munich Agreement of 1938—in which Britain, France, and Italy formally accepted Germany's forced annexation of parts of Czechoslovakia—dramatically illustrated Wilson's point. Historian Barry Posen argues that European political leaders viewed Britain's acquiescence as largely a means of warding off the threat of German bombing.[42] Although it may be a stretch to view German airpower alone as the reason for the concessions at Munich, later events confirmed the impact of this perception in persuading U.S. political and military leaders to bolster American airpower and to create a strategic bombing force.

On November 14 Roosevelt met with his national security team to delineate a new defense policy in the wake of the Munich accord. The president now saw an immediate need for rebuilding the armed services, both to defend the Western Hemisphere and to deter Hitler from further aggression. America's military forces had atrophied during the two preceding decades. The question now was, what military strength could the United States develop rapidly that would cause Hitler to take notice?

To Roosevelt the answer was clear. He told the group that he wanted a force of 20,000 airplanes for hemispheric defense, but he feared that a still-skittish Congress would approve only 10,000.[43] After a long discussion, the advisers suggested ordering a staff study.

Arnold stood ready to take advantage of the situation. In conversations over the next few days, he briefed Craig in detail about how creating a strong strategic bombing force could help provide what Roosevelt had in mind.[44] At Craig's request, Arnold worked with ACTS on a study that called for a bomber-heavy force comprising 5,500 aircraft. The estimated cost: $550 million.[45]

The General Staff's opposition to a bomber-centric air force did not die out after Roosevelt changed his strategic focus. Indeed, the group mounted an effective campaign to convince Craig that growth should be spread across all elements of the Army. Craig returned to the White House with a plan that balanced expansion of the Air Corps with a rebuilding of the traditional ground combat forces and a boost in Army infrastructure.

Roosevelt promptly rejected the plan to build additional infrastructure. "America could not influence Hitler with barracks, runways, and schools," he said. What it needed instead was aircraft.[46] The decision set the tone for the next round of military appropriations. On January 12, 1939, Roosevelt asked Congress for a $300 million expansion of the Air Corps to a new level of 5,500 aircraft, involving the purchase of 3,251 new airplanes, including many heavy bombers.[47] Congress approved the request three months later, beginning the next phase in the strategic bombing saga.

Three other important events in 1939 also had an impact on the future of strategic bombing. The first came in a critical report by the newly expanded Air Corps Material Division that helped spur a new round of technological innovation that made American heavy bombers read for their combat debut. Completed in August, the document—entitled "Future Aeronautical Research and Development problems"—warned military aviation technology in America had fallen behind that of other advanced countries, a slippage that it called "a deplorable situation that could not be tolerated."[48] It castigated the Air Corps for failing to place defensive gun turrets on either the B-17 or the newer B-24 bomber still in development and questioned why neither aircraft carried more than rudimentary navigation or communications equipment.[49]

The second, in September, was the appointment of Gen. George C. Marshall as Army Chief of Staff. Not only was Marshall in favor of beefing up U.S. airpower, but he also worked to strengthen the Air Corps' organizational structure. A month later, convinced that the creation of the GHQ AF had created confusion in the command structure, he established a new post of deputy chief of staff for air, appointing Arnold to the position.[50] The new office oversaw both the chief of the Air Corps and the GHQ AF commander, effectively creating a staff directorate to command both the support and combat elements of the aviation component. The step also alleviated many of the previous personnel and budgetary conflicts between the two elements. By June, he had formally combined the GHQ AF and Air Corps into a single organization called the Army Air Forces (AAF), with its own air staff to coordinate airpower issues in Washington.[51] The timely creation of the AFF ensured strategic bombing would have the proper command, planning, and logistics support in place as the United States entered World War II.

The third event to shape the future of strategic bombing was the start of World War II, in which the German invasion of Poland gave U.S. airpower strategists a window on what their own theories could accomplish. German aircraft seemed to rule the skies from the start, bringing destruction and terror to European industries and cities, and reinforcing the American conviction that strategic bombing forces could disrupt an enemy's infrastructure without concern about a threat from fighter aircraft. Wilson, now the director of the Department of Air Tactics at ACTS, wrote that "[H]itler is our greatest booster, without even so much as a request from us he has voluntarily undertaken the job of demonstrating our theories."[52]

Perhaps more telling were the lessons that the Americans drew from the Battle of Britain. Spaatz, who served as an observer in Britain from May to September 1940, recalled that the Air Corps had expected a close fight at the start of the battle, but were confident that the Germans would emerge victorious. Yet, the Germans failed to overpower the Royal Air Force fighters. Spaatz believed that the Americans' observations were colored by preconceived notions that were shaped by already accepted American aviation doctrine.[53] To offset that bias, Air Corps analysts adopted two alternative explanations for the Germans' poor showing: first, the Luftwaffe was too laden with ground-support aircraft and lacked heavy bombers, or second, the German defeat came because Luftwaffe leaders did not have a good understanding of strategic airpower.[54] In retrospect, the Americans' assessment techniques, which effectively allowed Air Corps analysts to craft after-action assessments that suited the goals of the service, without challenging their own assumptions, were risky—and potentially dangerous. Although their explanations may have helped to promote the role of strategic bombing in the short run, over the longer term they failed to identify important flaws in the current Air Corps theory. Correctly understanding the role of the British integrated air-defense system in stopping the Luftwaffe, for example, might have shed light on potential shortcomings in discussions about American bombing doctrine, such as the lack of a long-range escort fighter to help the bombers penetrate a similarly structured German air-defense system.

The catalyst for developing a formal aviation doctrine came on July 9, 1941, when Roosevelt asked the military to develop a production plan for the weapons and equipment it would need if the United States went to war with Germany. The first step in determining how many aircraft American industry should be asked to produce was for authorities to agree on a plan for the defeat of Germany and to work out a formal aviation strategy. With that accomplished, the Army could then establish the types and numbers of aircraft it would need—a job that fell to the Air War Plans Division of the Air Corps staff.

Although the Air War Plans Division comprised only four officers, they all had been key figures in the development of strategic bombing theory. The division chief, Lt. Col. Harold L. George, had served as both a student and instructor at ACTS from 1931 to 1935, including two years as the chief of the Department of Air Strategy and Tactics. His staff, Lt. Col. Orvil Anderson, Lt. Col. Kenneth Walker, and Maj. Haywood S. Hansell, also had been associated with ACTS, part of a group of instructors known as the "Bomber Mafia" for their vocal support of strategic bombing. To this team, George added Lt. Cols. Max F. Schneider and Arthur W. Vanaman and Majs. Hoyt S. Vandenberg, Laurence S. Kuter, and Samuel E. Anderson. All but Anderson had passed through ACTS during the rise of strategic bombing theory.[55]

The plan, completed in nine days and known as AWPD-1 (for Air War Plans Division No. 1), went far beyond a production schedule and offered a comprehensive plan for the defeat of Germany. The three-part proposal first outlined a strategic air campaign designed to destroy German war-related industries. Next came a plan to achieve air superiority to help blunt German air operations. Finally, the scheme included a ground-support element to ensure success during the final invasion of Germany.[56] The three-section format enabled the authors to portray the strategic air campaign as only one element in a broader war plan—an effort to allay objections by the Army that the Air Corps was abandoning its mission of providing close-air support for ground troops.

Not surprisingly the strategic air campaign portion of the plan closely followed the tenets that had been forged and burnished at ACTS. It incorporated Wilson's Industrial Web Theory, identifying 154 potential targets in the electrical, transportation, oil, and aircraft production industries that its authors concluded would "virtually destroy the source of military strength of the German state."[57] It ended by estimating the force needed to meet all three military objectives: a bomber component comprising ten groups of medium bombers, twenty groups of heavy bombers, and twenty-four groups of super-heavy bombers.

With the plan contained in AWPD-1 the American military had come full circle from the aviation thinking and strategy that prevailed twenty years before. America had entered the Great War with a poorly prepared air force. The questions of what types of aircraft it needed, how many of each, and how best to use them had largely evolved from French and British suggestions or from trial-and-error in combat. The lessons had penetrated deep into the American aviators' psyche, beckoning them to use the next two decades to explore options for the structure of a military aviation component, for technological advancements, and for the drafting of doctrine. In AWPD-1 they finally had a plan that began with a strategy and then figured out organizational and technological questions based on implementing the plan. With AWPD-1, the American strategic bombing effort was now ready for its moment in the sun.

CONCLUSION

The period between 1934 and 1941 represents a nice bookend for the birth and early development of American strategic bombing theory. In effect strategic bombing went through its adolescence during those critical years. It no longer was a new idea nor was it in the early development stages. By the second half of the 1930s, strategic bombing theory was starting to take its adult form with the beginnings of high-attitude daylight bombing, precision bombing, industrial web theory, and finally to heavy bombers. Even so, much as a human faces tremendous challenges between adolescence and adulthood, so too did strategic bombing. The forces of rivalry, jealousy, and budget problems all threatened to end the concept before it could prove itself during war.

Facing external and internal opposition, the founding fathers of strategic bombing established strong theoretical, organizational, and technological foundations that helped weather the storms of the pre–World War II environment. Although strategic bombing was still largely a theoretical exercise during World War I, it rapidly matured into a doctrine and then to a war plan.

This was not a simple linear transition. There were many obstacles that might have relegated strategic bombing to nothing more than an experimental theory. The General Staff's challenge could have removed the key technology required to carry out the concept. General Craig's new vision for the Army threatened to downgrade bombardment aviation to just another part of a rebuilt Army focused on ground offensives. The Navy, too, challenged the justification for heavy bombers by trying to take away the Air Corps' mission for coastal defense.

In the end, though, World War II and President Roosevelt's support for military aviation set the stage for strategic bombing to move from the theoretical to the operational. With this political support, the bomber advocates were ready to accept the challenge. As luck would have it, these men were transitioning from ACTS into critical Air Corps staff billets. When the order came to develop a war plan, men with years of experience developing strategic bombing theory were now in the right spot at the right time to implement their ideas.

CONCLUSION

S trategic bombing theory continued to develop in the years after AWPD-1 was issued and underwent several modifications during the early American and British bombing campaigns of World War II. The Air Corps—and after it the Army Air Forces—fashioned a servicewide doctrine that guided the enormous bomber fleets that played such a major role in helping to defeat Nazi Germany. Strategic bombing had come of age.

The evolution did not stop with the end of World War II. The dawn of nuclear weapons demanded further modifications to bring the doctrine into line with new domestic and international political realities, but the four major factors influencing the evolution of strategic bombing remained integral to the military doctrine and planning processes. Developments in airpower theory, technological advances, organizational structure, and political and economic context still shape America's military and aviation policies. As such, understanding them gives us keen insight into forces that still are at work in our present military systems.

It is clear that none of these factors in itself can explain the rise of strategic bombing. The idea that great men posited strategic bombing and then ushered it to prominence is perhaps the easiest explanation to debunk. Although some aviation leaders have drawn the attention of historians and the public, none of them would have been able to create strategic bombing by himself. A review of the three most important American strategic bombing theorists shows their limitations.

Edgar Gorrell may be the best candidate for consideration as the father of strategic bombing, because of his November 1917 bombing plan and his efforts to embed bombing theory into the official history of the war. His bombardment plan modified a British theory to draft a proposal that would be more acceptable to the American Army. Had the strategic bombing campaign planned for 1919 been carried out, Gorrell might have achieved military stardom, but the war's conclusion in November 1918 forever consigned him to the back pages of military aviation history. Indeed, he might have only been a minor footnote but for his work in compiling an official history of the AEF Air Service that contained the core elements of strategic bombing theory. Gorrell returned to the story in the 1930s through his correspondence with Air Corps officers and his participation in the investigations of aviation boards. Although the concept of strategic bombing could not have developed as it did without Gorrell, he cannot claim to have created it, either.

Despite Gorrell's efforts, Billy Mitchell is the American most associated with creating the independent air force and strategic bombing doctrine, but a close look at his contributions shows that much of that credit was misplaced. Although Mitchell's early writings from the summer of 1917 seem to support the British concept of strategic bombing, his later air campaigns at St. Mihiel and the Meuse-Argonne were more in line with providing air support for ground troops. His plans called for deploying bombers, but their missions were to disrupt railway stations, interdict lines of communications, and destroy supply depots. Mitchell did support a bomber-centric Air Service after the war, but he did not envision using it to attack the industrial heart of an enemy. Instead, bending to political and organizational realities, he opted for assigning long-range bombers to a coastal defense role, which he thought met military necessity and bolstered the argument for airpower independence. Rather than serving as the father of strategic bombing, he adjusted his vision of airpower to match the political and military needs of the moment.

Still, even with those caveats, Mitchell's role in molding strategic bombing theory was too important to ignore. He became an early acolyte of British bombing theory, which remained part of his strategic thinking throughout his professional life. His insistence on using semi-autonomous bomber units in his World War I air offensives introduced the concept of an independent strategical air campaign to the Army lexicon. He played an even more important role after the war. When massive military budget cuts seemed to spell doom for long-range bombers, he almost single-handedly created a new mission for them: coastal defense. In doing so, he helped create a requirement for long-range bombers that eventually led to the B-17, B-24, and B-29 aircraft.

Finally, the group of officers known as the Bomber Mafia is often credited with the success of strategic bombing. There is plenty to support this conclusion. As instructors and staff members at ACTS, these men fleshed out the concept for years before turning their theoretical work into an operational plan in 1941. Yet, for much of the 1930s, the Bomber Mafia was virtually separated from the larger debates on budget, strategy, and organizational structure. Their isolation in Montgomery, Alabama, enabled them to work on airpower theories without interference, but it also meant they had little ability to shape the larger thinking of the Air Corps, the Army, and, especially, politicians.

Citing advancing technology as the major factor in creating strategic airpower also runs into difficulties. Although technological innovations helped shape military aviation, they did not determine the success of the strategic bombing concept. The B-17 represents a historical anomaly. When it first flew, in July 1935, the new heavy bomber seemed to herald the ascendance of strategic bombing, since it provided the Air Corps the range and payload capacity it needed to meet its doctrinal vision. Yet, the opposite occurred. In the late 1930s, the combination of organizational rivalries and a lack of political support almost doomed the heavy bomber to the budgetary scrap heap. Still, without the technological breakthroughs incorporated into the B-17 there could never have been a strategic bombing campaign. The combination of range, accuracy, payload, and defensive firepower provided the weapon needed to carry out the strategy. The technology itself played an important role, but it was only one factor.

The same is true of organizational structure. Both internal dynamics and interservice rivalries shaped aviation budgets, technology, and strategy, but this influence alone cannot explain strategic bombing's evolution either. Two examples illustrate that point: first, despite the public attention to Mitchell's fight with the Navy, interservice rivalries remained tense but largely irrelevant for most of the interwar years. The competition never dramatically affected Air Corps budgets or the service's ability to acquire new aircraft. National economic pressures were much more important in determining military aviation budgets than interservice conflicts were. The same is true for the long-standing dispute between the Army and the Air Service over autonomy of the aviation component. Some senior army leaders (such as MacArthur) supported bombers while others (such as Craig) opposed them. Pershing appeared to bend both ways. Early on he accepted Gorrell's strategic bombing plan, but later he refused to send American squadrons to fight alongside the British Independence Force, which had been sent to France to serve as the catalyst for an Allied bombing campaign against Germany in late 1918 or 1919. While these factors definitely shaped the evolution of airpower, they were not the driving force.

The impact of political pressure in shaping the development of strategic bombing was mixed. Roosevelt's policies from 1939 to the start of World War II demonstrated his critical role in bringing strategic bombing to the forefront of national strategy, yet his earlier political decisions often limited the development of long-range bombers and strategic bombing theory. The effect of isolationism and progressivism also seems overstated. Both influenced political decisions, but they can only explain so much. Despite the national pressure for isolationism in the early 1920s, the Air Service never experienced the drastic budget cuts that other military branches felt. Similarly, it is difficult to prove that progressivism had anything but a minor effect on the mindsets of military planners.

So, what does explain the success of strategic bombing theory? The simple answer is that there is no simple answer. Instead, it was the complex interaction among the disparate forces that pushed and pulled American airpower toward long-range strategic bombing. The process evolved in many steps, from the invention of the airplane to the approval of AWPD-1.

In some ways, the origins of strategic bombing started with the Wright brothers' first flight in 1903. This technological leap not only made modern military aviation possible, but it also stimulated thinking about how to use aviation in warfare. Still, it was the use of the fledgling technology in combat, first in Mexico and then in France, that spurred leaders of the American Army to explore new uses for airpower. Raynal Bolling, Edgar Gorrell, and Billy Mitchell all played roles in shaping the early debate concerning the use of airpower. These men were not alone, though; they learned from and incorporated the earlier work of Allied airmen such as Caproni, Tiverton, Grey, and Trenchard. In this way, key individuals transformed the early technology into a potentially devastating, although not decisive, new type of warfare.

Airpower's path to success was not that simple. The new idea faced organizational, political, and technological complications that prevented its full acceptance by the eve of World War II. First, an Army that was resistant to change limited independent long-range bombing operations. Next, political exigencies hampered the use of aviation in a strategic context. The pressure came from all directions: the French professsed caution, fearing German retaliation for Allied bombing raids; the British clamored for revenge after the Germans bombed London and other cities; and American politicians were loathe to bomb civilian population centers. Finally, the technology itself proved a deterrence. There was simply not enough industrial or engineering capability to produce the required bombers before 1919. Even when aircraft production began to improve, the shortcomings in the range, payload, and accuracy of the early bombers hindered any real chance of success.

Ironically, in the end, the Armistice may have saved strategic bombing. Without an actual campaign to assess the success of the strategic bombing concept, the idea survived, to be nurtured and enhanced in coming years. Early on, Edgar Gorrell was a central figure. His decision to include a bombing plan in the official Air Service history formally embedded the core concepts of strategic bombing in a volume that would be relatively easy for future aviation theorists to find.

Gorrell's actions proved timely. The changing political context of the 1920s saw strategic bombing almost completely disappear from the military vocabulary. With the war over and Germany defeated there was no longer a potential major adversary whose actions would justify the tremendous cost of large bomber fleets. Political leaders faced pressure to deal with domestic priorities, forcing a rapid military drawdown and extremely tight Army budgets. In this environment, airpower had to adapt to survive, and one of the first casualties was strategic bombing. The Air Service quickly realized that it would have to find new missions for long-range heavy bombers in order to build political support for spending on new bombers. Mitchell provided that with his claim that airplanes could protect American coastlines more effectively than costly Navy fleets. His brash posture and skill at capturing the public's imagination worked. The Air Service grew larger during the 1920s.

The new coastal defense mission provided the justification for continued military investment in long-range bombers. Although budget realities kept such outlays small, it meant two important steps for strategic bombing. First, bomber technology continued to advance even if it took small steps. Next, bomber strategy also continued to evolve, primarily at ACTS.

In the late 1920s the strategic bombing story took an interesting turn. The civilian aviation industry became a key shaping force. Charles Lindbergh's famous flight across the Atlantic helped create a public fascination with the potential of civilian aviation, spawning a demand for safe and reliable long-range aircraft. That in turn spurred a series of technical and organizational advances that coincided with the military's requirement for a capable long-range bomber. Meantime, at ACTS, the school's policy of encouraging discussions and critical debates led a small group of instructors and students to rediscover strategic bombing theory. Working without the theoretical limitations of budgetary or political realities, they explored the potential uses of long-range bombers, and updated Gorrell's ideas to include Industrial Web Theory, centralized control, and high-altitude precision daylight bombing.

With the theoretical underpinnings completed, all that remained was for the political will, both inside the Army and out, to put the strategic bombing concept into practice. The changing world situation of the mid-1930s played the largest role in removing both of these hurdles. European fascism and Japanese expansionism in Asia forced a major rethinking of American national defense policy. Convinced that the United States needed a strong, but affordable counterweight to Axis aggression, President Roosevelt turned to airpower, but the military itself was slow to adapt. The traditional fight between the Army General Staff and the Air Corps continued well into the 1930s. As late as 1939, the General Staff appeared to have the upper hand, canceling all heavy bomber procurement plans. Then, suddenly, the threat of war with Nazi Germany subdued opposition to strategic bombing. First subtly in verbal support and later in direct orders, the president ensured that America focused on building a large heavy bomber force.

With the direction of American airpower assured, the final step was to turn theory into an actual war plan. Once again the role of the individual rose to prominence, as the members of the Bomber Mafia who had spent much of the last decade theorizing, debating, and working out the details of strategic bombing were now in the right place at the right moment. Having moved to planning assignments on the Air Corps staff, men such as Harold George, Kenneth Walker, Haywood Hansell, Hoyt Vandenberg, and Laurence Kuter became the instruments of strategic bombing's final triumph when they turned a decade of theoretical work into the first American operational strategic bombing plan in August 1941.

In sum, the story of strategic bombing is not that of any one person or any one factor. It is a twisting tale of individual efforts, competing priorities, organizational infighting, budget limitations, and technological integration. At no point was strategic bombing predestined to succeed. The theory continually had to survive critical challenges. In the end, technological innovations, doctrinal advances, changes in the military structure, and improved civilian production capability all came together, galvanized by the threat of another world war.

Now it would be time to turn the nation's attention to the final test of this aviation doctrine in a fully planned and well-supported combat operation in the skies over Germany and Japan.

EPILOGUE

By design, this book ends with the history of military aviation from 1917 through late 1941, a defined time period that takes the reader from the Army's first use of airplanes in the Mexican Expedition through World War I and the postwar era, when the Army Air Corps— and later the Army Air Forces—were formed. But the evolution of the strategic bombing mission and the military component that would be assigned to carry it out did not end there. During World War II, the United States and its major Allies conducted thousands of strategic bombing raids that played a significant role in the defeat of Nazi Germany and Imperial Japan. And in September 1947 the Army's air component, which had undergone several iterations between 1917 and 1941, finally was weaned from its parent service and reconstituted as the modern United States Air Force, a separate branch of the armed forces that achieved the ultimate in the structural autonomy that early aviators had sought. It was the aviation officers on active duty during the years covered by this book who laid the groundwork for these achievements.

NOTES

Introduction

1. Geoffrey Perret, *Winged Victory: The Army Air Forces in World War II* (New York: Random House, 1993), 240.
2. Robert F. Futrell, *Ideas, Concepts, and Doctrine: A History of Basic Thinking in the United States Air Force, 1907–1964* (Maxwell AFB: Air University Press, 1989), 4.
3. David Hackett Fischer, *Historians' Fallacies: Toward a Logic of Historical Thought* (New York: Harper Torchbooks, 1970), 210–13.

Chapter 1. A Late-Night Wake-Up Call in Mexico

1. Roger G. Miller, *A Preliminary to War: The 1st Aero Squadron and the Mexican Punitive Expedition of 1916* (Washington, D.C.: Air Force History and Museum Program, 2003), 29.
2. Capt. Benjamin D. Foulois, *Report of the Operations of the First Aero Squadron, Signal Corps, with the Mexican Punitive Expedition, for Period March 15 to August 15, 1916, Call# 168.68 IRIS# 125302,* Air Force Historical Research Agency, Maxwell AFB, Ala., 1–2.
3. Mark Clodfelter, *Beneficial Bombing: The Progressive Foundations of American Air Power, 1917–1945* (Lincoln: University of Nebraska Press, 2010), 8.
4. Edgar S. Gorrell Obituary, United States Military Academy, Cullum No. 5049, March 5, 1945.
5. Ibid.
6. Miller, *Preliminary to War*, 8.

7. Ibid., 13.

8. Ibid., 10.

9. Ibid., 13.

10. Ibid., 14–16.

11. Foulois, *Report of the Operations*, 1–2.

12. Edgar S. Gorrell, "Why Riding Boots Sometimes Irritate an Aviator's Feet," *U.S. Air Services.*

13. Charles deForest Chandler and Frank P. Lahm, *How Our Army Grew Wings* (New York: Arno Press, 1979), 160–61.

14. Benjamin D. Foulois, *From the Wright Brothers to the Astronauts* (New York: Arno Press, 1980), 70–71.

15. Chandler and Lahm, *How our Army Grew Wings*, 182–83.

16. Foulois, *From the Wright Brothers*, 75.

17. "Report of the Chief Signal Officer to the Secretary of War" (Washington, D.C.: Government Printing Office, 1908), 6–7.

18. Chandler and Lahm, *How Our Army Grew Wings*, 182–83.

19. Ibid., 187.

20. Foulois, *From the Wright Brothers*, 116.

21. Chandler and Lahm, *How Our Army Grew Wings*, 195–99.

22. Ibid., 206.

23. Foulois, *From the Wright Brothers*, 101.

24. House Resolution 5304: Act to Increase the Efficiency of the Aviation Section of the Army, July 18, 1914 (Washington, D.C.: Government Printing Office, 1914).

25. Signal Corps General Order #10, August 5, 1914, Record Group 18.2, National Archives.

26. Foulois, *From the Wright Brothers*, 119.

27. Gorrell, "Riding Boots," 22.

28. Miller, *Preliminary to War*, 20.

29. Ibid., 27–28.

30. Foulois, *Report of the Operations*, 2.

31. Miller, *Preliminary to War*, 32.

32. Ibid., 29.

33. Foulois, *Report of the Operations,* 9–10.

34. "Aviators in Mexico Tell World," *New York World*, April 3, 1916.

35. Miller, *Preliminary to War*, 34–35.

36. Ibid., 8.

37. National Defense Act as amended, June 3, 1916 (Washington, D.C.: Government Printing Office, 1921), 5, 14, 48.

38. Lauren Clark and Eric Feron, "A Century of Aerospace Education at MIT" (paper presented at the annual meeting of MIT's Tech Aero Conference, Cambridge, Mass., 2001), 1.

39. Edgar S. Gorrell, "Aerofoils and Aerofoil Structural Combination" (M.S. thesis), MIT, 1917.

40. "Scientific School Gives Stamp of Approval Upon Seven," *Washington Times*, June 12, 1917.

41. Edgar S. Gorrell Obituary, March 5, 1945.

42. Report of the Chief Signal Officer, United States Army, to the Secretary of War, 1915 (Washington, D.C.: Government Printing Office, 1915), 37.

43. Rebecca Grant, "The Real Billy Mitchell," *Air Force Magazine* 84 (2001): 67.

Chapter 2. The War in Europe

1. L. T. C. Rolt, *The Aeronauts: A History of Ballooning, 1783–1903* (New York: Walker and Company, 1966), 137.

2. John H. Morrow Jr., *The Great War in the Air: Military Aviation from 1909 to 1921* (Washington, D.C.: Smithsonian Institution Press, 1993), 21.

3. Lee Kennett, *A History of Strategic Bombing* (New York: Charles Scribner's Sons, 1982), 7.

4. Ibid., 10.

5. Neville Jones, *The Origins of Strategic Bombing: A Study of the Development of British Air Strategic Thought and Practice up to 1918* (London: William Kimber, 1973), 25–26.

6. Morrow, *Great War in the Air*, 4.

7. S. W. Roskill, ed., *Documents Relating to the Naval Air Service*, vol. 1, *1908–1918* (London: Naval Records Society, 1969), 14–18.

8. Morrow, *Great War in the Air*, 18.

9. Edmond Petit, *La Vie quotidienne dans l'aviation in France au debut du XXe siècle, 1900–1935* (Paris: Hachette, 1977), 79.

10. Morrow, *Great War in the Air*, 11.

11. Louis Morgat, "L'aviation en Berry avant la Grande Guerre," *Revue Historique des Armees* 1 (1980): 199.

12. Morrow, *Great War in the Air*, 35.
13. *Report of the Esher Committee*, 28 January 1909, AIR 1/2100, 207/28/1, The National Archives of the U.K.
14. Jones, *Strategic Bombing*, 38.
15. Robin Cross, *The Bombers: The Illustrated Story of Offensive Strategy and Tactics in the Twentieth Century* (New York: Macmillan Publishing Company, 1987), 8.
16. Jones, *Strategic Bombing*, 43.
17. Morrow, *Great War in the Air*, 45–46.
18. Michael Sharpe, *Biplanes, Triplanes, and Seaplanes* (London: Friedman/Fairfax Books, 2000), 43.
19. Cross, *The Bombers*, 7.
20. Sergei I. Sikorsky, *The Sikorsky Legacy* (Charleston, S.C.: Acadia Publishing, 2007), 10.
21. Ibid., 34.
22. Kennett, *History of Strategic Bombing*, 19.
23. Cross, *The Bombers*, 10.
24. Ibid, 12–13.
25. Jones, *Strategic Bombing*, 51.
26. Cross, *The Bombers*, 15.
27. Ibid., 16.
28. Ibid,
29. Morrow, *Great War in the Air*, 93.
30. Douglas H. Robinson, *The Zeppelin in Combat: A History of the German Naval Airship Division, 1912–1918* (Seattle: University of Washington Press, 1980), 49–50.
31. Ibid., 95.
32. Cross, *The Bombers*, 24.
33. Despite the Ilya Mouromets preceding the Ca-1, the IM was originally designed as a passenger plane and later was converted to a long-range bomber.
34. Frank J. Cappelluti, "The Life and Thought of Giulio Douhet" (PhD dissertation, Rutgers University, 1967), 3.
35. Morrow, *Great War in the Air*, 129.
36. Ibid., 132–33.
37. Ibid., 135.
38. Cross, *The Bombers*, 34.

39. Morrow, *Great War in the Air*, 138.

40. Cross, *The Bombers*, 33.

41. Policy Statement on Air Bombing, GHQ, 3 June 1916, AIR 1/978, 204/5/1139, NAUK.

42. Jones, *Strategic Bombing*, 85.

43. "Memorandum in response to Captain C. L. Lambe's Assessment on Air Warfare," Admiral R. H. Bacon, 1 June 1916. AIR 1/633, 17/122/90, NAUK.

44. Jones, *Strategic Bombing*, 104.

45. Ibid., 107.

46. Morrow, *Great War in the Air*, 173.

47. Jones, *Strategic Bombing*, 90.

48. Morrow, *Great War in the Air*, 175–76.

49. Cross, *The Bombers*, 36.

50. Robinson, *Zeppelin in Combat*, 128–29.

51. Ibid., 165.

52. Ibid., 203.

53. Cross, *The Bombers*, 41.

54. Harvey B. Tress, *British Strategic Bombing Policy through 1940* (Lewiston: The Edwin Mellen Press, 1988), 34–35.

55. Ibid., 132.

56. Ibid., 134.

57. Kennett, *History of Strategic Bombing*, 26.

58. Reprint of the Smuts Report in, H. A. Jones, *The Official History of the War Volume VI: The War in the Air* (Oxford: Clarendon Press, 1937), Appendix II, 2.

59. Ibid., Appendix II, 7.

60. George K. Williams, "The Shank of the Drill: Americans and Strategical Aviation in the Great War," *The Journal of Strategic Studies* 19 (Sept. 1996): 384.

61. Jones, *Strategic Bombing*, 142–44.

62. Kennett, *History of Strategic Bombing*, 29.

Chapter 3. The Birth of American Strategic Bombing Theory

1. Mason Patrick, The *United States in the Air* (Garden City, N.J.: Doubleday, 1928), 7.

2. War Department, *Field Service Regulations*, United States Army, 1914.

3. Maurer Maurer, ed., *U.S. Air Service in World War I* (Washington, D.C.: Office of Air Force History, 1978), 29.

4. War College Division, *Military Aviation Study* (Washington, D.C., September 11, 1915).

5. Cable from Premier Ribot to French Ambassador in Washington, May 23, 1917, BAP Hist. box 6, 311.2, National Archives.

6. I. B. Holley, *Ideas and Weapons: Exploitation of the Aerial Weapon by the United States During World War I: A Study in the Relationship of Technological Advances, Military Doctrine, and the Development of Weapons* (Washington, D.C.: Office of Air Force History, 1953), 40.

7. Contribution to Aviation to be Demanded of the United States, translation from French Army General Staff Study, April 1917, BAP Hist. 311.2, box 6, National Archives.

8. Holley, *Ideas and Weapons*, 43.

9. Report of the Joint Army-Navy Technical Aircraft Board, May 29, 1917, Sec A11, in Gorrell History, 11–12.

10. Maurer, *U.S. Air Service in World War I*, 105.

11. Charles C. Mooney and Martha E. Layman, "Organization of Military Aeronautics, 1907–1935," Army Air Forces Historical Study No. 25 (1944), accessed online at http://www.afhra.af.mil, 28–29.

12. "General Squier and Howard Coffin Discuss Opportunity This Country Has," *The Sun*, New York: New York, June 16, 1917, 3.

13. History of the Civilian Motor Mechanics Group, December 18, 1918, Sec A-2, in Gorrell History, 21.

14. George K. Williams, "The Shank of the Drill: Americans and Strategical Aviation in the Great War," *The Journal of Strategic Studies* 19 (Sept. 1996): 384.

15. Holley, *Ideas and Weapons*, 54.

16. "The Men and Machines: Air Operations in World War I, Part V," *Air Power Historian* 5 (Jan. 1958): 42.

17. History of the Civilian Motor Mechanics Group, Gorrell History, Sec A-2, 21.

18. Report by Maj. Raynal C. Bolling, August 15, 1917, Section A-23, in Gorrell History, 80.

19. Bolling Commission Report, August 15, 1917, Gorrell History, I-1, 82.

20. Memorandum Bolling to Coffin, October 15, 1917, Bolling Collection, box 1, folder 9, Greenwich, Conn., Historical Society, 3.

21. Ibid., 4.

22. James J. Cooke, *Billy Mitchell* (Boulder, Colo.: Lynne Rienner Publishers, 2002), 46–47.

23. Ibid., 48.

24. Memo, Mitchell for the Chief of Staff, U.S. Expeditionary Forces, June 13, 1917, contained in Gorrell History, Sec A-23, 81.

25. Ibid., 82.

26. Ibid., 81.

27. Neville Jones, *The Origins of Strategic Bombing: A Study of the Development of British Air Strategic Thought and Practice up to 1918* (London: William Kimber, 1973), 205.

28. Maurer, *U.S. Air Service in World War I*, 123.

29. "The Role of Aviation," report by Maj. Frank Parker, July 2, 1917, Sec A-23, in Gorrell History, 194.

30. Maurer, *U.S. Air Service in World War I*, 123.

31. Holley, *Ideas and Weapons*, 83–84.

32. Edgar S. Gorrell Biography, undated, Call #168.7006–47, IRIS# 125903, in Maj. Gen. (Ret.) Orvil A. Anderson Papers, AFHRA, Maxwell AFB, Ala.

33. Memo, Bolling to the AEF Air Service Chief, October 9, 1917, box 1, folder 9, Greenwich, Conn., Historical Society.

34. Williams, "Shank of the Drill," 384.

35. Neville Jones, *The Origins of Strategic Bombing*, 22.

36. Bob Pearson, "More Than Would be Reasonably Anticipated: The Story of 3 Wing, RNAS," *Over The Front* 13 (Winter 1998): 284.

37. Jones, *The Origins of Strategic Bombing*, 93.

38. Ibid., 24.

39. Williams, "Shank of the Drill," 391–94.

40. J. L. Boone, "Italian Influence on the Origins of the American Concept of Strategic Bombardment," *Air Power Historian* 22 (July 1957): 142.

41. Ibid., 145.

42. Gorrell Memorandum on the Caproni Contract, October 15, 1917, Bureau of Aircraft Production Hist. box 21, 425.1, National Archives.

43. Boone, "Italian Influence," 146.

44. Gorrell to Caproni, November 17, 1917, Call #168.661–86, IRIS #125201, AFHRA, Maxwell AFB, Ala.

45. Maurer, *U.S. Air Service in World War I*, 131–32.

46. Early History of the Strategical Section, by Col. Edgar S. Gorrell, December 28, 1919, Sec B-6, in Gorrell History, 374.

47. John H. Morrow Jr., *German Air Power in World War I* (Lincoln: University of Nebraska Press, 1982), 136.

48. Holley, *Ideas and Weapons*, 41.

49. Memo, Bolling to Coffin, November 17, 1917, Bolling Collection, box 1, folder 9, Greenwich, Conn., Historical Society, 2.

50. Williams, "Shank of the Drill," 398.

51. Early History, November 28, 1917, Gorrell History, B-6, 373.

52. Memo, Foulois to AEF Chief of Staff, December 1, 1917, Sec A-1, in Gorrell History, 9.

53. Williams, "Shank of the Drill," 403.

54. Early History, November 28, 1917, Gorrell History, B-6, 373.

55. Ibid., 376–78.

56. Ibid., 380.

57. Morrow, *German Air Power*, 162.

58. Williams, "Shank of the Drill," 401.

59. Memorandum to Air Service Chief of Staff, January 18, 1918, A-15, in Gorrell History, 122.

60. Early History, November 28, 1917, Gorrell History, B-6, 401.

61. Ibid., 371.

62. Alfred Goldberg, ed., *A History of the United States Air Force, 1907–1957* (Princeton, N.J.: Van Nostrand, 1957), 30.

Chapter 4. The Hard Realities of War

1. Harold S. Fowler Biography, undated, Call# 168.7006–47, IRIS# 125903, in Maj. Gen. (Ret.) Orvil A. Anderson Papers, AFHRA, Maxwell AFB, Ala.

2. Geoffrey Rossano and Thomas Wildenberg, *Striking the Hornet's Nest: Naval Aviation and Origins of Strategic Bombing in World War I.* (Annapolis: Naval Institute Press, 2015), 90–91.

3. Ibid., 371.

4. Neville Jones, *The Origins of Strategic Bombing: A Study of the Development of British Air Strategic Thought and Practice up to 1918* (London: William Kimber, 1973), 135.

5. H. A. Jones, *The Official History of the War Volume VI: The War in the Air* (Oxford: Clarendon Press, 1937), 16–17.

6. Jones, *Origins of Strategic Bombing*, 149.

7. Sir Douglas Haig's 4th Annual Dispatch (1917 Campaigns), December 25, 1917, accessed online at firstworldwar.com.

8. Andrew Boyle, *Trenchard* (London: Collins, 1962), 239.

9. Early History of the Strategical Section, by Col. Edgar S. Gorrell, December 28, 1919, Sec B-6, in Gorrell History, 401.

10. Ibid., 391.

11. Maurer Maurer, *U.S. Air Service in World War I* (Washington, D.C.: Office of Air Force History, 1978), 152.

12. Memo, Foulois to Chief of Staff, December 23, 1917, Sec A-1, in Gorrell History, 135.

13. Early History, December 28, 1918, 395.

14. Ibid., 396–98.

15. Original contains no date. Note: Mark Clodfelter, *Beneficial Bombing* footnote 46 indicates it was likely written in February or March 1918, but this would push the document's origins beyond Gorrell's tenure as Chief of Strategical Aviation in the Zone of Advance, which ended on January 21, 1918.

16. The Future Role of American Bombardment Aviation, by Edgar S. Gorrell, circa December 1917 to January 1918, Call# 248.222-78, IRIS# 00161162, AFHRA, Maxwell AFB, Ala., 1.

17. Ibid., 4.

18. Ibid., 10.

19. Ibid., 15.

20. Early History, November 28, 1917, Sec B-6, 398.

21. John H. Morrow Jr, *The Great War in the Air: Military Aviation from 1909 to 1921* (Washington, D.C.: Smithsonian Institution Press, 1993), 331.

22. Bulletin of the Information Section, Air Service, AEF, Vol, III, No. 132, 30 April 1918, Muir Library Special Collections, Maxwell AFB, Ala.

23. Ibid.

24. Robert P. White, *Mason Patrick and the Fight for Air Service Independence* (Washington, D.C.: Smithsonian Institution Press, 2001), 33.

25. Alfred F. Hurley, *Billy Mitchell: Crusader for Air Power* (Bloomington Indiana University Press, 1975), 26.

26. Thomas Wildenberg, *Billy Mitchell's War with the Navy: The Interwar Rivalry over Air Power* (Annapolis, Md.: Naval Institute Press, 2013), 12.

27. General Order No. 81, General Pershing, May 29, 1918, reprinted in Maurer, *U.S. Air Service* in World War 1, 187–89.

28. Ibid., 189.

29. Foulois, *From the Wright Brothers to the Astronauts*, 169–70.

30. White, *Mason Patrick*, 20.

31. Hurley, *Billy Mitchell*, 34.

32. Ibid.

33. Memorandum to Air Service Chief of Staff, January 18, 1918, A-15, in Gorrell History, 122.

34. Early History of the Strategical Section, December 28, 1919, Sec B-6, 401.

35. Aviation Annex to First Army Field Order, September 17, 1918, Gorrell History, Sec N-2, 330–35.

36. Jones, *Origins of Strategic Bombing*, 178.

37. Richard J. Overy, "Strategic Bombardment before 1939: Doctrine, Planning, and Operations," *Case Studies in Strategic Bombing*, eEdited by Cargill R. Hall, 11–90 (Washington, D.C.: Government Printing Office, 1998), 20–21.

38. Memo, Tiverton to Chief of the Air Staff, 22 May 1918, AIR 1/460, 15/312/101, NAUK.

39. The Scientific and Methodical Attack of Vital Industries, staff study by Brig. Gen. C.L.N. Newall, May 27, 1918, AIR 1/460, 15/312/101, NAUK.

40. Jones, *Origins of Strategic Bombing*, 190.

41. Patrick, *The United States in the Air*, 136–37.

42. Alan Morris, *First of the Many: The Story of Independent Force, RAF* (London: Jarrolds, 1968), 64.

43. Jones, *Origins of Strategic Bombing*, 191.

44. Lee Kennett, *A History of Strategic Bombing*, 75.

45. Ibid., 51.

46. Early History of the Strategical Section, by Col. Edgar S. Gorrell, December 28, 1918, Sec B-6, in Gorrell History, 1–4.

47. Maurer, *U.S. Air Service*, 365.

48. Ibid., 367.

49. Memo, McAndrew to CAS, June 18, 1918, Gorrell History, Sec B-6, 42.

50. Morrow, *Great War in the Air*, 321.

51. Memorandum on Bombing Strategy, by Newton Baker, October 6, 1918, Gorrell History, Sec A-23, 391.

52. Charles deForest Chandler and Frank P. Lahm, *How Our Army Grew Wings* (New York: Arno Press, 1979), 160–61.

53. Maurer, *U.S. Air Service in World War I*, 105.

54. Report of the Joint Army-Navy Technical Aircraft Board, May 29, 1917, Sec A11, in Gorrell History, 11–12.

55. Chief of the Air Service Annual Report, 1919, U.S. Air Force Academy Library, Colorado Springs, Colo., 225.

56. Jones, *The War in the Air*, 38.

57. HQ RFC Memorandum, January 13, 1918, AIR 1/925/204/5/812, London: NAUK.

58. Memo, MacAndrew to Patrick, June 18, 1918, in Gorrell History, Sec B-6, 42.

59. John J. Pershing, *My Experiences in the World War* (New York: Fredrick A. Stokes Company, 1931), 326.

60. White, *Mason Patrick*, 29.

61. Pershing to Trenchard, February 6, 1918, AIR 1/925/204/5/812, NAUK.

62. Patrick to his wife, May 11, 1918, Mason Patrick Collection, Fort Rucker Archives, Ala.

63. House Resolution 5304: Act to Increase the Efficiency of the Aviation Section of the Army, July 18, 1914 (Washington, D.C.: Government Printing Office, 1914).

Chapter 5. Solidifying Doctrine through History

1. National Archive's Introduction, 1974, in Gorrell History, 2.

2. James J. Cooke, *Billy Mitchell* (Boulder, Colo.: Lynne Rienner Publishers, 2002), 186.

3. Provisional Manual of Operations of Air Service Units, December 23, 1918, Call# 248.211–61s, IRIS# 124603, AFHRA, Maxwell AFB, Ala., paragraph 1.

4. Ibid., paragraph 68.

5. Ibid., paragraph 78.

6. Bulletin of the Information Section, Air Service, AEF, Vol. III, No. 132, April 30, 1918, Muir Library Special Collection, Maxwell AFB, Ala.

7. Memorandum for the Chief of Staff, U.S. Expeditionary Forces, by Lt. Col. William Mitchell, June 13, 1917, Sec A-23, in Gorrell History, 81.

8. Maurer, *U.S. Air Service in World War I*, 267.

9. Ibid., 313.

10. *Tentative Manual for the Employment of Air Services*, by Lt. Col. William C. Sherman, undated, Sec D-1, in Gorrell History, 234.

11. Marvin L. Skelton, "Colonel Gorrell and His Nearly Forgotten Records," *Over the Front* 5 (Spring 1990): 59.

12. Introduction, Gorrell History, 2.

13. Ibid.

14. Skelton, "Colonel Gorrell's Records," 60.

15. Ibid., 61.

16. Boone, "Italian Influence, 49–50.

17. Early History of the Strategical Section, by Col. Edgar S. Gorrell, December 28, 1918, Sec B-6, in Gorrell History, 400–1.

18. Ibid., 401.

19. Maurer, *U.S. Air Service in World War I*, vol. III, 1.

20. Milling Biographical Note, undated, Call# 168.7006–47, IRIS# 125903, in the Maj. Gen. Orvil A. Anderson (Ret.) papers, AFHRA, Maxwell AFB, Ala.

21. Memorandum to the Chief of the Air Service, January 9, 1919, Sec A-15, in Gorrell History, 5.

22. Ibid., 6.

23. Ibid.

24. Second Bomb Group Lessons from the War in the Air, December 18, 1918, Sec A-15, in Gorrell History, 209.

25. Ibid., 211.

26. Ibid., 212.

27. Memorandum to Air Service Chief of Staff, January 18, 1918, Sec A-15, in Gorrell History, 122.

28. *Results of the Air Service Efforts as Determined by Investigation of Damage Done in Occupied Territories,* Vol 1: *General Effects of Allied Bombing,* 1919, Sec R-1, in Gorrell History, 1.

29. Ibid.

30. All translations of 1918 marks into 2014 U.S. dollars accomplished through Measuring Worth, 2014, http://measuringworth.com/exchangeglobal/.

31. Results of Bombing, Gorrell History, R-1, 3.

32. Ibid.

33. Ibid., 4–5.

34. Ibid., 6.

35. Although the report included data on eighty cities, only sixty-six were deemed verifiable enough to include in damage calculations.

36. Results of Bombing, Gorrell History, R-1, 3.

37. Ibid.

38. Edgar S. Gorrell Biography, undated, Call# 168.7006–47, IRIS# 125903, in the Maj. Gen. Orvil A. Anderson (Ret.) papers, AFHRA, Maxwell AFB, Ala.

39. Convention Relating to the Regulation of Aerial Navigation, October 13, 1919, http://www.spacelaw.olemiss.edu/library/aviation/intagr/multilateral/1919_paris_convention.pdf.

40. Patrick, *The United States in the Air,* 57.

41. *Army Air Forces Historical Studies no. 25: Organization of Military Aeronautics, 1907–1935.* Prepared by Assistant Chief of the Air Service: Intelligence Division, December 1944, Call# 168.67, RIS# 0467617, AFHRA, Maxwell AFB, Ala.

42. Memo, Patrick to Pershing, Mason M. Patrick Papers, SMS 198, Special Collections, U.S. Air Force Academy Library, Colorado Springs, Colo.

43. *AAF Historical Study 25,* 39.

44. Patrick Diary, June 21, 1919, Mason M. Patrick Papers, SMS 198, Special Collections, U.S. Air Force Academy Library, Colorado Springs, Colo.

45. Gorrell Biography, Anderson Papers, Maxwell AFB, Ala.

46. Ibid.

47. Edgar S. Gorrell Obituary, United States Military Academy, Cullum No. 5049, March 5, 1945.

Chapter 6. Strategic Bombing to the Periphery

1. H. W. Brands, *Woodrow Wilson* (New York: Henry Holt and Co., 2003), 100.

2. Robert F. Futrell, *Ideas, Concepts, and Doctrines: Basic Thinking in the United States Air Force, 1907–1960* (Maxwell AFB, Ala.: Air University Press, 1989), 31.

3. Foulois, *From the Wright Brothers to the Astronauts*, 112.

4. *War Department Annual Report, 1919* (Washington, D.C.: Government Printing Office, 1920), 74–75.

5. Robert P. White, *Mason Patrick and the Fight for Air Service Independence* (Washington, D.C.: Smithsonian Institution Press, 2001), 45.

6. Report of Board of Officers, October 27, 1919, Call# 168.1–6B, IRIS# 00122088, AFHRA, Maxwell AFB, Ala., 2.

7. Ibid., 6.

8. Edgar S. Gorrell, *The Measure of America's World War Aeronautical Effort* (Northfield Vt. Norwich University Press, 1940), 123–25.

9. William C. Sherman, *Air Warfare* (New York: The Ronald Press Co., 1926), 41.

10. Oral History Interview, February 1967, Call# K239.0512–573, IRIS# 00904575, AFHRA, Maxwell AFB, Ala., 3.

11. Ibid., 7.

12. Ibid., 8.

13. J. E. Kaufmann and H. W. Kaufmann, *The Sleeping Giant: American Armed Forces Between the Wars* (London: Praeger, 1996), 129.

14. Kernan to Patrick, 18 September 1921, box 5, RG 18, 228/229, National Archives.

15. Patrick to Kernan, 2 November 1921, box 5, RG 18, 228/229, National Archives.

16. Kaufmann and Kaufmann, *The Sleeping Giant*, 15.

17. Martha E. Layman, *Air Force Historical Study No. 39: Legislation Relating to the Air Corps Personnel and Training Programs, 1907–1939* (Washington, D.C.: Army Air Force Historical Office, 1945), 117–20.

18. Memo, Maj. Gen. Haan to Gen. Pershing, July 6, 1921, Call# 145.93–101, IRIS# 00119243, AFHRA, Maxwell AFB, Ala.

19. Ronald R. Rice, *The Politics of Air Power: From Confrontation to Cooperation in Army Aviation Civil-Military Relations* (Lincoln University of Nebraska Press, 2004), 16.

20. Ibid., 26.

21. Tami Davis Biddle, *Rhetoric and Reality in Air Warfare: The Evolution of British and American Ideas about Strategic Bombing, 1914–1945* (Princeton, N.J.: Princeton University Press, 2002), 132.

22. Alfred F. Hurley, *Billy Mitchell: Crusader for Air Power* (Bloomington Indiana University Press, 1975), 41.

23. Williamson Murray and Allan R. Millett, *Military Innovation in the Interwar Period* (Cambridge: Cambridge University Press, 1996), 123–24.

24. Oral History Interview of Maj. Gen. James P. Hodges, January 1966, Call# K239.0512–565, AFHRA, Maxwell AFB, Ala., 4.

25. *Tactical Application of Military Aeronautics Manual,* January 9, 1920, Call# 167.4–1, IRIS# 00120667, AFHRA, Maxwell AFB, Ala., 2.

26. Ibid., 22.

27. William Mitchell, *Our Air Force: The Keystone of National Defense* (New York: E. P. Dutton, 1921), 200–1.

28. White, *Mason Patrick*, 49.

29. Patrick, *The United States in the Air*, 76.

30. Army Reorganization Hearings before the Committee of Military Affairs, 66th Congress, 1919, Call# 168.68–3a, IRIS# 00125299, AFHRA, Maxwell AFB, Ala., 907–8.

31. White, *Mason Patrick*, 50.

32. Biddle, *Rhetoric and Reality*, 129.

33. Air Service Information Circular: Aerial Bombardment Manual, April 1920, Call# 167.42–1, IRIS# 00121030, AFHRA, Maxwell AFB, Ala., 2.

34. Futrell, *Ideas, Concepts, and Doctrines*, 40.

35. Robert T. Finney, *History of the Air Corps Tactical School, 1920–1940* (Maxwell AFB: Air University Press, 1955), 15.

36. Futrell, *Ideas, Concepts, and Doctrine*, 40–41.

37. Air Tactics and Training Regulation 440–15, 1922, Call# 248.101– 4A, IRIS# 00127532, AFHRA, Maxwell AFB, Ala.

38. Lecture at Fort Leavenworth, March 27, 1924, Mason Patrick Papers, Special Collections, U.S. Air Force Academy Library, Colorado Springs, Colo.

39. Air Service Tactical School Bombardment Course Text, 1924, Call# 248.101–9, IRIS# 00157203, AFHRA, Maxwell AFB, Ala.

40. Sherman, *Air Warfare*, 190.

41. Ibid., 197.

42. Training Regulation 440–15 draft, 1922.

43. Lassiter Board Meeting Minutes, March 22, 1923, Call# 145.93–102, IRIS# 00119243, AFHRA, Maxwell AFB, Ala., 5–7.

44. Ibid., 3.

45. Lassiter Board Final Report, March 17, 1923, Call# 145.93–102, IRIS# 00119242, AFHRA, Maxwell AFB, Ala. .

46. Ibid.

47. Morrow Board Testimony Minutes, Call# 248.211–61V, IRIS# 00159949, AFHRA, Maxwell AFB, Ala. .

48. Report of the President's Aircraft Board, December 2, 1925, Call# 168.65411–3, IRIS# 00124933, Maxwell AFB, Ala., 3.

49. Ibid., 6–7.

50. Harry H. Ransom, "Air Corps Act of 1926: A Study in the Legislative Process" (PhD dissertation, Princeton University, 1954), 66.

51. Ibid., 78.

Chapter 7. Marrying Technology and Doctrine

1. *Employment of Combined Air Forces Manual*, 1926, Call# 168.7045–28, IRIS# 00127160, AFHRA, Maxwell AFB, Ala.

2. ACTS Pursuit Text, 1926, Call# 248.282–13A, IRIS# 00162278, AFHRA, Maxwell AFB, Ala., 53.

3. Jean H. Dubuque and Robert F. Gleckner, *The Development of the Heavy Bomber, 1918–1944* (Air Historical Study No. 6, Historical Division Air University, 1951), 7.

4. Thomas Kessner, *The Flight of the Century: Charles Lindbergh and the Rise of American Aviation* (Oxford: Oxford University Press, 2010), 122–23.

5. T. A. Heppenheimer, *Turbulent Skies: The History of Commercial Aviation* (New York: John Wiley & Sons, 1995), 25–26.

6. Kessner, *Flight of the Century,* 146–47.

7. Futrell, *Ideas, Concepts, and Doctrines,* 55.

8. Official Biography, Maj. Gen James E. Fechet, available online at http://archive.today/20121213031717/http://www.af.mil/information/bios/bio.asp?bioID=5401.

9. Futrell, *Ideas, Concepts, and Doctrine,* 57.

10. Air Corps Act of 1926, Call# 248.211–61E, IRIS# 00159929, AFHRA, Maxwell AFB, Ala., 7.

11. Dubuque and Gleckner, *Heavy Bomber,* 8.

12. Memo, Knerr to Fechet, May 28, 1928, as cited in Dubuque and Gleckner, *Heavy Bomber,* 57.

13. Rice, *Politics of Air Power,* 80.

14. David E. Johnson, *Fast Tanks and Heavy Bombers: Innovation in the U.S. Army, 1917–1945* (Ithaca, N.Y. Cornell University Press, 2003), 67.

15. Robert H. Ferrell, *Peace in Their Time: The Origins of the Kellogg-Briand Pact* (New Haven, Conn. Yale University Press, 1952), 219.

16. Air Corps Annual Report, 1928, Call# 168.7330–1286, IRIS# 02053550, AFHRA, Maxwell AFB, Ala.

17. Biddle, *Rhetoric and Reality in Air Warfare,* 144–46.

18. Rice, *Politics of Air Power,* 87.

19. Wildenberg, *Mitchell's War with the Navy,* 155.

20. Oral History, Maj. Gen. James P. Hodges, January 1966, Call# K239.0512–565, AFHRA, Maxwell AFB, Ala.

21. Dubuque and Gleckner, *Heavy Bomber,* 11.

22. Futrell, *Ideas, Concepts, and Doctrines,* 57.

23. Memo, Culver to Fechet, August 30, 1928, Call# K239.293, IRIS# 00481811, AFHRA, Maxwell AFB, Ala.

24. Memo, Fechet to Culver, September 9, 1928, Call# K239.293, IRIS# 004881811, AFHRA, Maxwell AFB, Ala.

25. Finney, *History of ACTS*, 28.

26. ACTS Commandant's Annual Report, 1929, Call# 245–111, IRIS# 00155806, AFHRA, Maxwell AFB, Ala.

27. Wildenberg, *Mitchell's War with the* Navy, 156.

28. Report of V Corps Maneuvers, 1929, Call# 248.2122, IRIS# 00160361, AFHRA, Maxwell AFB, Ala., 8.

29. Student Paper, Capt. Charles W. Walton, May 1, 1929, Call# 248–11–16F, AFHRA, Maxwell AFB, Ala., 19.

30. Maj. Gen. Haywood Hansell, "Pre-World War II Evaluation of the Air Weapon," Air War College lecture, November 16, 1953, Call# K239.716253–36, IRIS# 00483446, AFHRA, Maxwell AFB, Ala.

31. Dubuque and Gleckner, *Heavy Bombers*, 8.

32. Futrell, *Ideas, Concepts, and Doctrine*, 58.

33. Memo, ACTS Commandant to Chief of the Air Corps, March 19, 1930, as cited in Dubuque and Gleckner, *Heavy Bomber*, 10.

34. John W. Killigrew, "The Impact of the Great Depression on the Army, 1929–1936" (PhD dissertation, Indiana University, 1960), 11.

35. Dubuque and Gleckner, *Heavy Bombers*, 8.

36. Rice, *Politics of Air Power*, 96.

37. Biddle, *Rhetoric and Reality*, 147.

38. Stephen L. MacFarland, *America's Pursuit of Precision Bombing, 1910–1945* (Washington, D.C.: Smithsonian Institution Press, 1995), 92.

39. Finney, *History of ACTS*, 14.

40. U.S. Air Force Bio, https://www.af.mil/information/bios/bio.asp?bioID=10216.

41. Memo, Curry to Chief of the Air Corps, April 8, 1932, Call# 248.192, IRIS# 00158554, AFHRA, Maxwell AFB, Ala.

42. Oral History Interview of Hume Peabody, September 30, 1974, Call# K239.0512–810, IRIS# 01029101, AFHRA, Maxwell AFB, Ala.

43. Finney, *History of ACTS*, 16.

44. ACTS Bombardment Text, 1933, Call# 241.111, IRIS# 468620, AFHRA, Maxwell AFB, Ala.

45. Memo, Walker to Curry, September 24, 1932, Call# 248.211–13, IRIS# 00159577, AFHRA, Maxwell AFB, Ala.

46. Memo, MacArthur to Commanding Generals, Armies, Corps, and Departments, January 13, 1931, Call# 168.3952–91, IRIS# 00123080, AFHRA, Maxwell AFB, Ala.

47. Maurer Maurer, *Aviation in the U.S. Army 1919–1939* (Washington, D.C.: Office of Air Force History, 1987), 289.

48. Kaufmann and Kaufmann, *The Sleeping Giant*, 122.

49. Maurer, *Aviation in the U.S. Army*, 289.

50. MacFarland, *Precision Bombing*, 72–73.

51. Futrell, *Ideas, Concepts, and Doctrine*, 60–62.

52. Memo, Foulois to Killbourne, February 8, 1933, Call# 168.68, IRIS# 125297, AFHRA, Maxwell AFB, Ala., 2.

53. Ibid., 8.

54. Drum Board Report, October 11, 1933, Call# 168.7130–5, IRIS# 01034484, AFHRA, Maxwell AFB, Ala., 1.

55. Ibid., 12.

56. Doctrine for Employment of the GHQ Air Force, October 17, 1934, Call# 145.93–95, IRIS# 00119236, AFHRA, Maxwell, AFB, Ala., 3.

57. Ibid., 4.

58. John F. Shiner, *Foulois and the U. S. Army Air Corps, 1931–1935* (Washington, D.C.: Office of Air Force History, 1983), 212.

Chapter 8. The Triumph of the Bomber Advocates

1. Kaufmann and Kaufmann, *The Sleeping Giant*, 88–89.

2. Futrell, *Ideas, Concepts, and Doctrines*, 64.

3. Congressional Record, 73rd Congress, 2nd session, Vol. 78, pt 3, 3144–3145.

4. Meeting Minutes of the Special Committee on Army Air Corps and the Air Mail, April 17, 1934, Call# 167.66–1, IRIS# 121594, AFHRA, Maxwell AFB, Ala., 2.

5. Ibid., 17–19.

6. Report of War Department Special Committee on Army Air Corps, July 18, 1934, Call# 145.93–94A, IRIS# 00119235, AFHRA, Maxwell AFB, Ala., 14, 75.

7. Ibid., 26.

8. Ibid., 21.

9. Memo, Foulois to Assistant Chief of Staff G-3, January 8, 1935, Call# 145.93–94, IRIS# 125295, AFHRA, Maxwell AFB, Ala.

10. "2nd Bombardment Wing Exercise Report," Col. John Curry, April 19, 1935, Call# 248.224 1932, IRIS# 00161170, AFHRA Maxwell AFB, Ala., 2–3.

11. Finney, *History of the ACTS*, 17.

12. Memo, Commander ACTS to Chief of the Air Corps, August 14, 1934, Call# 145.91–409, IRIS# 118861, AFHRA, Maxwell AFB, Ala.

13. ACTS Instructors Memo #10, February 12, 1935, Call# 248.126, IRIS# 157746, AFHRA, Maxwell AFB, Ala.

14. Finney, *History of ACTS*, 20.

15. Richard J. Overy, "Strategic Bombardment before 1939: Doctrine, Planning, and Operations," *Case Studies in Strategic Bombing* (Washington, D.C.: Government Printing Office, 1998), 57.

16. H. H. Arnold, *Global Mission* (New York: Harper & Bros., 1949), 155.

17. Maurer, *Aviation in the U.S. Army*, 354.

18. Dubuque and Gleckner, *Heavy Bomber*, 22.

19. Memo, MacArthur to War Department Staff, August 13, 1935, in AAG321.9A, box#2583, RG#407, National Archives.

20. Memo, Westover to Adjutant General, November 8, 1935, AG452.1, box#2583, RG#407, National Archives.

21. Oral History Interview, Maj. Gen. Donald Wilson, Call# K239.0512–878, IRIS# 01103263, AFHRA, Maxwell, AFB, Ala., 6.

22. Ibid., 8.

23. "Student Research Project on New York City Statistical Data," Capt. Robert M. Webster, Call# 248–211–28, IRIS# 159749, AFHRA, Maxwell, AFB, Ala.

24. Futrell, *Ideas, Concepts, and Doctrines*, 83.

25. Ibid., 79.

26. War Department Staff Study: Augmentation in Aircraft to be included in FY 1938 Estimates, June 25, 1936, included in Arnold Papers, Call# 28211, IRIS# 089007, AFHRA, Maxwell AFB, Ala.

27. Ibid., 79.

28. Memo, Andrews to Chief of Staff, September 14, 1936, AG452.1, box#2583, RG#407, National Archives.

29. Maj. Gen. Frank Andrews lecture, "The GHQ AF" at the Army War College, October 9, 1937, Call# 248.211–62G, IRIS# 00159966, AFHRA, Maxwell AFB, Ala., 20–21.

30. Thomas H. Greer, *The Development of Air Doctrine in the Army Air Arm, 1917–1941* (Washington, D.C.: Office of Air Force History, 1985), 76.

31. Report of the Air Corps Board No. 44, October 17 1938, Call# 3794–44, IRIS# 121165, AFHRA, Maxwell AFB, Ala., 3.

32. "A Study of Air Defense of the Western Hemisphere," May 12, 1939, Call# 145.93–141, IRIS# 00119305, AFHRA, Maxwell, AFB, Ala., 7.

33. Andrews lecture, "The GHQ AF," 8.

34. Memorandum, Knerr to Andrews, July 31 1937, Call# 168.7028–11, IRIS# 126511, AFHRA, Maxwell AFB, Ala.

35. Memo, Deputy Chief of Staff to Chief of Staff, November 29, 1938, AAG 452.1b, box#2583, RG#407, National Archives.

36. Army War College report: "Air Forces and War," September 1937, Call# 168.7330–1501, IRIS# 2053765, AFHRA, Maxwell AFB, Ala.

37. Arnold, *Global Mission*, 176–79.

38. Memo, Spalding to Craig, July 19, 1938, AG452.1, box#2583, RG#407, National Archives.

39. Greer, *Development of Air Doctrine*, 93.

40. Directive for Chief of the Air Corps from Adjutant General for the Secretary of War, October 19, 1937 AAG451a, box#2583, RG#407, National Archives.

41. Futrell, *Ideas, Concepts, and Doctrines*, 95.

42. Barry R. Posen, *The Source of Military Doctrine: France, Britain, and Germany between the World Wars* (Ithaca, N.Y.: Cornell University Press, 1984), 136–37.

43. Mark S. Watson, *Prewar Plans and Preparations, U.S. Army in World War II* (Washington, D.C.: Office of the Chief of Military History, Department of the Army, 1950), 136–39.

44. Arnold, *Global Mission*, 177–80.

45. Futrell, *Ideas, Concepts, and Doctrine*, 87.

46. Robert Dallek, *Franklin D. Roosevelt and American Foreign Policy, 1932–1945* (Oxford: Oxford University Press, 1981), 173.

47. Futrell, *Ideas, Concepts, and Doctrine*, 88.

48. "ESMR No. 50–41–351: Future Aeronautical Research and Development Problems," August 18 1939, Call# 204–2 V.1 PT.1, IRIS# 00142378, AFHRA, Maxwell, AFB, Ala., 3.

49. Ibid., 34–36.

50. Watson, *Prewar Plans and Preparations*, 280–81.

51. Haywood S. Hanswell, *The Air Plan that Defeated Hitler* (New York: Arno Press, 1980), 155–57.

52. Wilson to Lt. Col. L. F. Stone (instructor at the Army Command and General Staff College), September 23 1939, in USAFHD 4633–37, as quoted in Greer, *Development of Air Doctrine*, 131.

53. Gen. Carl Spaatz, "Strategic Air Power," *Foreign Affairs*, (April 1941): 386–88.

54. Greer, *Development of Air Doctrine*, 117.

55. Donald L. Miller, *Masters of the Air: America's Bomber Boys Who Fought the Air War Against Nazi Germany* (New York: Simon & Schuster, 2006), 48–52.

56. AWPD-1, Munitions Requirements of the Army Air Forces to Defeat our Potential Enemies, August 12, 1941, Chapter 2, Sec 1, Part 3, Call# 145.82.1, IRIS# 00118160, AFHRA, Maxwell AFB, Ala.

57. Ibid., tab 1, 1–2.

BIBLIOGRAPHY

MANUSCRIPT AND ARCHIVAL MATERIAL

Air Force Historical Research Agency, Maxwell AFB, Ala.
Anderson, Orvil A. Papers.
Andrews, Frank M. Papers.
Arnold, Henry H. Papers.
Caproni, Gianni Papers.
Fairchild, Muir S. Papers.
Foulois, Benjamin D. Papers.
Hansell, Haywood S., Jr. Papers.
Kuter, Laurence S. Papers.
Records of the United States Air Force.

British National Archives, London
Air Ministry and Royal Air Force Records, reference AIR 1.

National Archives and Records Administration, Washington, D.C.
Records of the Army Adjutant General, Record Group 407.
Records of the Army Air Forces, Record Group 18.

Other

Bolling, Raynal C. Papers, Greenwich Historical Society, Greenwich, Conn.

Gorrell, Edgar S. Papers, National Air and Space Museum, Washington, D.C.

Gorrell, Edgar S. Writings, Norwich University Archives, Kreitzberg Library, Northfield, Vt.

Gorrell's "History of the American Expeditionary Air Service, 1917–1919," Fold3.com.

United States Air Force Academy, Colorado Springs, Colo.

Air Service Annual Reports, U.S. Air Force Academy Library.

Patrick, Mason M. Papers, U.S. Air Force Academy Library.

United States Congress

Hearings before the Committee on Military Affairs, House of Representatives, To Increase the Efficiency of the Military Establishment of the United States, 64th Congress, 1st session, vol. 1, January 18, 1916.

Hearings before the Select Committee on Expenditures in the War Department, Subcommittee on Aviation, House of Representatives, 66th Congress, 1st session, March 6, 1920.

National Defense Act, June 3, 1916. Washington, D.C.: Government Printing Office.

War Department Annual Reports, Washington, D.C.: Government Printing Office

United States Military Academy, WestPoint, N.Y.

Edgar S. Gorrell Obituary, United States Military Academy, Cullum No. 5049, March 5, 1945.

Newspapers and Periodicals

Air Force
Air Power Historian
Journal of Strategic Studies
Military Affairs
Over the Front

The Sun (New York newspaper)
U. S. Air Service
Washington Times

Books

Arnold, H. H. *Global Mission*. New York: Harper and Bros., 1949.

Biddle, Tami Davis. *Rhetoric and Reality in Air Warfare: The Evolution of British and American Ideas about Strategic Bombing, 1914–1945*. Princeton: Princeton University Press, 2002.

Boyle, Andrew. *Trenchard*. London: Collins, 1962.

Brands, H. W. *Woodrow Wilson*. New York: Henry Holt and Co., 2003.

Byrd, Martha. *Kenneth N. Walker: Air Power's Untempered Crusader*. Maxwell AFB, Ala.: Air University Press, 1997.

Chandler, Charles deForest, and Frank P. Lahm. *How Our Army Grew Wings*. New York: Arno Press, 1979.

Claussen, Martin P. *U.S. Army Air Force Historical Study No. 20: Comparative History of Research and Development Policies Affecting Air Material, 1915–1944*. Washington, D.C.: AAF Historical Office, 1945.

Clodfelter, Mark. *Beneficial Bombing: The Progressive Foundations of American Air Power, 1917–1945*. Lincoln: University of Nebraska Press, 2010.

Cooke, James J. *Billy Mitchell*. Boulder, Colo.: Lynne Rienner Publishers, 2002.

Cross, Robin. *The Bombers: The Illustrated Story of Offensive Strategy and Tactics in the Twentieth Century*. New York: Macmillan Publishing Company, 1987.

Dallek, Robert. *Franklin D. Roosevelt and American Foreign Policy, 1932–1945*. New York: Oxford University Press, 1981.

Dubuque, Jean H., and Robert F. Gleckner. *The Development of the Heavy Bomber, 1918–1944*. Air Historical Study No. 6. Maxwell AFB, Ala.: Historical Division Air University, 1951.

Ferrell, Robert H. *Peace in Their Time: The Origins of the Kellogg-Briand Pact*. New Haven: Yale University Press, 1952.

Finney, Robert T. *History of the Air Corps Tactical School, 1920–1940*. Maxwell AFB, Ala.: Air University Press, 1955.

Fonck, Rene. *L'Aviation et la Securite Francaise.* Paris: Bossard, 1924.

Foulois, Benjamin D. *From the Wright Brothers to the Astronauts.* New York: Arno Press, 1968.

Futrell, Robert F. *Ideas, Concepts, and Doctrines: Basic Thinking in the United States Air Force, 1907–1964.* Maxwell AFB, Ala.: Air University Press, 1989.

Goldberg, Alfred. *A History of the United States Air Force, 1907–1957.* Princeton, N.J.: D. Van Nostrand, 1957.

Gorrell, Edgar S. *The Measure of America's World War Aeronautical Effort.* Northfield, Vt.: Norwich University Press, 1940.

Greer, Thomas H. *The Development of Air Doctrine in the Army Air Arm, 1917–1941.* Washington, D.C.: Office of Air Force History, 1985.

Griffith, Robert K., Jr. *Men Wanted for the U.S. Army.* Westport, Conn.: Greenwood Press, 1982.

Hansell, Haywood S. *The Air Plan that Defeated Hitler.* New York: Ayer Publishing, 1980.

Heppenheimer, T. A. *Turbulent Skies: The History of Commercial Aviation.* New York: John Wiley and Sons, 1995.

Holley, I. B., Jr. *Ideas and Weapons: Exploitation of the Aerial Weapon by the United States During World War I: A Study in the Relationship of Technological Advances, Military Doctrine, and the Development of Weapons.* Washington, D.C.: Office of Air Force History, 1953.

Hurley, Alfred F. *Billy Mitchell: Crusader for Air Power.* Bloomington, Indiana University Press, 1975.

Johnson, David E. *Fast Tanks and Heavy Bombers: Innovation in the U.S. Army, 1917–1945.* Ithaca, N.Y.: Cornell University Press, 2003.

Jones, H. A. *The Official History of the War Volume VI: The War in the Air.* Oxford: Clarendon Press, 1937.

———. *The War in the Air: Being the Story of the Part Played in the Great War by the Royal Air Force.* Oxford: Clarendon Press, 1935.

Jones, Neville. *The Beginnings of Strategic Air Power: A History of the British Bomber Force 1923–1939.* New York: Frank Cass Publishers, 1987.

———. *The Origins of Strategic Bombing: A Study of the Development of British Air Strategic Thought and Practice up to 1918.* London: William Kimber, 1973.

Kaufmann, J. E., and H. W. Kaufmann. *The Sleeping Giant: American Armed Forces Between the Wars.* London: Praeger, 1996.

Kennett, Lee. *A History of Strategic Bombing.* New York: Charles Scribner's Sons, 1982.

Kessner, Thomas. *The Flight of the Century: Charles Lindbergh and the Rise of American Aviation.* Oxford: Oxford University Press, 2010.

Layman, Martha E. *Air Force Historical Study No. 39: Legislation Relating to the Air Corps Personnel and Training Programs, 1907–1939.* Washington, D.C.: Army Air Force Historical Office, 1945.

Loening, Grover. *Our Wings Grow Faster.* New York: Doubleday, Doran and Co., 1935.

Mahon, John K. *History of the Militia and the National Guard.* New York: Macmillan Publishing Co., 1983.

Maurer, Maurer. *Aviation in the U.S. Army 1919–1939.* Washington, D.C.: Office of Air Force History, 1987.

———. *U.S. Air Service in World War I.* Washington, D.C.: Office of Air Force History, 1978.

McFarland, Stephen L. *America's Pursuit of Precision Bombing, 1910–1945.* Washington, D.C.: Smithsonian Institution Press, 1995.

Miller, Donald L. *Masters of the Air: America's Bomber Boys Who Fought the Air War Against Nazi Germany.* New York: Simon & Schuster, 2006.

Miller, Roger G. *A Preliminary to War: The 1st Aero Squadron and the Mexican Punitive Expedition of 1916.* Washington, D.C.: Air Force History and Museum Program, 2003.

Mitchell, William. *Our Air Force: The Keystone of National Defense.* New York: E. P. Dutton, 1921.

Mooney, Chase C. *AAF Historical Study No. 46: Organization of Military Aeronautics, 1935–1945.* Washington, D.C.: Army Air Force Historical Office, 1946.

Morris, Alan. *First of the Many: The Story of the Independent Force, RAF.* London: Jarrolds, 1968.

Morrow, John H., Jr. *German Air Power in World War I.* Lincoln: University of Nebraska Press, 1982.

———. *The Great War in the Air: Military Aviation from 1909 to 1921.* Washington, D.C.: Smithsonian Institution Press, 1993.

Murray, Williamson, and Allan R. Millett. *Military Innovation in the Interwar Period*. Cambridge: Cambridge University Press, 1996.

Nalty, Bernard C. *Winged Shield, Winged Sword: A History of the United States Air Force*. Washington, D.C.: Office of Air Force History, 1997.

Overy, Richard J. "Strategic Bombardment before 1939: Doctrine, Planning, and Operations." *Case Studies in Strategic Bombing*, edited by Cargill R. Hall, 11–90. Washington, D.C.: Office of Air Force History, 1998.

Patrick, Mason. *The United States in the Air*. Garden City, N.J.: Doubleday, 1928.

Perret, Geoffrey. *Winged Victory: The Army Air Forces in World War II*. New York: Random House, 1993.

Petit, Edmond. *La Vie quotidienne dans l'aviation in France au debut du XXe siècle, 1900–1935*. Paris: Hachette, 1977.

Posen, Barry R. *The Source of Military Doctrine: France, Britain, and Germany between the World Wars*. Ithaca, N.Y.: Cornell University Press, 1984.

Pryor, Robin, and Trevor Wilson. *The Somme*. New Haven, Conn.: Yale University Press, 2005.

Rice, Ronald R. *The Politics of Air Power: From Confrontation to Cooperation in Army Aviation Civil-Military Relations*. Lincoln: University of Nebraska Press, 2004.

Robinson, Douglas H. *The Zeppelin in Combat: A History of the German Naval Airship Division, 1912–1919*. Seattle: University of Washington Press, 1980.

Rolt, L.T. C. *The Aeronauts: A History of Ballooning 1783–1903*. New York: Walker and Company 1966.

Roskill, S.W. *Documents Relating to the Naval Air Service, vol. 1: 1908–1918*. London: Naval Records Society, 1969.

Sharpe, Michael. *Biplanes, Triplanes, and Seaplanes*. London: Friedman/Fairfax Books, 2000.

Sherman, William C. *Air Warfare*. New York: The Ronald Press Co., 1926.

Shiner, John F. *Foulois and the U.S. Army Air Corps, 1931–1935*. Washington, D.C.: Office of Air Force History, 1983.

Sikorsky, Sergei I. *The Sikorsky Legacy*. Charleston, S.C.: Acadia Publishing, 2007.

Simpson, Albert F. *The World War I Diary of Col. Frank P. Lahm*. Maxwell AFB, Ala.: Historical Research Division, 1970.

Tompkins, Frank. *Chasing Villa: The Story Behind the Story of Pershing's Expedition into Mexico*. Harrisburg, Pa.: The Military Service Publishing Company, 1934.

Tress, Harvey B. *British Strategic Bombing Policy through 1940*. Lewiston: The Edwin Mellen Press, 1988.

Watson, Mark S. *Chief of Staff: Prewar Plans and Preparations, U.S. Army in World War II*. Washington, D.C.: Office of the Chief of Military History, Department of the Army, 1950.

White, Robert P. *Mason Patrick and the Fight for Air Service Independence*. Washington, D.C.: Smithsonian Institution Press, 2001.

Wildenberg, Thomas. *Billy Mitchell's War with the Navy: The Interwar Rivalry over Air Power*. Annapolis, Md.: Naval Institute Press, 2013.

Yenne, Bill. *Big Week: Six Days that Changed the Course of World War II*. New York: Penguin Group, 2012.

Articles

Boone, J. L. "Italian Influence on the Origins of the American Concept of Strategic Bombardment." *Air Power Historian* 22 (1957): 141–50.

Gorrell, Edgar S. "Why Riding Boots Sometimes Irritate an Aviator's Feet." *U.S. Air Services* 12 (1932): 24–32.

Krauskopt, Robert W. "The Army and the Strategic Bomber, 1930–1939." *Military Affairs* 73 (1958), 208–21.

"The Men and Machines: Air Operations in World War I, Part V." *Air Power Historian* 5 (1958): 37–54.

Morgat, Louis. "L'aviation en Berry avant la Grande Guerre." *Revue Historique des Armees* 1 (1980): 158–216.

Pearson, Bob. "More Than would be Reasonably Anticipated: The Story of No. 3 Wing, RNAS." *Over the Front* 13 (1998): 281–98.

Pool, William C. "The Origin of Military Aviation in Texas, 1910–1913." *The Southwestern Historical Quarterly* 59 (1956): 342–71.

Skelton, Marvin L. "Colonel Gorrell and His Nearly Forgotten Records." *Over the Front* 5 (1990): 56–71.

Williams, George K. "The Shank of the Drill: Americans and Strategical Aviation in the Great War." *Journal of Strategic Studies* 19 (1996): 381–431.

Dissertations, Papers, and Other Unpublished Materials

Cappelluti, Frank J. "The Life and Thought of Giulio Douhet." PhD dissertation, Rutgers University, 1967.

Clark, Lauren, and Eric Feron. "A Century of Aerospace Education at MIT." Paper presented at the Annual Meeting of MIT's Tech Aero Conference, Cambridge, Mass., 2001.

Gorrell, Edgar S. "Aerofoils and Aerofoil Structural Combination." MA thesis, Massachusetts Institute of Technology, 1917.

Killigrew, John W. "The Impact of the Great Depression on the Army, 1929–1936." PhD dissertation, Indiana University, 1960.

Ransom, Harry H. "Air Corps Act of 1926: A Study in the Legislative Process." PhD dissertation, Princeton University, 1954.

INDEX

Lt. Col. Craig F. Morris is an assistant professor of history at the U.S. Air Force Academy where he teaches courses on world history, aviation history, military history, and the history of technology. He is a twenty-five-year veteran of the U.S. Air Force with assignments in intelligence and air campaign planning.

The Naval Institute Press is the book-publishing arm of the U.S. Naval Institute, a private, nonprofit, membership society for sea service professionals and others who share an interest in naval and maritime affairs. Established in 1873 at the U.S. Naval Academy in Annapolis, Maryland, where its offices remain today, the Naval Institute has members worldwide.

Members of the Naval Institute support the education programs of the society and receive the influential monthly magazine *Proceedings* or the colorful bimonthly magazine *Naval History* and discounts on fine nautical prints and on ship and aircraft photos. They also have access to the transcripts of the Institute's Oral History Program and get discounted admission to any of the Institute-sponsored seminars offered around the country.

The Naval Institute's book-publishing program, begun in 1898 with basic guides to naval practices, has broadened its scope to include books of more general interest. Now the Naval Institute Press publishes about seventy titles each year, ranging from how-to books on boating and navigation to battle histories, biographies, ship and aircraft guides, and novels. Institute members receive significant discounts on the Press's more than eight hundred books in print.

Full-time students are eligible for special half-price membership rates. Life memberships are also available.

For a free catalog describing Naval Institute Press books currently available, and for further information about joining the U.S. Naval Institute, please write to:

Member Services
U.S. Naval Institute
291 Wood Road
Annapolis, MD 21402-5034
Telephone: (800) 233-8764
Fax: (410) 571-1703
Web address: www.usni.org